Beyond Emancipation

SUNY series in Multiethnic Literatures

Mary Jo Bona, editor

Beyond Emancipation

Maroon Freedoms in US Literature, 1850–1862

SEAN GERRITY

Published by State University of New York Press, Albany

© 2025 State University of New York

All rights reserved

Printed in the United States of America

No part of this book may be used or reproduced in any manner whatsoever without written permission. No part of this book may be stored in a retrieval system or transmitted in any form or by any means including electronic, electrostatic, magnetic tape, mechanical, photocopying, recording, or otherwise without the prior permission in writing of the publisher.

Links to third-party websites are provided as a convenience and for informational purposes only. They do not constitute an endorsement or an approval of any of the products, services, or opinions of the organization, companies, or individuals. SUNY Press bears no responsibility for the accuracy, legality, or content of a URL, the external website, or for that of subsequent websites.

EU GPSR Authorised Representative:
Logos Europe, 9 rue Nicolas Poussin, 17000, La Rochelle, France
contact@logoseurope.eu

For information, contact State University of New York Press, Albany, NY
www.sunypress.edu

Library of Congress Cataloging-in-Publication Data

Name: Gerrity, Sean, 1986– author.
Title: Beyond emancipation : Maroon freedoms in US literature, 1850–1862 / Sean Gerrity.
Description: Albany : State University of New York Press, [2025]. | Series: SUNY series in multiethnic literatures | Includes bibliographical references and index.
Identifiers: LCCN 2024044097 | ISBN 9798855802580 (hardcover : alk. paper) | ISBN 9798855802603 (ebook) | ISBN 9798855802597 (pbk. : alk. paper)
Subjects: LCSH: American literature—19th century—History and criticism. | American literature—African American authors—History and criticism. | Maroons in literature. | Liberty in literature | Fugitive slaves in literature. | African Americans in literature. | LCGFT: Literary criticism.
Classification: LCC PS153.B35 G47 2025 | DDC 810.8/0896073—dc23/eng/20241118
LC record available at https://lccn.loc.gov/2024044097

To Megan, Cooper, Emilia, and Colin

Contents

Acknowledgments	ix
Introduction: Canadas in the South	1
Chapter One: Swamp Things	29
Chapter Two: Beyond Revolt	61
Chapter Three: Toward Stillness	97
Chapter Four: Emancipation, Interrupted	121
Coda: Maroon Pasts, Maroon Futures	157
Notes	161
Bibliography	183
Index	193

Acknowledgments

An earlier version of chapter 2 was originally published as "Freedom on the Move: Marronage in Martin Delany's *Blake; or, The Huts of America*," *MELUS: The Society for the Study of the Multi-Ethnic Literature of the United States* 43, no. 3 (Fall 2018): 1–18.

An earlier version of chapter 3 was originally published as "Harriet Jacobs, Marronage, and Alternative Freedoms in *Incidents in the Life of a Slave Girl*," *Legacy: A Journal of American Women Writers* 38, nos. 1–2 (2021): 67–89.

This book has been nearly ten years in the making, and so the list of people to thank is a long one. First and foremost, it would not exist without the constant support and encouragement of my dissertation committee at the CUNY Graduate Center: Eric Lott, Duncan Faherty, and Robert Reid-Pharr. I will never be able to repay Duncan for the amount of drafts he has read over the years (I'm trying!). Eric opened every door he could for me as a budding scholar. Robert telling me my reading of *Incidents in the Life of a Slave Girl* changed the way he understood that text shocked me into thinking I might actually have something worthwhile to say. The earliest inklings of this project arose in a course with David Reynolds where I first read Harriet Beecher Stowe's *Dred* and learned about maroons. He pushed me to read deeply into primary sources on the subject, and a 2014 seminar paper on *Dred* marks the beginning of my fascination with marronage in literature. Kandice Chuh encouraged me to go all in on this project as a dissertation when I was nervous about committing to something. I am ever grateful for her sage advice. At the Graduate Center, Hildegard Hoeller, Marc Dolan, David Humphries, and Ammiel Alcalay helped me round out my studies and provided crucial feedback on my developing writing. Nancy Silverman helped me keep my life in order as a graduate student, and Carrie Hintz and Anne Ellis made sure I had the funding to keep going. Phyllis Van Slyck taught me how to be a college teacher in my very first semester as a graduate student. Jenny LeRoy was always there to commiserate when the going got tough. Research grants and fellowships from the Advanced Research Collaborative (ARC) and the Institute for Research on the African Diaspora in the Americas and the Caribbean (IRADAC) as well as time spent at the Futures of American Studies Institute at Dartmouth gave me critical research time and space to focus on this work. Summer fellowships at the University of Virginia and Virginia Historical Society helped me learn archival research methods that have been vital to this project.

At Hostos, Andrea Fabrizio, Linda Hirsch, Greg Marks, Heidi Bollinger, Tram Nguyen, Alex Milsom, Krysia Michael, Vicky Munoz, Liz Porter, Anne Rounds, Lou Bury, and Andy Connolly have supported me in more capacities than I can count. I owe Andy an enormous debt for his mentorship and encouragement to keep on keeping on with the writing. He believed in me and in this book from the moment he dropped by to introduce himself. Alex and I began this odyssey into professorial life together, and she has spent years lifting me up. Generous funding from the Professional Staff Congress at CUNY helped me keep the research going in the summers, as did time with the invaluable scholarly mentorship of Kelly Baker Josephs.

I began my journey with literary studies as an English major at Lafayette College and am thankful a hundred times over to Steve Belletto, who opened up what literary studies could actually mean and guided me through the intricacies and minutiae of successfully applying to graduate school. Chris Phillips and the late Bryan Washington formed the rest of my "committee" at Lafayette, and it's been an honor to go from their students to their colleagues. I would be remiss if I didn't thank some friends from over the years: Kyle Lynch, Mike Milea, Paul Montgomery, Dillon Malar, Chris Milea, JP Lynch, Jessica Buzzell, Marissa Halderman, Steve Koppel, Jamie Markle, Steve Holzer, Eric Wilson, Pat McGuire, and Chris Velderman. You've enabled and sustained a life that led me here, even if you don't realize it.

There were times, especially during the chaos of 2020 through 2022, when I didn't think I'd be able to finish this book. It would quite simply not exist had it not been for an incredibly generous Community College Faculty Fellowship from the American Council of Learned Societies and Andrew W. Mellon Foundation in 2020, which gave me the time and space to focus on the project with little other professional distraction. Before that, a chance Twitter ("X") exchange with Rebecca Colesworthy actually brought this project to life as a book. Unwavering support from my wife, Megan; daughter, Emilia; and ever-faithful companion, Cooper, is what ultimately made this possible. And Colin Gerrity, my son, who arrived later and was very cooperative. But of course there has always also been my family, to whom I am eternally grateful: Mom, Dad, Ryan, Carly, Murphy, Frank—thank you for always being there. And same with my other family: Cathy, Ben, Jen, Ryan—you're the best. In many ways this all began with my grandma, the late Lois Hildebrant. I hope this would make her proud.

Introduction

Canadas in the South

Slave resistance, not bourgeois liberalism, lay at the heart of the abolition movement.

—Manisha Sinha, *The Slave's Cause*

The maroons know something about possibility.

—Fred Moten and Stefano Harney, *The Undercommons*

The maroon is Sisyphus escaped.

—Yannick Marshall, "An Appeal"

In his 1859 travel narrative *The Roving Editor; or, Talks with Slaves in the Southern States*, Scottish-born abolitionist James Redpath shares the following recalibration of operant understandings of spaces of freedom from a formerly enslaved man:

> There is a Canada in the Southern States. It is the Dismal Swamp. It is the dreariest and most repulsive of American possessions. It is the favorite resort of wild animals and reptiles; the paradise of serpents and poisonous vegetation. No human being, one would think, would voluntarily live there; and yet, from time immemorial, it has been the chosen asylum of hundreds of our race. It has been the earthly heaven of the negro slave; the place "where the wicked cease from troubling, and the weary are at rest."[1]

Redpath credits a friend, a Mrs. Knox of Boston, with relating this information to him, which had been "narrated by a fugitive slave in Canada, whose words, as he uttered them, she reported *verbatim*."[2] While the unidentified (and perhaps unidentifiable) speaker remains unregistered, the concept he is credited with articulating—a notion of a Canada in the South, both a place and an idea—provides a generative starting point for this book's study of representations of marronage in nineteenth-century African American literature. To read for "Canadas in the South" is to read for articulations of Black freedom-making in constant, unsettled tension with the prevailing white abolitionist sensibility and publishing industry. It is crucial to be clear about the fact that all of the authors studied in this book wrote within and in relation to the white publishing industry. To suggest that we may somehow entirely disentangle their work from it would be disingenuous and would diminish the efforts of those Black writers to be heard and published in the first place. This is the opposite of what I hope to accomplish here. As a white scholar working in Black literary studies, I have tried to remain aware and to work against a tendency among white writers to romanticize maroons and, in analyzing marronage in the realm of literary scholarship, to conflate ideas about marronage in fiction with the material realities of maroons fighting daily for their freedom. By reading the way I will suggest, indexing possibilities for freedom without white abolitionists even as we know Black authors are writing knowingly under the constraints of a white publishing industry and set of expectations, we can locate formations of peripheral, alternative constructions of freedom *within* slaveholding US Southern states and within those publishing constraints—parasocial, paranational, and extranational conceptions of Black freedom that do not depend upon recourse to the state for legitimation. They are ideas of freedom, fragile as they may often be, willed into existence and fashioned into a source of sustenance by the enslaved person turned maroon. That the Dismal Swamp has existed as a site of refuge "since time immemorial" reveals a concept of maroon time that is separate from and contests a sense of national time and history in the United States, a collective consciousness and ideology that circumscribes the limits of possibility for Black freedom. Radical antislavery activist John Brown's description of the Virginia mountains as "created, from the foundation of the world, as a place of refuge for fugitive slaves" provides further credence to this particular idea of a sense of space and time out of sync with, but still in relation to, dominant modes of thinking in the context of the United States as a geopolitical entity.³ As a "chosen asylum,"⁴ the swamp provides a sense of agency for enslaved people, and it puts the lie to arguments about slavery's benevolence and enslaved people's supposed satisfaction with their circumstances. The swamp is always already and perpetually in the process of becoming a site of refuge geographically within the United States, and it stretches the limits of time and place as constructed and maintained by a white colonizer history. In nineteenth-century African American literature, we find representations of maroons and marronage that build on and complicate imaginaries of Canada(s) in the South, pushing beyond the limits of what white authors could possibly know or understand about Black experiences in the United States.

How did major African American writers in the North during the 1850s and '60s represent and frame maroon communities, acts of marronage, and knowledge about both for a predominantly white reading public? How can we read this body of literature to better see the possibilities for alternative freedoms offered by their representations of marronage? How does a focus on marronage in this literature allow us to register Black freedom-seeking tactics and imaginaries that do not fit neatly into a liberal philosophical paradigm? What happens when we purposefully attend to, and attune ourselves to, the "lower frequencies" and disruptive temporalities of Black life and Black thought as manifested through marronage?⁵

These are the primary overarching questions that animate *Beyond Emancipation*'s exploration of portrayals of maroons: enslaved people who self-exiled—some alone and others together, some temporarily and others permanently—and sought refuge in remote places like swamps, woods, forests, and mountains in the southeastern United States, forging lives and socialities within a regime that sought to crush them out of existence. Historically, from the seventeenth century through the end of the American Civil War, marronage was a consistent feature of plantation society, the true extent of which has only relatively recently been discovered and more fully acknowledged by historians, geographers, and archaeologists studying it, mostly in the context of swamps in the southern United States—the Great Dismal Swamp of Virginia and North Carolina in particular.⁶ Much of the writing that exists—but also, importantly, that which has been selected and curated over the past 170 years—about maroons and marronage in the nineteenth century focuses on the Great Dismal Swamp, and much of the scholarship since has done the same. The simplest explanation for this fact is that this massive swamp landscape was, according to the information we have, the most common and long-standing destination for maroons from the seventeenth through the nineteenth century, especially those who fled for longer periods of time or did not return at all.

Marronage in what would become the United States arose concomitantly with European colonization of the North American continent and the beginning of the transatlantic slave trade as it began to formally develop in the seventeenth century. Captive and enslaved Africans began to flee immediately, at the first opportunity, into a vast unknown and unfamiliar landscape. The swamps of the American Southeast were inhabited and traversed at times prior and during by indigenous peoples and sometimes also by white laborers like indentured servants and deported convicts sent over from Europe who fled life among the colonizers. This took on various forms, but the most common was short-term flight born of desperate circumstances, as scholars like Sylviane Diouf, Marcus Nevius, Christy Hyman, J. Brent Morris, Daniel Sayers, Herbert Aptheker, Richard Price, and many others have described over the past several decades. Diouf's work charts the development of US marronage from the seventeenth through the nineteenth century in what was the first documentary history to attempt such a vast undertaking. Her *Slavery's Exiles: The Story of the American Maroons* laid the groundwork for more in-depth studies that would focus on the swamps of Virginia, North Carolina, South Carolina, Louisiana, and what at the time was Spanish Florida. Timothy James Lockley's *Maroon Communities in South Carolina: A Documentary Record*, Sayers's *A Desolate Place for a Defiant People: The Archaeology of Maroons, Indigenous Americans, and Enslaved Laborers in the Great Dismal Swamp*, Nevius's *City of Refuge: Slavery and Petit Marronage in the Great Dismal Swamp, 1763–1856*, and, most recently, Morris's *Dismal Freedom: A History of the Maroons of the Great Dismal Swamp* continued and dug deeper into the hidden histories of maroons throughout the southeastern United States. Prior to these, Richard Price's *Maroon Societies: Rebel Slave Communities in the Americas* established the sustained presence of US maroons and opened avenues to further study.[7]

Like elsewhere in the Western Hemisphere, where marronage also began with the arrival of the very first captive Africans, the practice took on various forms influenced by many factors in North America related to geography, African cultural influence, population density of both white and enslaved people, the structure and organization of colonial regimes and authority, and the gradual development of laws about slavery and more localized versions of slavery that emerged from them. Through careful attention to hundreds of previously unexamined documentary sources, Diouf uncovered evidence of sustained communities, some likely numbering in the hundreds and remaining for several decades, especially in the Great Dismal Swamp. But those were outliers; far more common were individual and small-group flights with more fleeting existences. These, referred to as *petit marronage*, are the subject of Nevius's extensive historical work, and literary representations of them in various configurations will in large part be the focus of mine. Nevius charts the various ways in which the swamp served as a "city of refuge" for enslaved people who took flight and found some measure of asylum there from the middle of the eighteenth to middle of the nineteenth century. That hundred-year span saw significant changes in the extent to and means by which the swamp was turned to for colonial resource extraction and surveilled as a site of enslaved resistance.

Attention to marronage increased as white settler-colonizer encroachment on the swamp increased, its hidden inhabitants coming into greater focus. Beginning in the mid-eighteenth century, states passed laws designed to deter and punish marronage, even as informal networks of trade and labor between white, Black, free, and enslaved people would go on existing there until the formal abolition of slavery in the United States. These networks arose largely along the borders of the swamp. Deeper in the swamp interior, some maroons established sophisticated encampments with homes, farming plots, and hidden paths for entrance and exit, along with hunting practices and ways to work in concert with Africans enslaved on the plantations abutting the swamps. Less common were maroons who managed to survive deep in the swamps without contact with the outside to sustain basic necessities of life with supplies like food, tools, clothing, and blankets. Stories of their lives from their perspectives remain almost entirely impossible to access in detail. Work like Lockley's, Diouf's, and Nevius's has at least been able to establish documentary proof and record of those lives having existed.

Sayers and others have worked over the past two decades to uncover physical evidence of maroons in the Great Dismal Swamp in an effort to reconstruct the nature of their lives and means of survival and sustenance there over generations. Some of what he has found has been exhibited in the Smithsonian's National Museum of African American History and Culture, bringing the lives and histories of maroons to a public audience who has been eager to learn about these hidden and obscured histories. Diouf even located examples of maroons who had dug underground hideouts complete with trap doors and small chimneys where fires for cooking could burn in the darkest middle of the night. All maroons had to be immensely careful and constantly on guard for slave patrols and what were sometimes organized, concerted slave hunts sent into the swamps at the order of local governments and officials. Dogs were of particular concern, and maroons developed creative ways of misdirecting them from their trail. They nearly always remained at the ready to move quickly from wherever they had taken refuge, knowing that at any moment they may need to escape again with urgency. Maroons came to understand over time the landscapes of the swamps in ways that the white planter class and their hired slave hunters, who seldom ventured into swamps without necessity, could not, ways of transforming and reimagining these spaces that will be explored more closely in the chapters that follow.

As the colonies became more populated over the course of the eighteenth century, both with European settler-colonizers and with an always increasing number of enslaved captives, maroon tactics grew in sophistication and variety, adapting to new circumstances and forging ever-changing ways to survive, subvert, and resist the vicious circumstances into which the maroons had been thrown. There are stories of generations of maroons living in the swamps, of children who were born and died there, never knowing a life of slavery quite like what we usually imagine was the experience of enslaved Black people in the South, whether on the plantation or otherwise. We know now of maroons who remained in the swamps after legal emancipation, not knowing they had been legally freed or in some cases simply choosing to remain where they were regardless, rejecting emancipation as a form of "true" liberation from slavery. Many of the details of all these kinds of marronage will be explored throughout the chapters of this book, but stories of short-term flight, which were most common and are ultimately the most well documented in the histories and in the African American literatures available to us, are the focus of my work. Many of these stories center and coalesce around the Great Dismal Swamp as a site of prolonged escape, resistance, survival, and alternative varieties of African American and Black life. Aptheker in the 1930s estimated that the maroons in that swamp, which was massive during early settlement and shrunk over time as colonizer imposition increased, numbered in the thousands at times during the eighteenth century. However, these numbers, of course, are impossible to know or chart with any certainty.[8]

Attention to how white writers represented maroons provides a clearer picture of the limited and flawed ways in which those writers engaged with marronage as a literary trope. While Harriet Beecher Stowe's writing about maroons comes chronologically after some of that by Black writers considered in this book, her thinking aggregates the dominant, white modes of deploying maroons and marronage as didactic abolitionist figurations in the literary realm. Along with Stowe, whose second and less-studied novel *Dred: A Tale of the Great Dismal Swamp* (1856) deals extensively with maroons in the Great Dismal Swamp, well-known nineteenth-century writers like Thomas Wentworth Higginson, David Hunter Strother, and the architect Frederick Law Olmsted all wrote about the Great Dismal Swamp and specifically about marronage there.[9] Their writings brought mainstream attention to marronage for white readers and exerted a strong influence over how maroons were imagined, which could vary depending on whether those readers were in the North or the South—but usually with some combination of curiosity, romanticization, pity, and fear. These representations were both documentary and literary in nature, with writers like Strother in particular adding flourish and sensation to what, in his case, he claims to have actually witnessed in the swamp. In a *Harper's New Monthly Magazine* piece titled "The Dismal Swamp" from 1856, Strother describes an encounter with a maroon named Osman, portrayed in an accompanying illustration emerging from entangled roots and vegetation clutching a rifle. Strother's writing is designed to offer a glimpse into a hidden and alternative world deep in the seemingly uninhabitable morass and to portray it as resistant and defiant of white authority. The abolitionist writer Edmund Jackson published a short article called "The Virginia Maroons" in the *National Anti-Slavery Standard* in 1852, which begins by invoking the maroons of the West Indies, particularly Jamaica, Cuba, and Santo Domingo, and the battles for autonomy and agreements they established with colonial powers. Jackson moves into a detailed account of the existence of maroon communities in US southern swamps, describing the small, elevated plots of dry land where maroons built shelters and where archaeologist Daniel Sayers has found evidence of life as part of his fieldwork in the Great Dismal Swamp over the past two decades.[10]

The swamp appeared in African American writing earlier too, perhaps most notably Moses Grandy's *Narrative of the Life of Moses Grandy; Late a Slave in the United States of America* (1843), which describes Grandy's time working in the swamp and encountering some of its maroon inhabitants.[11]

Such encounters were not uncommon, and in some cases fugitives turned maroons themselves took on paid work in the Dismal Swamp, where few questions were asked by companies looking to profit by extracting wood from the swamp for shingle making, among other things. Beginning in the eighteenth century, following William Byrd II's expeditions in the swamp in the 1730s and '40s, when its landscape began to be officially charted and surveyed for extractive purposes, companies began to find ways to make us of what otherwise often appeared to be an impenetrable world: "The reeds which grew about 12 feet high, were so thick, & so interlaced with Bamboe-Briars, that our Pioneers were forc't to open a Passage. The Ground, if I may properly call it so, was so spongy, that the Prints of our Feet were instantly fill'd with Water."[12] Later, the Dismal Swamp Company was founded in 1763 to attempt to drain parts of the swamp and extract its resources within a developing capitalist economy. In the 1790s, the Dismal Swamp Canal Company (in which George Washington was a major founding investor) managed to dig out a canal system linking the Chesapeake Bay and Albemarle Sound, near where Harriet Jacobs was born and lived in the early nineteenth century. Nearly all of this early work was conducted by hired-out enslaved men, some of whom Washington was responsible for acquiring. Still, progress was slow, and the business of lumbering was less profitable than had been hoped. It wouldn't be until 1814 that the newly incorporated Dismal Swamp Land Company actually made money. By this time, however, Washington had sold his shares in the company and had largely moved on from involvement in its endeavors.

Beginning in the 1930s and '40s with Herbert Aptheker's pioneering historical research into US marronage and moving into Richard and Sally Price's anthropological work in the 1970s and '80s, and more recently to that of scholars across several disciplines including Sylviane Diouf, Timothy James Lockley, Ted Maris-Wolf, Daniel Sayers, Martha Schoolman, Neil S. Roberts, Marcus Nevius, Kathryn E. B. Golden, Christy Hyman, and J. T. Roane, a multidisciplinary tradition of maroon studies in the United States has emerged with increased urgency and relevance to our own time.[13] Work on marronage in US literatures has, however, received considerably less attention, though important work by critics like William Tynes Cowan and especially Schoolman, Richard Bodek, and Joseph Kelly has pushed us to consider what literary marronage can mean for our understanding of received traditions of US literary history, periodization, aesthetics, and politics.[14] This book's primary departure from their work involves studying literary representations of maroons as registering a sustained tradition of Black thought about imaginaries of alternative freedom in the 1850s and early 1860s. While maroons and marronage were of course real-world people and practices, my focus in this book is on their aesthetic depictions in largely Black literature as moments through which we might venture to better see and understand possibilities for Black freedom-making being articulated and speculated upon by those writers in the print public discourse of the time period. Describing the history is necessary to provide context and historical background for my work, but those histories themselves are not the focus of it. I read for and use these articulations as sites of aesthetic study informed and often constituted by historical practice but present for our access only through the textual record. It is these aesthetic articulations that provide the material for seeing and using marronage as a hermeneutic through which to explore the maroons' alternative freedoms, epistemologies, and ontologies.

This book argues that significant attention to maroons and marronage by African American writers in the United States emerged after the passage of the Fugitive Slave Act as part of the Compromise of 1850. African American literature from that decade offers an archive of myriad, rich representations of maroons and marronage that have yet to be analyzed together with the specific kind of sustained attention I have described and have the potential to reveal Black abolitionist thinking about freedom in more nuanced ways. *Beyond Emancipation* moves to recover these representations in order to better apprehend how African American writers understood marronage as part of a complex assemblage of freedom-seeking tactics—both means and ends—in the greater context of the 1850s and early 1860s as well as the longer *durée* of African American history. It asks how these understandings by Black writers gesture toward theorization of marronage as illuminative of a broader spectrum of ideas about freedom and unfreedom, about lives, spaces, practices, and ways of knowing and being within the context of chattel slavery that tries but fails to entirely circumscribe them within its own subjugating logics.

In the context of the British West Indies, Christopher Taylor has asked, "What happens . . . not simply when subjects are neglected, but when they come to conceive of themselves as being neglected?"[15] What began as neglect and deliberate subjugation of American colonizers by the British Empire in the second half of the eighteenth century had always been characterized by a double and violent neglect of African-descended subjects by the American colonizers under the British regime. Such neglect (to put it lightly) had always been painfully apparent, of course, to enslaved people. This neglect was codified and redoubled by those colonizers postindependence via the US Constitution's 1789 fugitive-slave provisions, followed by the 1850 Fugitive Slave Act and the Dred Scott decision legally denying African-descended people a route to citizenship or civil rights in 1857. Enslaved and nominally free Black people, Black maroons, and Black writers thus operated in a world that had definitively declared its lack of intention to acknowledge their existence as subjects but also its intention to deny them an identity or, most significantly, future route to an identity of subject*hood* as inhabitants of the United States. This fact fundamentally shaped and characterized the ways African-descended people could conceive of their place and imagine future possibilities of freedom in American society. For these people foreclosed from freedom granted, as the American colonizers had felt themselves, freedom taken became an increasingly urgent imperative. Maroons took it upon themselves to make and take freedoms unrecognized and unendorsed by the state, and Black writers increasingly located and explored the possibilities for those freedoms through acts of marronage. This is the backdrop within and against which the Black authors in this study wrote.

We don't have to go far to find some of the most significant and generative representations of marronage in the literature of this pivotal historical era: Frederick Douglass, Harriet Jacobs, and Harriet Beecher Stowe, some of the most canonical US authors of the nineteenth century, all incorporated stories of maroons and marronage into their writing in different ways, inflected by their racial positionality vis-à-vis the white-dominated publishing industry. Thanks to work by Floyd J. Miller in the 1970s and more recently by scholars like Jerome McGann, Robert Levine, Jean Lee Cole, Katy Chiles, Britt Rusert, Gregory Pierrot, and Martha Schoolman, among others, Martin Delany's *Blake; or, The Huts of America* (1859, 1861 to 1862) has begun to receive the kind of insistent critical attention it deserves as a crucial part of nineteenth-century Black literary history and the trajectory of a radical Black tradition in literary studies. Echoing Manisha Sinha's call to prioritize enslaved resistance in the abolitionist movement, I aim to read how these Black texts representing maroons should be understood as part of the this movement not just as antislavery works, literary texts, or didactic testimonials but as records of and unique contributions to abolitionist public discourse around the philosophy and meanings of freedom.[16] Read with attention to marronage, these works contest mainstream positions and ideologies, generating new horizons of possibility for Black freedom outside the confines of the white abolitionist imagination as represented by writers like Stowe. In other words, this Black literature should be read as contributing philosophically and aesthetically to debates about the nature of freedom and unfreedom that proliferated throughout the 1850s.[17]

Post-1850 African American literature is especially attuned to and concerned with notions of freedom that are not dependent on state intervention or the future possibility of legal emancipation. When the Fugitive Slave Law nationalized the legal imperative to capture and return runaways from slavery even if they had escaped to a free state, flight to the North became even more hazardous than it had already been, and its destination no longer considered a safe haven.[18] The devastating Dred Scott decision in 1857 exacerbated the issue, cutting African Americans off entirely from the possibility of freedom through state-granted means or recognized civil rights, both then and in the future.[19] Marronage, therefore, as a resistive tactic with no expectation or desire for state intervention, one unbeholden to state boundaries and the whims of white laws and extrajudicial justice, became a more pronounced part of African American literature's explorations of freedom and thus the basis from which this study takes its aims. This context is important, as these writers were all closely attuned to the print public discourse of their time as well as to each other's works and abolitionist textual production more generally.

Much important work, particularly that of Robert Levine beginning in the 1980s, has been done to uncover, recover, and situate these writers' works in relation to one another and to contemporaneous US political and social conditions in ways that move beyond neat correspondences between flattened organizing concepts like race, nation, nationalism(s), ethnicity, and identity.[20] Like Levine, I am interested in the value of "unknowingness" and "undoings," a focus that helps prevent us from "producing our own revisionary national narratives" at the expense of recognizing the fundamental uncertainty about the future with which writers in the 1850s (like writers at any point) lived.[21] Building from this recuperative and formative interpretive work, I intend to illuminate in more detail ways that Black writing about marronage registers a preoccupation with freedom-seeking decoupled and dislocated from attachments to normative, national temporalities and geographical imaginaries—even ones that are understood as contingent, uneven, and experienced unpredictably. I am less concerned with how we might map Black writers engaging marronage onto literary historical narratives invested in coming to terms with where their ideas fit into various nationalist and antinationalist registers, or into binaries of liberal freedom and unfreedom, and more concerned with how accessing lower frequencies of resistive life via marronage reveals often-speculative possibilities beyond what that kind of mapping allows to cohere.

To those ends, *Beyond Emancipation* argues that looking at marronage in this literature in part invites us to perceive possibilities for freedom that exist outside a unilateral South-to-North geographical axis hinging on the deepening sectionalist tensions that characterized the 1850s. This trajectory locates freedom in the North and unfreedom in the South, typically along the coordinates of the Underground Railroad, which has often exerted outsized power over the US American understanding of slavery.[22] Marronage instead links African American stories and histories with those around the hemisphere and within the circum-Atlantic exchange in human beings who rebelled and resisted in innumerable ways. Attention to marronage allows us to see in part how Black writers looked outward from the United States' normative geography rather than just inward, exceeding ideas of national time and space to gesture toward how freedom was fought for in a diasporic context across landscapes, continents, oceans, and centuries.

Ifeoma Kiddoe Nwankwo argues that "people of African descent's approaches to public self-representation were born, in significant part, of the Atlantic power structure's attempts to deny them access to cosmopolitan subjectivity."[23] She further contends that "this denial of access for people of African descent to cosmopolitan subjectivity coexisted with a denial of access for that same population to both national subjectivity and human subjectivity," which is relevant to my study because marronage represented an avenue toward possible affinities with diasporic Black people and realizations of more cosmopolitan subjectivity born out of and connected by diasporic marronage.[24] Though this study does not attend primarily or with detail to the specifics of these writers' definitive engagements with texts or populations outside the United States, it's important to note that their depictions of marronage gesture toward those possible identifications and subjectivities, registering a further threat to the organizing logics and disavowals of US chattel slavery via a construction of Black identity at odds with national subjectivity and thus some element of control within its socioracial logics. Struggles over and slippages between the ideas of subjectivity, subjecthood, personhood, and citizenship are central to the history of Blackness in the United States and to its aesthetic function and representation. Fred Moten registers Blackness as "the extended movement of a specific upheaval, an ongoing irruption that annaranges every line," a "strain that pressures the assumption of the equivalence of personhood and subjectivity."[25] Focusing on marronage invites us to privilege alternative and transitory movements *within* slaveholding states that both challenge the power of the slave system and provide examples of Black freedom-seeking strategies in tension with the concept of freedom in the tradition of liberal philosophy and the geographical confines of the United States. Marronage in this book becomes a focus of literary and aesthetic study through which I investigate and attempt to register the production of alternative, non- and illiberal forms of Black community, sociality, belonging, being, space, and ultimately geographies and freedoms. The texts under consideration form a constellation that articulates a Black-centered politics and praxis of resistance within and against the regime of chattel slavery. They provide a sense of how African American writers in the late pre–Civil War period navigated audience and aesthetics in their careful representations of marronage and how they themselves depicted marronage in ways that contested normative ideas of freedom and unfreedom in the context of an Atlantic world not entirely constitutive of the US national system of slavery.

In the United States—unlike in places such as Jamaica, Suriname, and Brazil, where maroon wars were fought; where large, organized maroon communities existed for many decades; and where maroon descendants live in often still resistive identification with that ancestry today—scholarship by the critics mentioned so far as well as by John Hope Franklin and Loren Schweninger has shown that most marronage was temporary and carried out by individuals or very small groups. These maroons rarely made it to the free states or Canada, and often, in the cases of those living in the deepest southern states, never set out for them in the first place. While there is historical evidence of larger and long-lasting US maroon communities, representations of them are rare in the African American print public sphere, in part for reasons that will be elaborated in the chapters that follow. While some Black people and communities in the United States today can and do trace their ancestry to maroons, these identifications are less centralized largely because US maroons did not forge officialized paranational communities acknowledged by the state.[26] This is not to say that US maroons tried and failed to accomplish that but instead speaks to contingencies of existence often having to do simply with geography and sociopolitical possibility. As Edmund Jackson and Thomas Wentworth Higginson noted in the 1850s and '60s and Diouf, Nevius, and Sayers have today, US maroons lacked access to spaces large, inhabitable, defensible, and remote enough, unlike, for example, the Jamaican maroons who created communities in places like the Cockpit Country and deep interior of the Blue Mountains.[27]

Beyond Emancipation suggests that focusing on small acts of marronage in literature (or *petit marronage*) that are not tied to imaginaries of political autonomy reveals contours and intricacies of freedom that an emphasis on marronage as a path to extensive community formation or negotiation with colonial powers obscures. Working in the field of critical Black geographies, Justin Hosbey and J. T. Roane "locate ongoing shared cultural histories of resistance through the matrix of Black ecologies in 'untamed' spaces," suggesting that "in swamps and forests, the enslaved formed a fleeting Black commons, whereby they used their unique knowledge of the landscapes and waterscapes to extend a fugitive and transient freedom."[28] Maroons renegotiated the nature of the landscapes they inhabited, even if—though maybe especially because—those renegotiations did not manifest with politically recognized permanence but instead as Black subaltern knowledge and resistant praxis. The meanings of freedom located and generated within "a fleeting Black commons" manifest in African American literary representations of marronage.

This book works to enhance understandings of marronage and of maroons to include what becomes available to us by looking at literary representations by Black writers in the pre–Civil War period in contrast to representations by white writers in the tradition of Harriet Beecher Stowe. Minor instances of marronage in literature should be considered major opportunities to study alternative practices and ideas about freedom. Over the course of the chapters that follow, I aim to generate a more nuanced conception of marronage, one that captures some of its most common and crucial elements like mobility, concealment, stillness, parasociality, disaffection, and disavowal of liberal state formations of freedom. My definition of marronage is not so much a definition as it is a constellatory set of freedom-seeking practices by which unregistered frequencies of Black life and proactive agency coursed beneath the radar of a white supremacist state. I take seriously Monique Allewaert's identification of "a process through which human agents found ways to interact with nonhuman forces and in so doing resisted the order of the plantation."[29] The swamp landscape in this literature is not simply a backdrop; rather, following Allewaert, it is a life-giving, complex ecology that provides for even as it also obstructs and interferes with human activity. While small acts of marronage may not have been a threat to the system of slavery, their presence threatened a prevailing *idea* of slavery as an all-encompassing system of domination and control.[30]

Judith Madera has drawn particular attention to the "spatial interruptions," "counter-geograph[ies]," and "alternate temporal[ities]" that are manifested through Black literature from this time period, suggesting that they are characteristic of its exploration of contested, destabilized Black notions of place and space.[31] She emphasizes that we should not "conceive of territory as a settled state of affairs or a bounded culture that deterritorialization undoes" but rather that "what African American narratives show us, quite explicitly, is that territory is unstable by its very constitution."[32] Each chapter builds upon the next in an episodic structure rather than chronological order as both a reflection of and critical movement toward imagining maroons as disruptors of commonplace organizing logics of temporality, spatiality, place, and territory along which US history has been narrativized to progress. These interlocking themes are developed over the course of the chapters and relational in ways that my interpretations of the major literary texts draw into focus as often discretely episodic rather than insistently linked.[33] Through episodic case-study-like readings of each major text the book considers, I show how Black thinking about marronage developed unevenly, without a clear linearity or stable possibilistic definition and without any sense of retroactive historical inevitability. What might be thought of as a definition of marronage arises with similar unevenness but reveals thematic threads that, when taken together, the texts work to articulate and these chapters draw into greater focus. Celeste Winston defines marronage as "flight from and placemaking beyond slavery."[34] It is the possibilities arising in and from the *beyond* that preoccupy my study. At its most fundamental level, this book understands marronage to be broadly characterized by proactively resistant acts of movement from the physical and psychic subjugation of chattel slavery toward moments that avow Black agency and potentiality on their own terms, catalyzing reconfigurations of normative freedoms in the realms of subjectivity, space, and place.

In her second but, as noted, much less studied antislavery novel, *Dred: A Tale of the Dismal Swamp*, Harriet Beecher Stowe paints a strikingly detailed portrait of marronage and maroon life in an established community encampment in the famed Great Dismal Swamp.[35] In African American literature, marronage tends to exist as hints, whispers, intimations, ephemeralities, at the very least both revealing and cautiously withheld. Diouf has shown that for white writers, particularly those in the tradition of northeastern abolitionists, marronage was seen as useful rhetorically, mostly because it suggested the horrors of slavery, that enslaved people would rather live in treacherous swamps than on brutally oppressive plantations. In these texts the desperate, temporary escapes of maroons are often presented as further proof of slavery's cruelty and the enslaved's relentless desire to be free. For Stowe, *Dred*'s titular insurrectionary maroon protagonist must be killed, his community destroyed, in order for the white abolitionist fantasy of Black liberation to be realized via a journey from the South to the North, to the "enlightened," free, and morally untainted world of the free states. Black narratives about marronage, on the other hand, contest geographical and ideological binaries between slavery and freedom and create narrative tension where Stowe otherwise ends such tension with Dred's death.

While other competing ideas about a path to Black freedom circulated with zeal prior to the Civil War among both Black and white abolitionists—such as colonization (famously supported by Stowe in her earlier work and heavily criticized later by Martin Delany) and relocation to the American West or West Indies—this book focuses on the Underground Railroad paradigm and the Northern states and Canada as sites of potential freedom because of the hold they have had on mainstream conceptions of African American literary history, which depends so heavily on the genre of the slave narrative as a site of origin and organizational departure. The slave narrative, of course, privileges the kind of unilateral geography of freedom this book is principally interested in contesting through marronage-focused rereadings of African American literature. This is why I focus on them, not at the deliberate expense of the others but because they are most relevant to this project's attention and concerns and they are the concerns of the literary works under study. Eric Gardner has invited us to look in "unexpected places" for the presence of both African Americans and African American literary formations in the nineteenth century, and this book heeds and expands upon his call by looking for and at maroons and marronage where they have been less studied in major African American literary texts.[36]

Delany's support of emigration to Liberia and Central America, and in *Blake* for the creation of a Black island nation founded on the illegality of slavery, fits into what he militated for as the more desirable aims of an ideology committed to a Black nationalist project of large-scale political liberation. But the small acts of marronage in his novel, and marronage more generally, are of particular interest here precisely because they contest and often reject community or sociality as a national project, instead exposing the inherently oppressive and racist organizing logics of the liberal nation-state as manifested from Enlightenment-based philosophy. Canonical African American literature and abolitionist literature—and the canonical ways in which they have been read and their meanings packaged and perpetuated over time—have often been fit into a framework in which the North (and Canada) is presented as a beacon of freedom as a way to foreclose slavery and the enslaved within the boundaries of the South, into the past, and as ultimately over in the North. This, of course, downplays the long history of de jure slavery in the Northern states along with their continued involvement in the slave economy after legal abolition in those states in the first few decades of the nineteenth century. The received, traditional ways of reading these canonical texts have had great staying power as a convenient and oversimplified means in the US popular imaginary of understanding a Black past as organized around reaction to oppression rather than proactive freedom-seeking and alternative ontological creation as realized through marronage.

Roland Leander Williams has forcefully averred that "scholars have suspected that Blacks were beaten and broken by bondage and accustomed to act full of folly and from fright fostered by the slave system. . . . The position at issue evokes an image of African Americans, bound by bondage, as mere puppets dangling from strings controlled by hands above their heads."[37] Like Williams, I am concerned with contesting the idea that African American resistance to enslavement was principally reactive, that modes of resistance arose in direct response and as foils to modes of white oppression. Indeed, Adam Bledsoe has gone so far to say that "more than simply a reaction to slavery and non-being, marronage was perhaps one of the most creative and emergent methods of life-building found in the modern world."[38] Instead, while marronage begins as a flight reaction to the bonds of slavery, the creative expressions of freedom that follow are not necessarily bound by liberal (white) ideologies and practices. While scholars of US slavery and African American literature have significantly complicated such a simplified idea about geographic imaginaries of freedom, marronage remains elusive in studies of this work and is the feature I attend to with sustained interest. Christina Sharpe asks, in the wake of but always perpetual present of transatlantic slavery, "How can we think (and rethink and rethink) care laterally, in the register of the intramural, in a different relation than that of the violence of the state?"[39] I take her question as one way to begin privileging marronage as a form of radically lateral sociality over a mostly longitudinal reaction to subjugation from above. It is both at once but should not be overdetermined by the latter. It is in and from the intramural space of that reaction that novel ways of living, being, and caring via marronage emerge.

Beyond Emancipation thus emphasizes, to return to the epigraph by Fred Moten and Stefano Harney that frames this introduction, what maroons know about possibility outside of received geographical and temporal refrains, and what they reveal, if we learn to read as I am arguing here, to attune ourselves to the lower frequencies decoupled from normative time and space, about possibility outside a limited understanding of the meanings and potentialities of Black freedom. Marronage reveals novel forms of subversion of white liberalism as possible or aspirational and also sustains nonnormative forms of belonging and freedom over and against assimilation and integration through state-sponsored legal emancipation. Black liberatory practices, epitomized by the self-liberation of maroons and their rejection of the system of slavery and the national regime that enables it, threaten to undermine the overarching logics and ideologies of liberalism, capitalism, and settler colonialism—that is, the very foundation of the United States and the liberal philosophy upon which it is based.

Marronage ultimately disputes the supposed coherence of liberalism as a political philosophy, ideology, and sociopolitical system, often contesting and disavowing even an aspirational liberalism like that frequently espoused by much of the mainstream abolitionist movement and its emphasis on moral suasion and sentimentalized refrains about the cruelty of slavery. The mobility exhibited by runaway enslaved people who fled north via what came to be known as the Underground Railroad has been comported into affirming a teleological narrative about possible trajectories of freedom. In essence, this narrative creates the appearance of those wrongfully denied liberal subjecthood valiantly striking out in search of it. Marronage, however, does not comport neatly with ideologies of assimilation, integration, emancipation, and aspirational citizenship or civil rights. This book insists that the recovery of the possibilities afforded by a serious consideration of marronage in African American literature is difficult but necessary.

Each of the major writers *Beyond Emancipation* focuses on—Frederick Douglass, Harriet Jacobs, Martin R. Delany, and Harriet Beecher Stowe—addressed the issue of writing about marronage for a majority-white reading public in different ways but also acknowledged readership outside that group in significant ways. Douglass, for example, tempers his only work of fiction, the novella *The Heroic Slave* (1852), by having it narrated by a white man to another white man, and much of the action in the story is also seen and interpreted through the eyes of a sympathetic white character, Mr. Listwell.[40] Madison Washington, the story's protagonist, tells this character of his five years of marronage but does not provide many details. What Douglass knows about possibilities for freedom via marronage remains elusive, concealed within Washington's statement that he lived for "five long years" "sustained by the promise that my good Susan [his wife] would meet me in the pine woods at least once a week."[41] How his wife contributed to his sustenance and concealment is never made clear, nor are any details provided about how he managed to survive for so long. The length of time thus becomes the focal point, and readers are left to understand that at least for a time Washington preferred this life to a life of enslavement. The horrors of slavery are amplified by his inclusion of this experience, and, at the same time, readers are presented with a possibility for Black self-determination and moments of autonomy that do not depend on the benevolence of a Mr. Listwell as representative of sentimental abolitionism. It is only once Washington is back under the control of the slave system that his insurrectionary plan takes full shape, suggesting that slavery creates the conditions for revolt, while marronage may also create alternative conditions for freedom that do not necessarily require recourse to further involvement with the slave state. By reading *The Heroic Slave* and pausing to analyze its representations of marronage, the idea emerges that marronage interrupts emancipation both as a historical event and as a conceptual framework for apprehending the struggle for Black freedom in the United States through literary analysis.

Harriet Jacobs wrote her narrative, *Incidents in the Life of a Slave Girl* (1861), under a pseudonym ("Linda Brent"), and it was edited by the well-known white abolitionist author and activist Lydia Maria Child.[42] Jacobs also changed the names of all the characters in the story to avoid, for her own safety and that of those still enslaved in the area, implicating the actual people involved. For much of the text's history, readers and scholars alike assumed that Child was the real author of the narrative and that it was, therefore, fictional. Jacobs's seven years spent in the tiny garret space above her grandmother's shed seemed to many a fantastical tale rather than a possible reality, more like a hyperbolic abolitionist rhetorical strategy for arguing against the tyranny of slavery than a true story of creative resistance through a form of what I read as marronage as stillness. So careful had Jacobs and Child been that it took until 1981 for enough evidence to be analyzed by the late historian and Jacobs biographer Jean Fagan Yellin to prove that Jacobs herself actually composed the narrative.[43] When Jacobs writes directly to a newspaper on the subject of slavery, as we will see in chapter 3, she also uses a pseudonym. Once again, the potentialities of marronage are hinted at rather than drawn out in their fuller complexity, which is what I attempt to do through my textual interpretations.

Unlike Douglass and Jacobs, Martin Delany is more explicitly radical in his presentation of an alternative to assimilation into white society or the creation of a Black society built on liberal principles. There is, after all, a reason why his serialized novel *Blake; or, The Huts of America* is not quite a canonical work outside African American literary studies and only reappeared in print during the height of the civil rights movement in the United States as the issue of Black self-determination entered the foreground of conversations about freedom on a national level.[44] Since then, critical attention to *Blake* has increased, but it remains mostly absent from a normative American literary canon. Like David Walker's *Appeal* (1831) and Henry Highland Garnet's "An Address to the Slaves of the United States of America" (1843),[45] *Blake* makes no apologies to white society and asks nothing of it. Instead, it articulates a vision of a hemispheric Black republic with, like postrevolutionary Haiti, the total illegality of slavery at its core. Delany makes no effort to disguise what he sees as the need for violence in achieving this end. Even so, we remain left with a text that is possibly unfinished; we do not know whether the insurrection of the titular character, Henry Blake, was carried out or whether or not it was successful. We do not and cannot know what reality manifested. The last chapter we have ends with the plan being set into motion. Readers are left to ponder this unknown and sit with that discomfort and ambiguity, with a sense of normative time and narrative disrupted, interrupted, and fragmented by maroon temporality of a perpetual present and unsettling futurity.

Even before *Dred*, which explicitly deals with maroons, Stowe's *Uncle Tom's Cabin* (1852) briefly raises the possibility of marronage but dismisses it in keeping with the white abolitionist strategy of using marronage as a sentimental rhetorical device aimed at garnering sympathy for the plight of the enslaved, who would consider life in the swamps preferable to a life on the plantation.[46] In a scene later in the book on Simon Legree's Louisiana plantation, the characters Cassy and Emmeline, long brutalized and sexually violated by Legree, take to planning their escape. In her desperation, Emmeline tells Cassy, "I'd be willing to live in the swamps, and gnaw the bark from trees. I an't afraid of snakes! I'd rather have one near me than him [Legree]."[47] The elder Cassy, however, warns her that "there have been a good many here of your opinion . . . but you couldn't stay in the swamps,—you'd be tracked by the dogs, and brought back, and then—then—."[48] Stowe, via Emmeline and Cassy, acknowledges the existence and practice of marronage in the swamps but does not present it is a realistic or sustainable possibility for freedom-seeking, even if temporary. Something similar will occur in *Dred*. In Stowe's imagination, at least in this text, only flight to and arrival in the North can achieve freedom for enslaved people. Only with the help of benevolent white actors, the logic goes, could enslaved people envision "true" freedom on the horizon of possibility. The same ultimately occurs in *Dred*, as Dred is killed and his maroon encampment destroyed, setting the remaining characters on the familiar, canonized route to freedom along the waypoints of the Underground Railroad. Stowe uses marronage to represent the plight of the runaway and to warn against the increasingly urgent possibility of violence if slavery is not done away with as a nationalized institution, but she is unable or unwilling to see possibilities beyond that even though maroons pervade her novel.

All of the Black writers under consideration here wrote against the normativized, sectionalized geography of freedom and unfreedom as apprehended through the logic of the Underground Railroad and the need for benevolent white actors to intercede on behalf of the enslaved. This triumphalist abolitionist narrative submerges white Northerner complicity in slavery via the Fugitive Slave Law and through production and commerce indelibly marked and propped up by slave labor all the way up to the Civil War and through the exploitative laws and labor practices that followed. This narrative others and demonizes the South as the morally bankrupt, greedy place from which slavery was established and maintained, further reinforcing the South-to-North trajectory to freedom so crucial to northern political interests.[49] The critic Jennifer Rae Greeson usefully illuminates the ways that a concept of "American literature" and by extension white American identity formed in large part through founding literature in opposition to the South as a geographical and social other. African American writers contest this official, national narrative of place and politics, thereby contesting how white abolitionists imagined emancipation in the context of US liberal democracy. In hindsight, Northern white abolitionists could congratulate themselves after legal emancipation for having developed and driven the prevailing narrative about that history, but maroons throw the stability and ostensible inevitability of that history into question.

This logic about white benevolence has contributed to slave narratives (a problematic genre convention retrofitted onto a strikingly diverse array of African American textual production) like Douglass's and Jacobs's being long-heralded as a starting point for the study of African American literature.[50] Carla Peterson has noted the problematic nature of Frederick Douglass's *Narrative* (1845) and Harriet Jacobs's *Incidents in the Life of a Slave Girl* being understood as metonymic for nineteenth-century African American literature. While this generic and temporal oversimplification has been challenged by critics like Vincent Carretta, the fact remains that the more mainstream study of African American literature, particularly in the popular imagination, exhibits an ongoing attachment to the slave narrative and its construction as the originary genre of an African American tradition of writing.[51] The shape of these narratives, heavily influenced by white editorial hands, presents the enslaved as unfree and voiceless in the South but free and heard (via the publication of the narratives and abolitionist circuit speeches) in the North. William L. Andrews, Robert B. Stepto, and James Olney are responsible for some of the foundational work on early Black autobiography that laid the groundwork for studying it as a body of autobiography and literature in its own right.[52] The narrative about these narratives was replicated and reified over time in the study of African American literature, ossifying for too long this limited way of reading and understanding Black literature like slave narratives and often ignoring more than a century of African American writing that precedes those narratives. Through the alternative reading practices that I am arguing African American writers reveal to us via marronage and that I am explicating in this book, we can uncover a fuller and more accurate sense of how these writers themselves understood the geographies, landscapes, and politics of freedom and unfreedom in the pre–Civil War period. This way, new, noncanonical readings of these touchstone texts of African American literature can be realized, readings that center Black writing, thinking, philosophy, and politics—readings that enable us to know something of the possibilities of marronage. Those readings make up the rest of this book.

The first chapter, "Swamp Things," focuses on the longest and most well-known representation of maroons and marronage in nineteenth-century American literature: Stowe's *Dred: A Tale of the Great Dismal*

Swamp. I interrogate Stowe's detailed depictions, suggesting that we must first understand the text as one in which representations of marronage are mediated through the perspective and articulation of white voices explicitly deployed by a white writer to garner white sympathy for the abolitionist cause. From this analysis emerges a clearer sense of how delimited white understandings of marronage were in contradistinction to the horizons of possibility opened by a study that privileges the Black experiences and perspectives explored in the subsequent chapters. Further, I focus the lens of marronage especially on how attentiveness to Black agency, autonomy, community building, resistive practices, and socialities leads to the emergence of possibilities for freedom that might be explored but are foreclosed by the boundaries of white understandings of what Black freedom(s) can look like. By pausing with these moments, this chapter closely examines representations of and gestures toward marronage, asking what we can make of the novel's interplay between maroon, Black, and poor, white worlds as imbricated in the pre–Civil War South's landscapes of freedom and unfreedom. *Dred* intimates ways that freedom could be provisional for poorer white characters and Southerners with antislavery leanings thanks to the system of chattel slavery and evokes the possibility of an interracial, interclass, and intersectional coalition-based politics of sentiment and action as a weapon against nationalized enslaver interests. It makes linkages between maroons, poor white people, and white Southern abolitionists that this chapter attempts to reckon with as potentially radical but also deeply problematic and reflective of Stowe's positionality as a white writer imagining Black experiences.

Chapter 2, "Beyond Revolt," argues that Delany's serialized novel *Blake; or, The Huts of America* focuses primarily on an individual enslaved male hero even while it elucidates how marronage is enabled by community and social relations and complex, intertwined geographies within the plantation landscape and the circum-Atlantic world. This chapter shows how marronage reveals alternative freedoms made possible by the maroon's mobility, adaptability, avoidance of detection, and survival strategies. Delany's protagonist demonstrates no interest in assimilation, integration, or reliance on the state for emancipation. Blake's notion of civil rights does not comport with the state's—especially in the context post–Fugitive Slave Law and post–Dred Scott case decision that Black people had no rights bound to be respected by the state in the form of individual actors and juridical maneuvering. The chapter ultimately shows how *Blake*—by virtue of being an unfinished work, the planned insurrection in the story never yet begun—allows us a window into freedom in perpetual process and becoming, into a temporally complex assemblage of self- and community-affirming Black resistant practices that can be valuably considered as marronage.

The third chapter, "Toward Stillness," interrogates what happens if we imagine Harriet Jacobs—or Linda Brent, her pseudonym in *Incidents in the Life of a Slave Girl*—as a maroon during her seven years famously immobilized and concealed in the garret above her grandmother's shed as well as in the events leading up to that concealment in the narrative. I argue that doing so is both accurate and generative, while illustrating that *Incidents* is pervaded by representations of all kinds of maroons and practices of marronage, expanding our understanding of marronage to include stillness along with the mobility examined in the previous chapter. I demonstrate how Jacobs even further complicates more traditional understandings of maroons, expanding in particular on the ways Black women played a role in enabling and sustaining marronage, especially forms of short-term marronage wherein maroons remained in close proximity to the places of enslavement they had fled and employed stillness as a resistive strategy. Through careful, deliberate attention to marronage in *Incidents*, this chapter identifies a constellation of alternative tactics and forms of nonliberal freedom recognized by Jacobs and locates these within the broader discourse on freedom and unfreedom throughout early and pre–Civil War African American literature with which this book is concerned overall. *Incidents* suggests that spaces of marronage are imbued with nonmaterial resources like the hopes, fears, aspirations, memories, desires, and epistemes of enslaved people—particularly of enslaved women. From these spaces of marronage, from the maroons who created and inhabited them, and from Jacobs's representation of them, there arise ways of being and knowing that are overlooked when critical focus remains attached to an imagined political and geographical trajectory that locates unfreedom in the South and freedom in the North or Canada. In approaching Jacobs's text in this way, we come to realize that *Incidents* is not just a text that exceptionalizes the individual experiences of its narrator (and author) but rather one that links those experiences with(in) a network of maroon activities and subject positions oriented toward alternative possibilities for freedom.

Chapter 4, "Emancipation, Interrupted," reads Frederick Douglass's novella *The Heroic Slave* for fissures in the text's otherwise overt emphasis on Madison Washington's individual Black revolutionary exceptionalism. In so doing, I argue that the text's representations of marronage unsettle the possibility of Black freedom via emancipation and integration within the United States and ultimately challenge the coherence of liberalism as an organizing sociopolitical logic. I show how the story poses a direct challenge to the notion that African Americans could depend upon recourse to the state for freedom as emancipation, instead offering possibilities that contest official, juridical, state-sponsored means of achieving freedom and even locate those possibilities outside of the United States. I argue that the liberatory practices of marronage usually underacknowledged in readings of the text in fact offer insight into freedom-making decoupled from teleologies of legal manumission and emancipation, thereby interrupting narratives of liberal freedom that frame Black textual and historical progress as linear and beholden to the logics of state-sponsored freedom. *The Heroic Slave* sometimes represents episodes of marronage as waypoints on the path toward violent revolt rather than as themselves moments of possibility that might be explored on their own terms, but this chapter shows how these can be generatively paused at to explore how they function within a greater landscape of insurgent and resistive freedom-seeking practices. The chapter illustrates how these episodes serve as interruptions and irruptions worth stopping at for a glimpse into alternative freedom-seeking tactics embedded within a more conventional and recognizable narrative arc. I explore how they reveal the ways attention to marronage in the archive of African American literature illuminates novel possibilities for resistance, survival, and freedom-making. By doing so, the chapter creates space for further and deeper exploration into nonliberal and illiberal practices of freedom-seeking and -making through marronage.

Marronage was a difficult choice in a spectrum of choices, but it was still a *choice*—an expression of self-determination, autonomy, and agency—and one that many enslaved people in the United States made at one point or another in their lives. There were many more acts of and attempts at short-term marronage than there were successful escapes to the North and Canada. We must reckon with that fact if we want to grasp the complexity with which African American authors were representing marronage as part of the bigger discourse on freedom and unfreedom in pre–Civil War literature. What *Beyond Emancipation* does not do, and in fact argues strongly against, is suggest that the relative, contingent freedoms gained through marronage and by maroons are somehow analogous to those accorded to legally emancipated Black people—they are most certainly not. But they are something other than legal enslavement and legal freedom thought as equality before the law; they sit somewhere in between these subject positions and state-recognized subjectivities, troubling and complicating, as Neil Roberts has suggested in *Freedom as Marronage*, a dichotomous basis for understanding African American history and literature through those two axes of apprehension. They exist in a space in fundamental tension with white hegemonic sovereignty, highlighting the ways that privileging legal freedom is another way of disavowing inequalities built into the US sociopolitical landscape and founding documents. This book attempts to avoid arguing that alternative freedoms through marronage are *better* but instead contends that they are both different and significant in the ways they not only contest enslavement but also reveal novel ways of thinking about freedom as a process of being and becoming through Black-centered outlooks.

In resisting the imposition of hermeneutics that have sometimes submerged the theoretical work nineteenth-century African American writers have done in articulating forms of freedom and belonging outside white authority, *Beyond Emancipation* creates space, to the extent that such a thing is possible, for exploration and speculation about marronage as freedom to emerge from literary texts, registering the African American writers under consideration as speaking to us in extreme tension with dominant white, Western philosophies of freedom in the tradition of liberal thought.[53] My approach is influenced by the work of David Kazanjian in his analysis of nineteenth-century letters written by Black settlers in Liberia to their former enslavers, friends, and family. Kazanjian describes this approach in the following way:

> By reading apparently descriptive texts as theoretical texts that speculate upon their own conjunctures, in addition to describing or witnessing them, I have been able to discern some profound challenges to classically liberal conceptions of freedom, conceptions that often go unquestioned and thus are perpetuated in work that attends principally to the questions of who did what, where, and when. These include, for instance, meliorist conceptions like the idea that movement from slavery to freedom is ideally progressive and developmental, the idea that subjects willfully desire and thus volitionally seek to be free, the idea of the individual will as such, the idea that subjects ought to have a desire they know and seek to realize or that citizenship is a desirable expression of freedom.[54]

Beyond Emancipation indexes the limitations of a history of freedom via textual selection that begins with white abolitionists like William Lloyd Garrison and Lydia Maria Child and still impacts the ways we read even the most canonical of nineteenth-century African American writers. My project in what follows is animated by Angela Davis's contention that "the history of Black Literature provides . . . a much more illuminating account of the nature of freedom, its extent and limits, than all the philosophical discourses on this theme in the history of Western society."[55] *Beyond Emancipation* insists that writers like Frederick Douglass, Harriet Jacobs, and Martin Delany were engaged in philosophical and critical theorizing of Black freedoms in their writings about and depictions of marronage.

Chapter One

Swamp Things

> There is a coal-black Angel
> With a thick Afric lip,
> And he dwells (like the hunted and harried)
> In a swamp where the green frogs dip.
> But his face is against a City
> Which is over a bay of the sea,
> And he breathes with a breath that is blastment,
> And dooms by a far decree.
>
> —Herman Melville, "The Swamp Angel"

When white writers in the nineteenth century depicted maroons and the swamps they inhabited, they usually did so in one of three ways: as pitiful, as romanticized, or as threatening.[1] In "The Swamp Angel," Herman Melville does all three. The Angel, "like the hunted and harried," inhabits a swamp full of dangerous creatures.[2] He evokes great fear in "the City," which white people live in and believe that they control, and Melville heavily romanticizes this aspect using Christian tropes about avenging angels. Like Harriet Beecher Stowe, Melville in part invokes marronage to serve as a warning to Southern society and to suggest that, should its white population not free the enslaved Black people who live among them and find true meaning in Christ, they may face dire, violent consequences. In the poem, the angel Michael "(The white man's seraph . . .)" does not come to their aid; rather, he flees their societal turpitude "to the Angel over the sea."[3] The title of this chapter has a twofold meaning: First, it evokes the fact that white writers "thingified" enslaved people, particularly maroons, vacating them of complex subjectivity by using them as aesthetic and rhetorical devices to argue against slavery. Second, it broadly evokes the "things" that occurred in swamps and were represented by white authors but with marked limitations—things as considerations and subjects of study for those authors and, differently, for us today.

The novel as form and genre can be considered inherently hostile to marronage, which is, by nature, an always ongoing and open-ended process rather than something definitive, conclusive, and fixed. This leads to some of the tensions and limitations in the way maroons and marronage are deployed by Stowe as characters and tropes—tensions that play out in different ways for all of the writers who operated within the same white-dominated publishing and print public spheres. At the levels of both form and content, then, possibilities for freedom are fundamentally constrained in the novel. If one of the functions of the American novel has been to index the trajectory of an outsider figure into the supposed benevolence of liberal subjecthood, access to such a path is preconditionally foreclosed for the maroon. In Stowe's novelistic world, maroons must be unmarooned in order to become legible within the borders of the novel as a form for liberal subject making. That is, they must become unambiguous, either slave or free—or they must die. Such irreconcilable tension thus characterizes *Dred* from its very outset. In this chapter, I aim to locate and privilege Black subjectivity where it has often been disavowed, to address these tensions in order to begin the work of recovering and expanding the contours of Black life from within the bounds of the white abolitionist imaginary.

Harriet Beecher Stowe's *Dred* marks a significant departure from her rhetorical and didactic strategies for militating against slavery in *Uncle Tom's Cabin* (1852), which depended heavily upon sentimentalism and moral suasion as ways to garner sympathy from white readers for the plight of the enslaved. As Robert Levine and others have noted, Stowe took seriously the criticism leveled at *Uncle Tom's Cabin* by none other than African American writers and abolitionists like Martin Delany and Frederick Douglass, namely on the issue of her endorsement of colonization of Liberia as a solution to the nation's slavery problem. According to Levine, "Stowe's change of mind on Liberia is not an isolated instance of her willingness to attend to black writings and views, and it is precisely her effort to comprehend such views that makes *Dred* more black-centered, revolutionary, and morally challenging than *Uncle*

Tom's Cabin."[4] Levine's careful analysis of the African American presence in *Dred* has helped us better understand the sources from which and people from whom Stowe drew in an effort to understand, to the extent that could be possible, the experiences of previously enslaved people. This work has gone a long way toward revealing the inspirations behind Stowe's Black characters but has not accounted in kind for how we might make sense out of her representations of Black-centered spaces and the unique relationships Black people—particularly maroons—had to Southern spaces more broadly conceived. Levine's points about the connection Stowe explicitly makes between Dred and Nat Turner, and between Dred and Denmark Vesey, are convincing: "Sympathetic to and aligned with the prophetic Nat Turner, the ultimate African American presence in the novel, Stowe in *Dred* anticipates, promotes, and helps to supply the terms for understanding the bloodshed of the Civil War."[5] Instead of focusing on thwarted Black revolutionary potential, however, this chapter dwells with Stowe's representations of the swamps, of maroons, and of acts of marronage in order to parse the limitations and possibilities inherent in her text. My goal is not to locate and discuss possible sources Stowe drew from to craft these depictions but instead to treat them as novelistic and part of her aesthetic and abolitionist project, with a focus on the world of the text itself.

While still a novel deeply characterized by the trappings of racial essentialism found in Stowe's previous work, *Dred*'s direct engagement with the subject of maroons and marronage was undoubtedly radical in the context of 1850s antislavery literature, especially that produced by white writers. Stowe was not alone in introducing more revolutionary fervor into her antislavery politics during this particular time period. Martha Schoolman calls the 1850s the "Maroon's Moment" in abolitionist literary discourse, arguing that "during the period that spanned John Brown's ascendancy and the start of the Civil War, white radical abolitionists discovered in the maroon an object of imaginative identification to guide their increasingly counternationalist and revolutionary conceptions of what would have to be done to end slavery in the United States."[6] In a sense, maroons function as the apotheosis of Black-centered ideologies. Self-exiled, self-determined, and largely operating autonomously, they are affirmations of Black collectivity and Black life within the material spaces of the very system that is designed at every level to negate Black humanity. Literary and historical marronage were affirmations of the enduring power of Black life in a system categorically committed to Black social death.

Dred's title can feel misleading: the maroon and titular tragic hero Dred is not a major character; he haunts the text, its characters, and the events that unfold throughout, stalking the margins of the story the same way he does the margins of the plantation landscape as it intersects with the ever-ominous Great Dismal Swamp. He does not appear until part two of the text, nearly two hundred pages into the six-hundred-page novel. In part, this chapter centers Dred in its analysis in a way that Stowe does not, making marronage—rather than the insurrection Dred plans that never comes to pass—the aesthetic focal point of analysis. I pause at depictions of maroons and marronage to consider these moments as interruptions of the conventional South-to-North narrative trajectory taken by slave narratives and by most white authors who portrayed enslaved people's quests for freedom. *Dred* links marronage with violent revolt, much like, as we will see, *The Heroic Slave* and *Blake* do, but, as with those works, we can read with attention to marronage on its own terms, separating it from associations with insurrection and counternationalisms that inevitably elide possibilities for freedom that do not require concerted violence or white, state intervention.

Representing and actually promoting a successful insurrection of the enslaved in the United States is beyond the horizon of possibility or desire for Stowe, as it is indeed for the vast majority of white abolitionist writers and thinkers other than John Brown. Jared Hickman has gone so far as to say that "the advent of the ontologically othered Afro-Atlantic slave rebel" came to "signify in the cosmos of globality as an affront to and limit on Euro-Christians' attempt to become the gods of this world."[7] The stakes of creating a sympathetic Black revolutionary hero, whose tactics were indelibly bound up in circum-Atlantic resistant maroon practices, were therefore about as high as can be imagined, especially for someone like Stowe, whose identity as an abolitionist writer was inextricably bound up with her identity as a white Christian and whose audience was also circum-Atlantic. One exception might appear to be Herman Melville in his novella *Benito Cereno* (1855),[8] but even there readers narratively witness the aftermath of a successful revolt, not the depiction of its unfolding.[9] In the story, Captain Amasa Delano and his ship, the *Bachelor's Delight*, come upon a Spanish slaver, the *San Dominick*, floating off the coast of Chile in apparent distress. Delano offers his assistance to the ship's captain, Benito Cereno, attended constantly by Babo, an enslaved Black man. Despite increasing signs that something is seriously awry aboard the ship, Delano does not suspect the shocking truth until Cereno attempts to dive aboard his boat as the men are returning to their ship. Readers, too, inhabiting Delano's viewpoint as the story progresses, never suspect that an insurrection had occurred aboard the *San Dominick* and that the enslaved were now in charge and dictating Benito Cereno's actions. In hindsight, the signs seem obvious, but the astonishment for first-time readers evokes the unthinkability of revolt by the enslaved as it was felt viscerally by Delano and would have been by the story's largely white reading audience as well. Whereas revolt generally marks an end point for enslaved resistance—or at least this is the way it is conceived of by white writers using it rhetorically and aesthetically as a warning against slavery—marronage evokes the possibilities that exist without attachment to a preconceived end point, almost always meaning death for the organizer and all presumed to be involved. In 1859, radical abolitionist James Redpath, whose words about marronage, shared by a formerly enslaved man, began this book, summed up nicely the unthinkability of enslaved insurrection in the minds of white readers:

> All other perils are understood. Fire upon land, or storm at sea, wrapping mortals in a wild or watery shroud, may be readily imagined. Pestilence walking abroad in the city, making the sultry air noisome and heavy, hushing the busy throng, aweing into silence heated avarice, and glooming the very haunts of civilization as if they were charnel-houses, can be quickly understood. But the appalling terror of a slave revolt, made instinct with life, and stunning as it pervades the community—the undescribed and indescribable horror which fills and sways every bosom as the word is whispered along the streets, or borne quickly from house to house, or speeded by fleetest couriers from plantation to plantation—"an insurrection"—"an insurrection"—must be *felt* and *seen* to be realized.[10]

Stowe imagines the fictional Dred as the son of the actual historical figure Denmark Vesey, an enslaved man from South Carolina who was implicated in the planning of a mass insurrection in 1822.[11] Vesey's insurrection was thwarted, as Dred's will also be because of his death, setting the stage for the fellow maroons in his swamp encampment, called Engedi, to head north in search of freedom. While no insurrection occurs within *Dred*, the threat of one haunts the text as a possibility, one designed to excite fear in the white imagination and further Stowe's argument that failing to abolish slavery will result in dire, violent consequences in the US South.

This chapter asks in part what *Dred* accomplishes by explicitly and directly depicting maroons in the Great Dismal Swamp, with the understanding that the novel must be read as one in which representations of marronage remain mediated by the perspective and articulation of white voices. Nevertheless, we can begin here by approaching the novel as I do all of the others in this book: through the lens of marronage and with particular attention to it in all of its multifaceted forms. From this emerges a clearer sense of how delimited white understandings of marronage were in contradistinction to the horizons of possibility opened by a study that privileges the Black experiences, perspectives, and aesthetic representations. Further, we can focus the lens of marronage especially on how attentiveness to Black agency, autonomy, community building, resistive practices, and socialities leads to the emergence of possibilities for freedom that might be explored but are foreclosed by the boundaries of white understandings of what Black freedom(s) can look like. By pausing with these moments, we can identify representations of and gestures toward marronage, tracing their trajectory and development across the story and ultimately focusing on maroons as a throughline for analysis and privileging a concerted focus on Black experiences and points of view.

I argue in this chapter that Stowe's depictions of maroons, a maroon community, and marronage in *Dred* work to elucidate the multifaceted self- and community-affirming potential of these peoples and practices as they relate to the causes of abolition, liberation, and Black self-determination from a white perspective though still informed by Black thought. By not entirely reducing marronage to its possibilities for actuating large-scale revolt and potential political autonomy, Stowe allows for a surprisingly nuanced exploration of the radical, subversive, and at times interracial and interclass potentialities, socialities, and collectivities manifested through these self-exiled people and their alternate community formations in the swamp and at the margins of the plantation zone. This depiction provides a sense of how freedom for enslaved people was understood by white people as an unstable and provisional concept in the United States during the 1850s. By demonstrating also how freedom could be provisional for poorer white characters and Southerners with antislavery leanings thanks to the system of chattel slavery, Stowe evokes the possibility of an interracial, interclass, and intersectional coalition-based politics of sentiment and action as a weapon against nationalized, elite enslavers' interests. She makes linkages between maroons, poor whites, and white Southern abolitionists to suggest that slavery degrades the entirety of the Southern social order, arguing to her readership that slavery consumes everything and everyone even tangentially connected to it. By doing so, she often submerges or sidelines the specificity of Black resistance to oppression, and so I move to recuperate that specificity and to show how and why its elision fit into the normative white abolitionist project.

Marronage as Interruption

Maroons chose a life of desperate peril in the insect- and reptile-infested morass of the Dismal Swamp, with the ever-present threat of being legally murdered as outlaws by any citizen, over life as a chattel slave. Such a choice flies in the face of proslavery claims that enslaved people were treated well, preferred life in servitude and as Christians, and did not desire to escape or obtain their freedom. Stowe capitalizes on this fact, and the wild, exotic, threatening, but intensely captivating Dismal Swamp comes to serve in *Dred* as a repository—a site of projection—for racially and religiously inflected fears, fantasies, and desires that exceed the parameters of normativized social, racial, and class relations in the white abolitionist imaginary.[12] The swamp's presence—along with that of Dred and the other maroon inhabitants—also exerts a complicated influence on the surrounding area and people, Black and white, free and enslaved, which Stowe explores throughout the novel. Maroons and marronage have the potential to interrupt the conventional, expected narrative progression of stories about enslaved people and their escapes from bondage in the South to nominal freedom in the North. In *The Heroic Slave*, Madison Washington's five-year marronage in the Dismal Swamp forestalls the historical fiction's teleological drive toward its end point: the slave-ship rebellion that we know from history Washington will ultimately carry out. Marronage interrupts the ideological coherency of Douglass's story through its interruptions of the narrative itself. And, as we will see in chapter 3, in *Incidents in the Life of a Slave Girl*, Linda Brent's seven years in the garret also interrupt the geographical progression of what, by 1861, had come to be expected of the fugitive slave narrative genre in the United States. Willingly and purposefully immobilized for seven years as a maroon, Brent hides in plain sight while family and friends work out plans for her eventual escape to the North.

But *Dred* differs from both of these texts in that it represents marronage directly and at some length—though carefully never using the word *maroon*, like Edmund Jackson and Thomas Wentworth Higginson did, which evoked the dreaded Black insurgents in the Caribbean. It takes marronage and maroons up as object and as theme, featuring a titular maroon protagonist and a maroon community in the Dismal Swamp complete with separate dwellings, agricultural plots, and hidden entrances and paths like those described by Sylviane Diouf from the historical record. In *Dred* too, however, marronage—specifically the presence and appearances of the maroon Dred—interrupt the text in a variety of ways that tie back to the idea of marronage as excess and thus often exceed perceived boundaries of genre, narrative, geography, space, race, and class. We must, however, reconfigure our reading practices in order to see things this way. By doing so, the particular possibilities and limitations of Stowe's ideas about freedom related to marronage come into clearer focus.

In simple terms, *Dred* might be best summed up as an experimentation with the tragic plantation romance genre, with two significant legal cases (based on actual events) serving as the basis for Stowe's examination of slavery's insidious destruction of the Southern social order. Her two didactic objectives in *Dred* are to continue to show the humanity of Black people, as she had in *Uncle Tom's Cabin*, and to reveal the extent to which slavery threatened the idea of whiteness by pitting enslavers and nonslaveholding, poorer white people against one another. This, by extension, threatened white society understood as a coherent whole. The main storyline follows Nina Gordon and her life at the plantation Canema in North Carolina, the estate of her father, the brutal Colonel Gordon. Her enslaved, Black half-brother, Harry, lives there as well, largely running the estate, and finds himself frequently in conflict with the even more brutal Tom, Nina and Harry's white half-brother. Nina receives suitors and becomes most enamored with local attorney Edward Clayton, portrayed as a "progressive" Southern enslaver who treats enslaved people with kindness and experiments with teaching them to read and write, much to the dismay and suspicion of the surrounding planter community. His antislavery views are well known and function in contradistinction to his local judge father's constitutional originalist views that, while he does not support slavery, lead him to make legal decisions that continue to uphold its power dynamics. Significantly, though, Clayton does not emancipate his enslaved people; that is not the route to freedom he imagines for them, but rather one in which his tutelage and benevolent guidance set them up to succeed in the context of a white society he imagines will someday integrate them. As readers, we are invited to see Clayton as a sympathetic character whose subversive ideas are worthy of our admiration. At the end of part 1 of the novel, Nina dies during a local cholera outbreak, and suddenly the storyline we thought would define the text fractures. The second half of the book focuses heavily on Clayton and his legal practices and also introduces the world of Dred and the swamp, bringing into orbit a cast of minor characters from various lots and stations who serve as ways for Stowe to explore Southern social relations as inflected by slavery and in tension with the strictures of the planation romance genre. These minor characters are in fact major players in the themes explored in part 2, the focus of this chapter.

Dred's liminal subject position as a maroon is reflected in the ways he momentarily becomes legible in the narrative before disappearing once again into the swamp. In his first two appearances to other characters, he lacks material form, a disembodied voice speaking from the shadows. The first time Dred appears to readers is in a scene where Harry is riding on horseback along a road bordering the swamp. Enslaved characters often take routes through the neighborhoods that border the swamp, for reasons that will soon become apparent. Dred has just been accosted by Tom, his half-brother, who demands that Harry tell him where he is going, which Harry refuses to do because Tom, Nina's ill-tempered and violent brother, does not own him. Tom strikes Harry in the face with a whip and threatens to purchase and sexually assault his enslaved wife who lives on another plantation nearby. Stowe cannily uses this scene to set up a moment that echoes and then revises Uncle Tom's brand of nonviolent noncompliance for the new rhetorical project at hand in this novel. Harry will not abide these threats and degradations without protest and his own threats of violence if need be, thus positioning him as a kind of radical foil to Uncle Tom—that is, until we meet Dred.

In this instance the maroon Dred—self-liberated and remaining that way, he says, by virtue of his rifle—interrupts Harry's "bitter cursing" at the violent humiliation he has just suffered at the hand of Tom Gordon, intervening in the narrative at a highly charged moment that comes to define the parameters of the dialectic in *Dred* whereby white characters and enslaved Black characters interact with one another. The terms of Dred's legibility to other characters are terms that he sets. Characters do not happen upon him; he appears to them when and where he chooses. He controls space and his embodied presence within it in ways that only a maroon can. For Dred, as for virtually any maroon, survival requires illegibility. Illegibility is a necessary precondition for the other characteristics we associate with maroons and maroon communities: namely, autonomy, agency, and self-determination. It is worth emphasizing why *illegible* is the most precise word to describe maroons, and what maroons must be, in the eyes of the slavocracy and of white society at large. Not just physically hidden or unseen, Dred's illegibility to the slavocracy renders him indecipherable and therefore unable to be *known* or *understood*. He exceeds the capacity of white imagination, to return to Redpath's excerpt above, one of the reasons Stowe cannot imagine or depict his full resistive potential, which threatens to push the limit of her white readership's actual tolerance for the idea of Black revolt. Dred uses the aura of mystery that surrounds him to his distinct advantage, and we can understand it in that way if we read against Stowe's aesthetic idealization for the traces of realism that undergird it. Dred maintains that aura partly intentionally and partly as a consequence of the way he must operate in relation to plantation society as he navigates through and between its landscapes, both material and perceptual.

Dred's second interruption comes during a lengthy camp meeting scene where, once again, we hear but do not see him, a disembodied voice this time seeming to emanate from the trees themselves as a metonym for nature and the natural world. The way the camp meeting is described and framed in the text makes his intervention into the meeting's discourse particularly charged. The camp meeting is a democratizing, carnivalesque affair in which, for a short time, racial and class divisions are to a certain extent temporarily suspended. This is not to say that enslaved people in attendance are free from the routine denigration and violence that characterizes their social station, but they are by and large allowed to attend and move about freely while there. As Anthony Kaye has noted, enslavers were often less apt to break with codes of civility and decorum in the company of their own, and thus at such a large-scale public event gave more leeway, and enslaved people took full advantage of this fact.[13] Clayton in particular expounds upon what he calls the "savage freedom" of the camp-meeting setting, championing the natural landscape of "flowers, festoons of vine . . . arches of green" and "underbrush, these dead limbs, these briers running riot over trees, sometimes choking and killing them."[14] Clayton goes on to compare the "savage freedom" and "grotesque growths" of this natural landscape to the "enthusiasms of the masses," declaring, "I reverence the people, as I do the woods, for the wild, grand freedom with which their humanity develops itself."[15]

This serves as a prime example of the problematic ways Stowe connects Black freedom and wilderness or wildness, playing into the trope of the "noble savage," and of the way she frequently submerges the specificities of Black resistive tactics and opportunities for freedom-seeking within situations that include white people and their own desires to escape the trappings of class and station that characterize the Southern social hierarchy. Her comparisons of the plights of poor white people to those of enslaved Black people read to us now as a form of deflection and whataboutism. For Stowe, however, they were a way to elicit sympathy from white people for other white people, across class and geographical lines. We might focus instead in this scene on Dred's disembodied, thunderous voice, which disrupts even the disordered order of the carnivalesque camp meeting. The disruption is auditory and also spatial and temporal.

Dred exists seemingly without physical form, everywhere and nowhere, as the crowd searches for the source of his ominous words. He invokes a sense of Christian and biblical time—tied closely to a sense of national time in the early formation of the United States—that recognizes a judgment day for all, suggesting that those who support slavery and seek that day with hope should instead fear it. He reconfigures the white Christian notion of salvation, implying as Melville did that those who support slavery are in fact not real Christians but people whose minds instead need conversion by Christ if they are to attain forgiveness for their earthly sins. This scene, then, interrupts the very foundations through which white Southerners perceive and order their world and their places within it. From it we glean a small sense of how Dred's position as a maroon creates a space of freedom from which he is able to "sermonize" himself, imposing his uninhibited speech on a gathering of white people in a way that would be otherwise impossible.

Suddenly, in the midst of the camp meeting, "every one was startled by a sound which seemed to come pealing down directly from the thick canopy of pines over the heads of the ministers," the voice of Dred exclaiming, "Woe unto you that desire the day of the Lord! To what end shall it be for you? The day of the Lord shall be darkness, and not light!"[16] His words echo the final lines of *Blake*, in which the enslaved cook Gopher Gondolier exclaims, "Woe be unto those whites, I say!,"[17] along with Melville's ominous warning that should enslavers fail to renounce slavery, Christianity may not save them. Dred soon retreats, and the camp meeting's reverie continues, but the interruption marks an intrusion into the otherwise balmy atmosphere of the event, shaking white meeting-goers out of the sense of communal comfort provided by prayer and their belief in salvation for themselves regardless of earthly actions. Readers are made to reckon with this interruption and discomfort, as well. It is an apt setting for Dred's intrusion, framed by Clayton's description of the wild landscape and "savage freedoms" it engenders, as problematic as that term is for us today. The meeting-goers, by setting up camp in the nearby vicinity of the swamp, have entered into Dred's domain, or at least a place where that domain overlaps with the landscape of the plantation zone and has the potential to interrupt it. The scene presents a striking instance of countersurveillance—of the typical, normative strictures of white social order being suddenly disturbed. Whereas the "planter gaze," following Rebecca Ginsburg's formulation, traditionally dominates seeing and interpreting the landscape, here Stowe reverses that gaze and Dred observers the gathering of enslavers without their seeing—and by extension interpreting or understanding—him.[18] Thus emerges a form of freedom through the maroon's reconfiguration of space and speech. Dred rails against slavery not from the northern speech circuit or abolitionist newspaper, but from within the ideological and geographical heart of slavery itself.

Dred again appears to Harry on his way home from the camp meeting, emerging on his own terms as a maroon as he approaches Harry's horse from behind and places a hand on the bridle. He speaks to Harry of the hypocrisy of the camp-meeting preachers, whom he calls "hunters of men, their hands red with blood of the poor, all seeking unto the Lord! Ministers who buy and sell us!"[19] By generalizing about the impacts of slavery on "the poor," Stowe, via Dred, brings poor white people as well as enslaved Black people into the sociopolitical consideration of slavery's impact on Southern life writ large. Harry agrees with Dred's assessment, and Dred continues to press him on his plans for a future course of action regarding his tenuous situation with his wife, Nina, and Tom. Dred warns him, "Now, hurry! Come to me, or he [Tom] will take thy wife for a prey!,"[20] but Harry does not yet fully understand the implications of Dred's warning. Here, though, the threat of rape appears as a catalyst for action on the part of the enslaved and their supporters both Black and white. This interruption, however, marks another moment in which Dred breaks the narrative momentarily out of its normative progression by stopping Harry and interjecting his alternative perspective on resistance and freedom-seeking into the story. From Dred's point of view from the swamps, Harry should end his servitude by self-exiling and joining Dred as a maroon as a way to save both himself and his wife—even if only temporarily. Harry appears increasingly convinced of the validity of this plan but remains in place so he can deal with the plantation's finances under Nina and with his wife's predicament.

Dred appears to Harry once more prior to the time when, ultimately, he will flee to the swamps after physically assaulting Tom. This time, Harry rides along the same "unfrequented path" where he had met Dred twice before, seeming desirous of another meeting, when Dred appears "standing silently, as if he had risen from the ground,"[21] a kind of "blooming idiosyncrasy,"[22] following Irène Mathieu and Monique Allewaert as a way of reclaiming wildness without attaching it to "noble savage" discourse. At this meeting, Dred speaks openly to Harry about the possibilities for violent revolt as a means for self-liberation and collective Black liberation, invoking the name of Nat Turner specifically and also of his father, Denmark Vesey. It is significant here that Stowe chooses the real historical figure of Denmark Vesey as Dred's father, as Vesey's planned rebellion never came to fruition. The gesture is at once radical and conservative, as readers familiar with Vesey's story may be put at some ease by the reference to an insurrection thwarted. Even so, readers are left to contend with Dred's desire to carry out what his father did not. Dred articulates here a point made earlier about the potency of the *fear* of slave revolt as a weapon against slavery. Harry fears that rising up will simply result in a "rush on to our own destruction," but Dred counters with an invocation of the Turner case: "Nat Turner—they killed him; but the fear of him almost drove them to set free their slaves! Yes, it was argued among them. They came within two or three votes of it in their assembly. A little more fear, and they would have done it. If my father had succeeded, the slaves in Carolina would be free to-day."[23] Dred understands a point that still needs to be articulated and reaffirmed in scholarship surrounding enslaved resistance today: that rebellions, conspiracies, and fear of both contributed in no uncertain terms to the goals of the abolitionist movement and to the driving of the nation to civil war over the question of slavery.[24] Fear, then, serves as a powerful tool when wielded by the maroon, a tool that can be used to interrupt the slavocracy's status quo in a variety of complex ways. As argued above, Stowe uses this fear as a way to argue that slavery should be ended by white people for their own protection and for the sake of their salvation as professed Christians. However, we can read this fear as a fear of the unknowability and unthinkability of maroon freedom that animates what often feel like paradoxical representations of marronage by white writers.

Marronage as Refuge

Dred's robust and varied cast of characters includes many whose subject positions exceed the limits of plantation-romance stereotypes or otherwise disrupt the conventional confines of those stereotypes with regard to stable, fixed positions of freedom and unfreedom in the slaveholding society of 1850s North Carolina. For poorer white characters like Abijah Skinflint and his family, the Cripps children under enslaved Old Tiff's care, the antislavery preacher Father Dickson, the slave catcher Ben Dakin with his pack of highly trained dogs, and even the upper-class, esteemed but openly abolitionist-leaning lawyer Edward Clayton, physical proximity to both the Dismal Swamp and its maroon inhabitants constitutes a threat to their whiteness and therefore unsettles their freedom in liberal terms, at least in the eyes of the slaveholding elite. The "Blackening" by Stowe of these characters and the spaces they inhabit leads to complications in the order of plantation-society social relations as they are organized around the constellating elements of space and race. Taken together, these situations reveal that, because of the constructedness of race and race's relationship to freedom, the presence of liminal maroon figures inhabiting and traversing liminal swamp spaces frustrates and complicates the concept of "freedom" itself. Though problematic because of the ways this can suggest that marronage can be carried out by white people or its subject position inhabited by them, it is nevertheless worth a further look because of how it draws the particularity of Black maroon practices into focus in ways that later chapters elaborate.

    Not much has been made of Stowe's depiction of poor whites, or "poor white trash," as they are frequently called in *Dred*, despite the fact that they play a substantial role in the narrative, far more so than in *Uncle Tom's Cabin*, where they are almost entirely absent in any significant sense. Allison Hurst has attempted to rectify this critical oversight, but where she sees Stowe uncritically participating in a long antebellum tradition of disparaging poor Southern whites as "lazy, shiftless, uninterested in culture and education, immoral, and oversexed," I see Stowe demonstrating an affinity between poor whites and Black maroons.[25] This affinity derives at its core, as I think Hurst aptly points out, from both groups' statuses as "masterless men" who occupy space outside the control of enslavers.[26] Closely examining this affinity provides more insight into how Stowe opens up possibilities for alternative Black freedoms but tempers them by connecting them to the plight and concerns of poor white characters.

Throughout the novel, members of the slaveholding elite disparage poor white characters. Even some enslaved characters, we are shown, look down upon them, particularly the indigent Cripps family. Nina's Aunt Nesbit believes that poor Southern whites would be better off enslaved, and she holds forth on this topic at length on several occasions. She subscribes to the essentialist, classist, and not-so-subtly racialized idea that, like those of African descent, poor whites are inherently unable to care for themselves and their children and elevate themselves in society through industry and hard work. The abject Cripps family has for some time "squatted," as Mrs. Nesbit says, "over in the pine woods, near the swamp,"[27] and proximity to known runaways and maroons, and to the swamp itself, inflects the way in which she describes and understands their character. They are, in her opinion, "all of them liars and thieves" who "always will steal from off the plantations, and corrupt the negroes, and get drunk, and everything else that's bad."[28]

In other words, Mrs. Nesbit accuses the Cripps—and poor whites in general—of the same kinds of things swamp-dwelling maroons like Dred and his compatriots are accused of throughout the novel and of which real, historical maroons were accused all the time: deception, thievery, and corruption of enslaved people still on the plantations. Poor whites and enslaved Black people lack access to the fertile grounds of crop production and extraction; instead, they inhabit the fluid and undesirable spaces that interfere with the logic of the white American capitalist project. To Aunt Nesbit's mind, poor whites are all the same and deserving of the same, as she sees it, "benevolent" fate: "O, I don't know that I know anything against this family [the Cripps] in particular; *but I know the whole race*. These squatters—I've known them ever since I was a girl in Virginia. . . . There isn't any help for them, unless, as I said before, they were made slaves; and then they could be kept decent" (emphasis mine).[29] As "a race" of interstitial figures who do not effectively "belong" and who do not exhibit the characteristics conventionally associated with whiteness in the context of Southern plantation society—property, education, refinement, virtue—Stowe suggests that the poor whites in *Dred* have more in common with maroons than with the likes of Mrs. Nesbit in the world of the text and according to its white characters. Because Stowe is so invested, as she was in *Uncle Tom's Cabin* and her larger oeuvre of antislavery writings, in arguing against slavery because of the ways it denigrates not only enslaved people but everyone involved, emphasis is drawn away from the centrality of Black experience and generalized to include white people with whom her readership could more readily connect. Of course, the fallacy of this comparison emerges from the realization that their situations remain otherwise incomparable. But understanding why Stowe makes these decisions helps us better understand white abolitionist tactics and motivations, and the expense at which they often came to the specific lived experience of Black people in the South.

Mrs. Nesbit's husband, Nina's Uncle John, takes the slavery-as-solution idea even further, all the while reinforcing the similarities in interstitial subject position between poor whites and maroons from the perspective of enslavers. According to John, "It's perfectly insufferable, what we proprietors have to bear from this tribe of creatures! . . . There ought to be hunting-parties got up to chase them down, and exterminate 'em, just as we do rats. It would be a kindness to them; the only thing you can do for them is to kill them."[30] Ratcheting down his rhetoric just a little, John concludes that "the government ought to pass laws—we will have laws, somehow or other,—and get them out of the state."[31] John's ideas, cruel and brutal as they may seem, are in fact exactly the legal solutions that had been arrived at in North Carolina and other Southern states for dealing with maroons (outlawing and killing them) and free Black people (deporting them from the state) at various times during the eighteenth and nineteenth centuries. To John, poor whites are, like maroons, a population at once threatening and disposable, both being outliers with whom the law should deal swiftly and harshly. And if it will not, as we will see in the case of another character, Father Dickson, extralegal violence must be employed to achieve the desired ends: expulsion or death. These threats were constant and visceral for maroons rather than hypothetical musings by a wealthy white woman. While all of this was an abstract, fictional thought experiment for Stowe, it was very dire and very real for enslaved people and maroons, a fact made evident in detail by Black writers in the 1850s.

Regarding the practice of outlawing runaway enslaved people and maroons, the narrator explains, "A provision of the Revised Statutes of North Carolina enacts that slaves thus secreted in the swamps, not returning within a given time, shall be considered outlawed," and that " 'it shall be lawful for any person or persons whatsoever to kill and destroy such slaves, by such ways and means as they shall think it, without any accusation or impeachment of crime for the same.' "[32] "It also provides," the narrator continues, "that when any slave shall be killed in consequence of such outlawry, the value of such slave shall be ascertained by a jury, and the owner entitled to receive two thirds of the valuation from the sheriff of the county wherein the slave was killed."[33] The "Revised Statutes" being referred to were revised in 1831 after the publication of David Walker's *Appeal to the Coloured Citizens of the World* (1829) and Nat Turner's Southampton rebellion in Virginia in 1831, but North Carolina had had statutes on the books for outlawing runaway slaves since 1741, though gestures toward the outlawing provisions existed even in the colony's first official Slave Code of 1715.[34]

These outlawing statutes officially criminalized acts of marronage in the eyes of the state and placed responsibility for punishment and restitution also in the state's or auxiliaries of the state's domain. Enslaved people who fled were generally outlawed once it was determined that they had engaged in more than an act of *petit marronage*, or short-term flight, and had instead left without any intention of returning on their own. But these decisions were of course arbitrary and decided by enslavers, often based on past behavior patterns of the enslaved people who had fled and on their own financial concerns. Outlawing led to a rise in the class of professional slave hunters with trained hunting dogs that are the subject of much terror and revulsion in the slave narratives of the nineteenth century. Outlawing also increased the stakes of any act of marronage, putting the maroon at risk for being mistaken for an outlawed slave and being chased, hunted, and shot at by slave catchers and ordinary citizens overzealously looking to cash in on posted reward money. The original outlawing clause from the 1741 Slave Code, titled "R'naway slaves may be outlawed in certain cases," establishes much of the language that would be used by slaveowners, authorities, and white observers to describe maroons and their activities for the next 120 years:

> Whereas many times slaves run away and lie out hid and lurking in swamps, woods, and other obscure places, killing cattle and hogs, and committing other injuries to the inhabitants of this State; in all such cases, upon intelligence of any slave or slaves, lying out as aforesaid, any two justices of the peace for the county wherein such slave or slaves is, or are supposed to lurk or do mischief, shall, and they are hereby empowered and required to issue proclamation against such slave or slaves (reciting his, or their names, and the name or names of the owner or owners, if known) thereby requiring him or them, and every of them forthwith to surrender him or themselves; and also to empower and require the sheriff of the said county

> to take such power with him as he shall think fit and necessary, for going in search and pursuit of, and effectual apprehending such outlying slave or slaves, which proclamation shall be published at the door of the court house, and at such other places as said justice shall direct. And if any slave or slaves against whom proclamation hath been thus issued, stay out and do not immediately return home, it shall be lawful for any person or persons, whatsoever to kill and destroy such slave or slaves, by such ways and means as he shall think fit, without accusation or impeachment of any crime for the same.[35]

The legal designation of "outlaw" is a curious one, as it seemingly admits and codifies the very agency and subjectivity denied to enslaved people by virtue of their status as property, or chattel. Above all else, the existence of such a detailed statute as this with precursors dating to the early seventeenth century and in many Southern states suggests in the strongest terms the fear that maroons occasioned in the minds of planter society. Making it lawful for "any person or persons, whatsoever to kill and destroy such slave or slaves, by such ways and means as he shall think fit, without accusation or impeachment of crime for same" served also as a means by which the planter class might enlist the assistance of poor whites in removing the scourge, as they saw it, of marronage from local neighborhoods and communities. For, as we will soon see, poor whites sometimes engaged in illicit trade with maroons that undercut planter control over the movements and activities of their enslaved populations. It was crucial to contain and control maroons, but so too was the need to keep maroon and poor white interests from intersecting in ways that subverted the regulatory mechanisms of the system of US chattel slavery. Stowe demonstrates this fact in *Dred*, underscoring how maroons used the arrangement to their benefit by acquiring supplies and materials crucial to their ongoing survival in the swamps. Whereas the novel represents it as a problem, we may read it is an opportunity for maroons to sustain resistive practices and social life. These kinds of opportunities are what the Black writers in the rest of the chapters that make up this book will capitalize on and explore.

The Cripps children, another group of characters representative of the class of "poor white trash" who are a problem population and a plague on white Southern elites, are left almost entirely in the care of the elderly, enslaved Old Tiff thanks to their mother's chronic sickliness and their father's itinerant drunkenness. Tiff, we are led to understand, has chosen to remain with the Cripps family out of genuine love and concern for the children as well as an allegiance to their mother's family name, that of Peyton, an old, monied Virginia family who has since, to his knowledge, lost their fortune. Tiff's "hut" near the swamp (which is technically the Cripps' but is tended to entirely by Tiff), we are told, "stands alone, in the heart of a dense pine forest, which shuts it in on every side."[36] Though we know from Nina's aunt and uncle that this hut stands quite near their home—on their property, in fact, but in the uncultivated pine woods—it is described as if it is very much isolated, "shut in on every side" where "no sound was heard but the shivering wind, swaying and surging in melancholy cadences through the long pine-leaves,—a lonesome, wailing, uncertain sound."[37] Again, Stowe uses a sympathetic, stereotypical Black character to highlight the plight of white characters. The interstitial, intermediary space these characters physically inhabit and which their subject positions reflect is, in Diouf's terms, a borderland space, meaning one close to and very often literally bordering plantations and developed landscapes. In the US context along with that of the prior British colonies, the Southern borderlands were the most common haunts of maroons—both short-term and longer-term—as opposed to the hinterlands (to use Diouf's other term), or highly remote areas distant from towns, cities, or villages, as in the examples of the Jamaican and Surinamese maroons who established communities in often distant mountains and jungles. In the description of Tiff's hut, then, we find a striking commonality with contemporaneous descriptions of maroons and maroon settlements, which were frequently understood as "hiding in plain sight," or rather paradoxically both present and absent, far and near, shifting and unpredictable. But more exists to Tiff and his relationship to marronage than Stowe initially presents, and not all of it is tied back to his relationship with the white Cripps children.

Much later in the novel, crisis strikes Tiff and the Cripps children when their father, drunk, brings home a new woman—a "low woman," in Tiff's estimation—to replace their mother who had finally succumbed to her illnesses. Sensing the impending threat to the children's livelihood, Tiff answers their repeated queries of "What shall we do? What shall we do?" with "I's a good mind to go off wid you in de wilderness, like de chil'en of Israel . . . though dere an't no manna falling nowadays."[38] Tiff thus proposes a version of marronage as it has thus far been constructed by the novel, a flight from danger into the wilderness, though it might at first appear quite strange to imagine an enslaved Black man and his two "poor white" charges undertaking a life of marronage. Tiff's alleged agency and desire to engage in a kind of marronage are worth a further look. In this case, the act of marronage would be an act of forced family separation enacted by a Black man on a white family—a reversal of the usual state of affairs. Though sentimentalized and problematically racialized by Stowe, Tiff remains a character who challenges normative white family structure and arrangement, offering protection and potential freedom to the white children who are largely abandoned by their parents. Tiff draws these white children into the orbit of the maroon world, employing Black and maroon knowledge to see the possibility of marronage as liberatory for himself and the children. Historically, the Great Dismal Swamp of Virginia and, in the case of *Dred*, North Carolina played home to all manner of exiles and outcasts—the dispossessed, oppressed, disenfranchised, outlawed, criminalized, and wanted. From the time of the first European surveys and explorations, beginning in earnest with William Byrd II in 1728, the swamp was characterized as a place of refuge for undesirables, whether they be indigenous people perceived as a threat or fugitives from labor or crime, Black and white.[39] But this context does not undermine the fact that escaped, enslaved Black people were far and away the most common inhabitants of the swamps and therefore the most commonly hunted, killed, and overall persecuted population there. While there is a clear romantic and stereotyped element to the way Stowe represents Tiff and his relationship with the white children under his care, as well as in the way she suggests they might participate in a form of marronage with him, the swamp world of *Dred* is undoubtedly a Black world first and foremost—it privileges Black agency, subjectivity, and ways of being and knowing that are not entirely beholden to white sensibilities about freedom. The communal life in Dred's encampment is multiracial, and a sense of community is established there that cannot exist in the white world.

Fearing the consequences of *two* drunken parents who are violent and unable to provide for the children, Tiff does indeed whisk them off into the woods, heading toward none other place than Dred's maroon encampment in the swamp "where he knew many fugitives were concealed,"[40] which, as was quite common among enslaved populations, was known to the local Black inhabitants by general location and as a site of refuge in a way that it simply was not known by whites—especially white enslavers. The contrast between the children's life at home and their life of flight or pseudo-marronage in the swamp (as Stowe represents it), even before they encounter Dred, is stark. As she does throughout the novel,

Stowe romanticizes the swamp landscape, emphasizing Fanny Cripps's peaceful delight at the "soft and fragrant pine-foliage" and the "still patter of falling dew-drops, and the tremulous whirr and flutter of leaves" about the makeshift shelter Tiff has constructed for them.[41]

That same night, on the outskirts of the swamp, Dred comes upon Tiff and the children as they sleep, and we learn more about the relationship between maroons and the enslaved, as well as between the swamp landscape and the nearby plantations:

> But, though Tiff and the children slept all night, we are under no obligations to keep our eyes shut to the fact that between three and four o'clock there came crackling through the swamps the dark figure of one whose journeyings were more often by night than by day. Dred had been out on one of his nightly excursions, carrying game, which he disposed of for powder and shot at one of the low stores we have alluded to. He came unexpectedly on the sleepers, while making his way back. His first movement, on seeing them, was that of surprise; then, stopping and examining the group more closely, he appeared to recognize them. Dred had known Old Tiff before; and had occasion to go to him more than once to beg supplies for fugitives in the swamps, or to get some errand performed which he could not himself venture abroad to attend to. Like others of his race, Tiff, on all such subjects, was so habitually and unfathomably secret, that the children, who knew him most intimately, had never received even a suggestion from him of the existence of any such person. Dred, whose eyes, sharpened by habitual caution, never lost sight of any change in his vicinity, had been observant of that which had taken place in Old Tiff's affairs. When, therefore, he saw him sleeping as we have described, he understood the whole matter at once.[42]

This scene and the narrator's reflections upon it reveal a great deal about the interplay between space and race in the world of the novel and within the context of the historical reality Stowe intends the novel to reflect. The narrative structure provides readers a glimpse into a world otherwise inaccessible to them by virtue of their position as largely white Northerners and inaccessible as well to white characters in the novel itself by virtue of the ways in which cognitive landscapes and their material projections manifest along racialized lines. Typical of maroons, even those living and moving about deep within the swamps, Dred conducts the majority of his business by cover of darkness. More importantly, though, the scene hints at two types of connections integral to the shadow networks and economies that helped sustain maroons and in some cases—like Tiff's here—provided temporary relief to the enslaved: connections between maroons and the still enslaved, and connections between maroons and the "poor white" population, which together reveal the multifaceted interconnectedness of all three groups. This interconnectedness only posed a further threat to elite, enslaver interests in the area, as the swamp space came to represent a space without control, one of discord, chaos, and ominous potential. The "we" at the beginning of the long quote above performs a lot of work here. Stowe speaks directly to white readers through the narrator, suggesting that, as white people, they "are under no obligation" to maintain secrecy surrounding maroons and tactics of marronage. Whereas Black writers largely traffic in whispers and intimations about maroons, Stowe's narrator speaks openly about them, and this frankness registers one of the reasons that Stowe's work serves as the primary conduit for "understanding" marronage in traditionally canonical nineteenth-century American writing.

We learn also that Dred knows Tiff, like he did Harry earlier, and has for quite some time. What's more, Tiff has apparently assisted Dred by providing him with hard-to-find supplies for the swamp-dwelling maroons and by performing unspecified "errands," which, we might imagine, involved communicating information to enslaved people further from the swamps or transacting business with merchants or traders on Dred's behalf to acquire particular supplies for his encampment. But, just as readers were earlier surprised by Harry's familiarity with Dred, we learn here that the Cripps children would be equally surprised to learn of Tiff's familiarity with him, for Tiff, like Harry, maintains true knowledge of Dred's existence as a closely guarded secret, while for white characters Dred remains shrouded in mystery, more myth than man, hovering at the margins of legibility.

Another poor white character in the novel, a keeper of one of the "low stores" alluded to in this same excerpt, Abijah Skinflint runs a small trading operation out of his log cabin, which stands between the large plantation estates of John Gordon, Nina's uncle, and Nina's own plantation, Canema. Already marginalized by his lower-class status, his position as an outsider to plantation society mirrors the space he physically inhabits:

a liminal space literally in between two plantations, on land that remains uncultivated for agricultural purposes and thus without usefulness in the realm of the plantation economy. The narrator informs us that Skinflint's establishment "was a nuisance in the eyes of neighboring planters, from the general apprehension entertained that [he] drove a brisk underhand trade with the negroes, and that the various articles which he disposed for sale were many of them surreptitiously conveyed to him in nightly installments from off their own plantations."[43] Not only does Skinflint conduct "underhand trade with the negroes," but the narrator also suggests that he can be counted among the "low white traders in the neighborhood" who "knew Dred well."[44] If as a poor white man living and conducting business in the interstices of plantation society, Skinflint has come to be seen as a nuisance, then his association with shadow networks of trade and especially with Dred and Dismal Swamp maroons elevates him to the level of a threat. The suspicion that Skinflint was pilfering items from the surrounding plantations to sell for himself was often a suspicion and accusation leveled at maroons inhabiting the swamps and borderland areas in the vicinity of plantation society—though maroons were more likely to pilfer items like food, blankets, or tools to use for themselves or to trade for things they needed rather than to sell for profit, as money generally served little purpose in the swamp. Stowe herself has the narrator explain these connections in a manner that has subsequently been supported by historians' assessments:

> The negroes lying out in the swamps are not so wholly cut off from society as might at first be imagined. The slaves of all the adjoining plantations, whatever they may pretend, to secure the good-will of their owners, are at heart secretly disposed, from motives both of compassion and policy, to favor the fugitives. They very readily perceive that, in the event of any difficulty occurring to themselves, it might be quite necessary to have a friend and protector in the swamp; and therefore they do not hesitate to supply these fugitives, so far as they are able, with anything which they may desire. The poor whites, also, who keep small shops in the neighborhood of plantations, are never particularly scrupulous, provided they can turn a penny to their own advantage; and willingly supply necessary wares in exchange for game, with which the swamp abounds.[45]

Stowe presents facts about maroons that are true, but any imagining of the possibilities actuated by these facts remains absent, as it does not suit her rhetorical purposes. In the eyes of the likes of Aunt Nesbit and Uncle John (and even sometimes Nina), then, Skinflint, despite his whiteness, potentially has more in common with maroons and the Black underclass than he does with enslavers. Skinflint poses a threat because he operates at least in part within the Black and maroon landscapes of *Dred*'s North Carolina. In the above description, the narrator intimates the existence of shadow networks of knowledge and communication among the enslaved population, the maroons, and to a certain extent the "low" whites who conduct business with them. These networks threaten white supremacy, like the maroons themselves, because they exceed the capacity of the slavocracy to police, control, and contain them. Stowe emphasizes this problem of lost control and the need to regain it by associating these characters with one another, though, not with what a lack of control could mean for possibilities for alternative freedoms through marronage.

"On the verge of the swamp, a little beyond Tiff's cabin, lived Ben Dakin," another poor white character who, despite his vocation as a slave catcher, tends to be, from the vantage point of social class, grouped together by Stowe with maroons and enslaved people rather than propertied, white enslavers. This emerges as undoubtedly Stowe's most problematic association between the stations and experiences of poor white people and enslaved Black people or maroons. The suggestion that a slave catcher has anything in common with the unfreedoms experienced by enslaved people is flatly wrong, and flatly offensive, but worth a further look in the context of Stowe's representation of liminal figures and the swamp. The paradox is in fact revealing of *Dred*'s inability to come to terms with what exactly to do with maroons in the contexts of both the novel as a genre and the publishing industry of which it was a part. The narrator describes Dakin thus: "Ben was a mighty hunter; he had the best pack of dogs within thirty miles round; and his advertisements . . . detailed with great accuracy the precise terms on which he would hunt down and capture any man, woman, or child, escaping from service and labor in that country."[46] Dakin represents a particularly interesting case because, unlike Skinflint or Cripps, his vocation makes him part of the economy of trade and labor in human beings, a necessary adjunct to an "imperfect" system in which the living chattel cannot always be forced into submission. Still, though Dakin has one foot in the world of the enslavers, he nevertheless occupies a marginal position relative to that class as well as to its "official" economy and plantation community. Like Cripps (and Tiff), he lives in close proximity to the swamp, though in his case this proximity provides obvious benefits to his profession, as many of the runaways he attempts to track down have sought refuge in the swamps. But he remains an outsider, a member of a poor, uneducated white underclass employed by enslavers but scorned by them, and rightfully feared and despised by the enslaved population and Black people in general. For Stowe, Dakin becomes "blackened" via his profession, which though it involves hunting down fugitive slaves still involves associating with them regularly, and via the space he inhabits near and in the swamp. For our purposes, we can read Stowe's depiction of Dakin as further evidence of the idea of the swamp as a site of projection for white fears and anxieties. For Stowe, slavery and the swamp—giving rise to the "necessity" of a person like Dakin—are problems to be addressed, reasons to end slavery so that the need for such low white persons ceases to exist. The connections she makes between them serve as further evidence of the need to abolish slavery rather than as revelatory of freedoms that may be achieved for enslaved people independent of white intervention.

The white preacher Father Dickson represents perhaps Stowe's most compelling didactic case illustrating the precarity of whiteness—and thus normative, liberal ideas of freedom—in swamp and maroon-inflected spaces. Father Dickson lacks pretensions to upward class mobility, seeming content to live without artifice or ostentation as a man of God. What sets him apart from other members of the local clergy and puts him at odds with some in the community, however, is the fact that he "had never yielded to the common customs and habits of the country in regard to the holding of slaves. A few, who had been left him by a relation, he had at great trouble and expense transported to a free state, and settled there comfortably."[47] Not only does Father Dickson refuse to enslave people himself or to engage in any aspect of the slave trade, he also actively, as the novel progresses, begins speaking out against the system and practice in his personal life and in his sermons. Like most of the other poorer white characters previously described, Father Dickson lives in a woodland hut near the outskirts of the swamp. What's more, he preaches in what the narrator describes as a "rude church which stood deep in the shadow of the wood."[48] He therefore comes to be seen by the slavocracy as a kind of triple threat: poor and white, living and preaching in woodland seclusion, and openly harboring antislavery opinions.

A common form of deflection on the part of enslavers was to blame white abolitionist sentiment for agitation among the enslaved population, as if the enslaved needed any other reason to be desirous of their freedom than the fact of enslavement itself. Father Dickson becomes the victim of such tactics later in the novel as tensions are rising between enslavers and Southerners with openly abolitionist sentiments. As Father Dickson rides up to his church one Sabbath day to preach his sermon, "a throng of men, armed with bludgeons and pistols"[49] accost him regarding his purported antislavery preachings. The men have come together to serve justice, as they perceive it, outside the realm of the law and without any legitimate authority, though with the informal social consent and prerogative of Southern society. In response to Father Dickson's query regarding whether the men "have any warrant from the civil authorities to stop [him]," he receives a telling response: " 'Now . . . you may as well know fust as last, that we don't care a cuss for the civil authorities, as you call them, 'cause we's going to do what we darn please; and we don't please have you yowping abolishionism round here, and putting deviltry in the heads of our niggers!"[50] As noted, this serves as a standard refrain, blaming abolitionism for enslaved unrest, and Father Dickson refuses to budge on the issue, standing his ground and indicating that he is determined to preach his sermon, even in the face of extrajudicial violence. Tom Gordon emerges as the leader and organizer of the group, and he informs Father Dickson that he "shall sign a pledge to leave North Carolina in three days, and never come back again, and take [his] whole spawn and litter with [him]."[51] Dickson refuses, the situation continues to escalate, and what follows is one of the more harrowing scenes in the novel, tellingly inflicted on a white person rather than a Black person as Stowe aims to garner maximal sympathy from her white reading audience. The men forcibly lead Father Dickson back to his home, where, in view of his sickly wife and two young children, they proceed to strip him down to his undergarments, bind him to a tree, and whip him. "He is so dreadful fond of the niggers, let him fare with them!"[52] is Tom's rallying cry to the inebriated, lurid mob as one of them begins delivering blows to the still unwavering Dickson.

Stowe uses this scene to demonstrate in no uncertain terms the fate that awaits white Southerners who publicly profess antislavery sentiments and refuse to disavow them. They will, ultimately, be punished like enslaved people: subjected to the extrajudicial violence of the lash. In this particular case, Father Dickson's proximity not only to enslaved people but also to maroons exacerbates the threat he poses and therefore the punishment he receives at the hand of Tom and his ilk. Father Dickson is a loner, an outlier; he lives in a shack near the swamp and preaches in a woodland church far from the town center. He cannot be monitored and controlled through the usual mechanisms of the slavocracy and as a result gets singled out for punishment in a way that resembles—though of course without the sentence of death—the way outlawed slaves were dealt with. Before the men can give Father Dickson the "six and thirty" they first set out to, Edward Clayton happens upon the scene and interrupts it. Though the interruption saves Father Dickson any further violence and humiliation, it turns the mob's increasing wrath on Clayton, already an unpopular figure in the neighborhood because of his own outspoken antislavery views and the radical experiments he is carrying out on his plantation, teaching enslaved people to read and write and allowing them to earn personal savings toward their eventual freedom. Soon enough, it will be Clayton's turn to feel the mob's fury, and in his time of need his proximity to maroons and spaces of marronage will be what save him.

Continuing his violent spree, Tom later finally pushes Harry to his breaking point, and in a heated argument at Canema, Harry strikes Tom and promptly flees out the window, headed, as we will learn, for the refuge of the swamp's maroon community. He flees on Tom's horse to his cottage and collects his wife, Lisette, and they ride immediately to "the place where he [Harry] had twice before met Dred," where Dred, with his characteristic prescience, already awaits them.[53] "And before sunset of that evening," the narrator proclaims, "Harry and Lisette were tenants of the wild vastness in the centre of the swamp."[54] Like Tiff before him, albeit for different reasons, Harry seeks the refuge of the swamp and the maroons he knows to inhabit it in his time of need. The Black socialities that extend through and within the spaces of both the swamp and the plantation zone enable Harry to call upon his affiliation with Dred and move himself and his wife to a space of relative safety when he knows his life is in immediate danger. By having Dred already waiting for Harry, improbable as it may be, Stowe reinforces the idea that clandestine networks of communication, intelligence, and sociality existed between enslaved people and maroons and outside the regulatory mechanisms of the slavocracy. At Engedi, Harry joins a growing group of self-exiled refugees, among them Old Tiff and the white Cripps children under his care.

In a final act of vicious brutality, Tom attacks Clayton. Clayton decides to ride over and spend the night at Father Dickson's cottage in order to provide him some measure of protection and reassurance after he had been assaulted by Tom and the mob. "Arming himself with a brace of pistols" and "riding deliberately through the woodland path in the vicinity of the swamp," Clayton is startled by three men on horseback, who approach him from behind, one striking him in the head with a gutta-percha cane before he can recognize any of them.[55] He rises to defend himself, but Tom strikes him once more, accusing him of being a "renegade abolitionist" who is "covertly undermining our institutions."[56] However, just as Tom prepares to strike again, "a violent blow from an unseen hand struck his right arm, and it fell, broken, at his side."[57] Tom calls out for his men to "look for the fellow," but the only answer they receive is "the crack of a rifle, and a bullet which passed right over his [Tom's] head . . . from the swamp."[58] Dred's rifle—which enacts a kind of freedom familiar to enslavers in its means, but contradicts their ends—is one of his catalysts for freedom. He has no right to bear arms; he has no rights at all other than those which he claims for himself in the swamp. Like other fictionalized maroons explored before him, Dred insists on defining freedoms on his own terms. He takes what he needs from white society and its corollaries but expects nothing from it and disavows its capacity to define and delimit his actions, potentials, and futures. There is not and never was a path to integration, assimilation, or emancipation for Dred. His fight is against the foundation of white American society itself, and so he must be killed in the story so that threat can be contained.

The rifle shot fired above came from Harry and Dred, who have been watching from the swamp, enacting reverse surveillance on the plantation zone from the liminal maroon space of the swamp. They decide the best course of action is to bring Clayton "to our stronghold of Engedi, even as Samson bore the gates of Gaza. Our women shall attend him, and when he is recovered we will set him on his journey."[59] With Clayton's admittance to Engedi, its interracial and interclass potentiality has reached its apotheosis for Stowe in the text. But it is at that apotheosis that the idea is ultimately exploded and set aside for Stowe. Indeed, we learn more in the chapter that follows about Dred's plan for insurrection than we have throughout the rest of the novel. As Denmark Vesey's son, Dred is motivated by a sense of personal and community vengeance, but he submerges this desire for the greater good of his people in bondage. Deriving his justification from the Bible, Dred, like Henry Blake, sent compatriots into the swamp whose job it was to prepare "the minds of the people, and he was traversing the swamp in different directions, holding nightly meetings, in which he read and expounded the prophecies to excited ears."[60] Dred takes the religion of the enslavers and uses it against them, speaks to them in a language they purportedly understand.

Mere pages later, however, in a chapter titled "All Over," Dred dies attempting to assist a fellow fugitive in the process of escaping slave hunters, and everything we have just learned about his plans becomes, at least for the narrative arc, moot. The question arises, then, as to whether Stowe's radical, coalitional politics of resistance articulated through representations of marronage in this text are suddenly contained, deflated, or negated by Dred's death and the concomitant death of his plan for insurrection. In what follows, I will suggest that, over the course of its narrative, *Dred* opens up many more possibilities for subversive action than it forecloses, despite Dred's death near the end of the story. While Dred's death does precipitate a movement northward by many of the inhabitants of Engedi, activating a more familiar storyline in which enslaved people flee captivity in the South to some form of nominal freedom in the North, readers are left to ponder both what will become of the other countless and nameless maroons dwelling in the swamps and the implications of the radical space- and race-upsetting politics of resistance indexed by practices of marronage throughout the text. They are left with possibilities that we might register even if Stowe could not or would not. What is "All Over" for Stowe conforms with a sense of normative temporality and linear forward movement. It is never over for maroons, whose lives and actions transcend the confines of Stowe's narrative and exceed white capacity for imagination and desire.

Marronage and Im/mobility

Maroons simultaneously run away and refuse to leave. In the eyes of the slavocracy, they simultaneously possess an unruly mobility and an infuriating stasis. *Dred* reveals the way in which maroons enact this dynamic in the setting of a series of overlapping and interrelated neighborhoods that border the Dismal Swamp and thus lie in proximity to its maroon inhabitants. Dred's appearances in the novel alternate between intruding into the borders of the plantation zone and hiding out in his swamp stronghold of Engedi. As readers, we become privy to both his extraordinary mobility and his ability to stay put, both results of the freedom he has obtained for himself by fleeing enslavement and taking up life as a maroon. Dred's mobility along with the freedom he has to remain in place when he so chooses make him a threat to the very cornerstone of freedom as understood through the political philosophy of liberal democracy that undergirds conceptions of citizenship and belonging in the United States. As Hagar Kotef argues in *Movement and the Ordering of Freedom*, "Africans, indigenous Americans . . . as well as women and paupers keep appearing in the texts of liberal thinkers as either too stagnant or too mobile."[61] Maroons, as I have argued, appear as both of these things together, and especially in *Dred*. Whereas Stowe ultimately represents this fact as a problem, the Black writers in the chapters that follow explore the ways in which it may serve instead as an opportunity.

Kotef further explains that "through the production of patterns of movement . . . different categories of subjectivity are produced. Regimes of movement are thus never simply a way to control, to regulate, or to incite movement. Regimes of movement are integral to the *formation of different modes of being*."[62] I submit that the regime of movement instantiated by maroons, one that upsets the hegemonic ordering and regulating of space and the bodies that exist in that space, in fact indexes a mode of *being* fundamentally at odds with the ordering of movement as it relates to freedom in conceptions of liberal subjecthood. Of course, anything like a liberal subject only exists in relation to its opposite, the illiberal or nonliberal subject, one who is unfree: the enslaved person. Articulating the freedoms of the liberal subject required the existence of a population who was denied and could never have those freedoms, and, as Kotef continues, "colonized subjects who were declared to be nomads, poor who were seen as vagabond or thrown into vagrancy as they lost access to lands, women whose presumed hysterical nature was attached to their inability to control bodily fluids, all were constituted (or rather deconstituted) as unruly subjects whose movement is a problem to be managed. This configuration was the grounds for justifying nonliberal moments—and spaces—within liberal regimes."[63]

But the situation with maroons does not constitute an example of a "nonliberal" moment within a liberal regime. The practice of outlawing fugitive enslaved people does, certainly, but maroons must be understood on their own terms as people who have rejected not only the condition of enslavement in its entirety but also the aspirational ontology of liberal subjecthood and its precursors altogether. Enslaved people, by virtue of their existence and of their perspective, fundamentally challenged dominant ways of seeing and being in the world, and in turn they challenged the hegemonic spatial representations that resulted from that dominance. Maroons compound the challenge by inhabiting and operating within spaces, like swamps, that always already exist outside the spatial order proclaimed and enacted by that hegemony. What's more, they move between the realms of what is ordered (the plantation zone) and what remains in disorder (the swamps), never allowing hegemonic spatial representations to be rendered fully coherent as a result. Stowe's work hints at these tensions but finds a way to resolve them through novelistic convention.

Maroons like Dred thus represent a singular threat in the sense that, as formerly enslaved people whose non–subject position was in some ways the foil against which something like the liberal subject could be imagined in the first place, they recorporealize the liberal subject and embody its founding tenet of freedom of movement in the face of one of the most repressive, controlling, containing systems ever designed to prohibit exactly that thing: race-based chattel slavery. Stowe's depiction of Dred theorizes via embodied representation the existence of liberal subjectivity in the place where it in theory could not be, in self-liberated, de facto free people: maroons, inhabitants of the very states that recognized them only as property. Taken up by Black writers, these kinds of representations can be understood to challenge the ideology, political philosophy, and legal mechanisms by which US hegemony organized normative conceptions of freedom, space, mobility, movement, and liberal subjecthood. Stowe can only imagine this subjecthood in a limited liberal/nonliberal binary, however, and it is life outside that binary that Black writers take up through their representations of marronage.

Thought this way, the interracial and interclass valences I have been elaborating throughout this chapter amplify the threat of marronage in *Dred*. But whereas Stowe largely stops at imagining and using marronage as a threat, the African American texts taken up in subsequent chapters imagine possibilities beyond that, possibilities outside binaristic frameworks like enslaved and free, liberal and nonliberal. Marronage not only rejects the conditions of enslavement; it also rejects the normativized aspiration of liberal subjecthood altogether. Maroons have no aspirations toward assimilation, recognition, citizenship, or subjecthood. Not only do they *not* aspire to these things, they actively *conspire against* them. The politics of marronage as they relate to "politics" understood as commonsense (read: white) are ultimately a politics of disaffiliation, disaffection, rejection, and unrecognition. While Dred must die, his plot for insurrection along with him, and the remaining maroons of Engedi flee the swamp toward various northern destinations at the conclusion of the novel, this conventional turn cannot negate the Black-centered, alternative politics of material and rhetorical resistance that characterizes maroons and marronage in tension with white and Black representations. Reading for the contours of that resistance in African American literature, which operate along lower frequencies and registers emerging from Black radical thought about marronage, makes up the chapters that follow.

Chapter Two

Beyond Revolt

... all sustained slave revolts must acquire a Maroon dimension.

—Orlando Patterson, "Slavery and Slave Revolts"

Martin R. Delany framed his serialized novel *Blake; or, The Huts of America* (1859, 1861 to 1862) as a direct response to Stowe's *Uncle Tom's Cabin*, which is in part evident in the similarity of construction of the titles. *Blake*'s epigraphs for both parts of the text are also drawn from Stowe's writing. At the most basic level, Delany's work replaces Stowe's timid martyr figure of Uncle Tom with the avowed insurrectionist Henry Blake, a radical Black revolutionary who seeks the destruction of slavery and slaveholders and, in keeping with parts of Delany's own political thought, plans the creation of a Black republic where the outlawing of slavery is the first decree. As Martha Schoolman has noted, Delany advocated specifically for Black emigration to Liberia both before the Civil War and later, "during the era of white-supremacist retrenchment" that arose during Reconstruction.[1] At other times in his career, he also focused his emigrationist energies on the West Indies and Central America, which he explored in several works published before and after *Blake*. While *Blake*'s ultimate liberatory scheme is a solidly Black nationalist one, my reading foregrounds the presence of marronage as a persistent locus of freedom-seeking practice that courses beneath and often interrupts the text's overall orientation toward Black communal futurity as necessarily nationalized in a liberal sense. While the novel is ultimately left unfinished, Blake's revolution yet to have begun, what we do find in the text, along with what I will argue is Blake's own marronage, is a thriving maroon community concealed deep within the Great Dismal Swamp. Blake is dismissive of the maroons and what he deems to be their superstitious and quasi-religious beliefs, as he is staunchly attached to a defiant mode of Christianity with many similarities to Stowe's Dred, but the fact remains that they have established a version of community and social organization within the heart of US slavery itself. My reading here is one that attunes to the possibilities inherent in what does happen in the novel rather than the realities of what ultimately does not.

This chapter examines the quest for freedom in *Blake* through the lens of marronage, arguing for Henry Blake as a maroon figure and suggesting that his peregrinations throughout the US South can be generatively understood as acts of marronage. Following Schoolman, I consider the national, transnational, and hemispheric valences of *Blake*, which Schoolman observes "may be . . . the quintessential North American geographic novel."[2] I contend that Henry's marronage draws other varieties of resistant practices into a sharper focus that reveals their association with marronage according to the more expansive parameters of the phenomenon articulated by Sylviane Diouf, Neil Roberts, Steven Hahn, and others—and upon which I am building further in this book. *Blake*—by virtue of being an unfinished work, the planned insurrection in the story never yet begun—allows us a window into freedom in perpetual process and becoming, into an assemblage of self- and community-affirming resistant practices that can be valuably considered as and through the analytic of marronage. This chapter's title, "Beyond Revolt," reflects the influence of Koritha Mitchell's thinking; Mitchell's framing of African American history "beyond protest" opens space to consider Black subjectivity and agency proactively—as something teeming with imagination, possibility, and creation—rather than as always simply reactive to the oppressive operations of white supremacy.[3] Maroons should be considered some of the most significant historical actors and literary figures who have provided us with insight into unexplored possibilities for freedom in this context, and here I aim to elucidate how and why via Delany's singular work of serialized fiction, one that is deserving of more mainstream scholarly consideration in general.

The Background of *Blake*

Blake was first published in a limited serial run in the *Anglo-African Magazine* in 1859 and then again in a more complete and somewhat modified run in the *Weekly Anglo-African* in 1861 and 1862; the now commonly indicated publication dates reflect that interruption. Critics remain unsure as to whether the text is unfinished, as the issue in which its potential final installment would have been published has been lost. While Henry Blake, the titular hero, spends almost the entirety of the story traveling and spreading his plan for mass insurrection to enslaved people all over the Southern states, and eventually into Cuba, the revolt never occurs. Intentional or not, the ending we do have, wherein revolution is deferred, allows us for my purposes to focus more closely on the elements of marronage and/as freedom that pervade the body of the narrative itself. Marronage emerges here as a set of practices untethered from the extremes, from the codified poles of enslavement as totalizing unfreedom and freedom as emancipation through the fantasy of revolutionary actualization or state-granted emancipation. Thus, *Blake*'s publication as a serial—a text in the process of realization, moving in different directions through each installment—mirrors the notion of marronage itself as freedom in continual process through movement, illegibility, and uncertainty.

In 1970, on the heels of the turmoil of the civil rights struggle in the United States, Floyd J. Miller edited the first version of *Blake* in book form—over one hundred years after it had first been released.[4] It was a fitting time for the text's publication, as *Blake* deals heavily with the themes of Black self-determination, self-reliance, pride, and militancy in the face of systemic white supremacy. While the 1970 publication slowly spawned a steady stream of interest and criticism, perhaps most notably for my purposes in work by Robert S. Levine and Martha Schoolman, among many others, *Blake* would not be republished until 2017, this time with Jerome McGann tackling the text's notoriously complicated publication history, printing, references, and orthography. The arrival of McGann's heavily revised and corrected edition means that, like marronage, *Blake* too is ripe for a new wave of scholarly reconsideration, particularly as it relates to freedom and to marronage as a kind of freedom in process rather than freedom achieved or given. Indeed, McGann insists that *Blake*'s "most 'solemn responsibility' is the quest for freedom" and that Delany's project depends upon an unwavering commitment to the project of "black self-reliance."[5]

The gestures here are toward new kinds of freedom(s). For McGann, the text's incompleteness only adds to the sense of its transhistorical applicability, as its characters' quest for freedom is one perpetually in process, always, for better or worse, in a state of becoming and possibility. In this sense, McGann echoes Floyd Miller's earlier thoughts regarding the novel's "inconclusiveness": "the rebellion in process . . . is perhaps more relevant today than any ending Delany could possibly have conceived."[6] This remains true into our own present critical and sociopolitical moment, as well. While for Orlando Patterson slave revolt requires a "Maroon dimension," *Blake* examines how a maroon dimension can also activate possibilities for freedom that need not end with an eruption of violence but may instead remain open to novel yet unrecovered iterations of alternative freedom in a state of perpetual, inconclusive becoming. That normative, national time is interrupted by the continuous presence of maroon life, and the lack of any definitive end to the possibilities inherent in marronage, is crucial to better apprehending the nebulous rhythms of Black life under slavery in the United States.

Many critics, beginning with Floyd Miller, Paul Gilroy, Eric Sundquist, and Robert Levine and more recently Martha Schoolman, have recognized *Blake*'s vision of a pan-African or hemispheric Black radicalism and internationalism that is disassociated from the structuring logic of the US South and of the traditional nation-state. Taking it a step further, Schoolman has argued that "unlike earlier expressions of abolitionist geography . . . that represented expansiveness in order to argue against it, *Blake*'s approach is by contrast to swallow the U.S. South whole, and then *surround it*."[7] With Schoolman, I aim to track the influence of literary works like Delany's as crucial to changing US geographical imaginaries in the 1850s and '60s, particularly those put forth by abolitionist writing and ideology. Building on the transnational and hemispheric turns in American studies and US literary studies, which have generated many insightful readings of *Blake*, Andy Doolen has made a compelling case for the text's wholesale rejection of the rhetoric and ideology of the American Revolution as a "failure that cannot serve as the ideological origin for a black independence struggle that exceeds national time and space" (very much unlike *The Heroic Slave*, as will be made evident later on).[8] All of these facets of *Blake*—its interest in the relationship between Black violence, conspiracy, and community; its negotiations of property (both person and otherwise) across state and national borders; Henry's mobility as a challenge to inscribed notions of limitations of enslaved movement; and its transnational or hemispheric declaration of Black radicalism and a struggle outside the constricting boundaries of national time and space—connect to and elaborate possibilities of freedom via marronage, which interrupts and exceeds the circumscribing logics of national time and space.

Rethinking Marronage and Imagining Henry Blake as a Maroon

If marronage has been a constituent but unappreciated feature of Henry's quest for freedom and of the landscape of enslaved resistance in *Blake* all along, I suggest that this is in part because we have been unable to fully recognize it thanks to the longstanding critical adherence in studies of US slavery to the Caribbean model of marronage, one that privileges its insurrectionary potential over its multidimensional project of interrelated resistant and life-affirming practices. Eugene Genovese exemplifies the former position on US maroons: "the question concern[ed] less the existence of *marronage*—it did exist—than of *marronage* on a scale that could affect the politics of the slave society, especially the politics inherent in any encouragement to slave revolt, in a manner comparable to that in Brazil, Surinam, or even Colombia or Venezuela."[9] Genovese concludes that US maroons "typically huddled in small units and may be called 'maroons' only as a courtesy."[10] *Blake*, like other works under consideration in this book, anticipates recent critical revisions of our understanding of marronage, especially in the US context, by not only decoupling marronage from insurrection and direct resistance but also revealing that marronage was in fact an ever-changing, multidimensional project and process of individual and collective resistance existing in the liminal space between the codified poles of "freedom" and "enslavement," one that cannot simply be reduced to a process of self-exile, autonomous community formation, fugitivity, or a mere waypoint on the path to potential future revolt.

Without question, Henry Blake's "plan for a general insurrection of the slaves in every state, and the successful overthrow of slavery"[11] looms large throughout the text, ostensibly acting as its organizing narrative impetus for Henry's journey throughout the Southern states and Cuba, where he locates his wife and continues organizing his plan. But, as McGann observes, the story "involves much more than insurrection."[12] As he sees it, Henry's quest for freedom is most significant, and "that quest has succeeded, has been succeeding, from Chapter VI forward."[13] Viewing that quest for freedom and the successes it achieves through the lens of marronage, we become privy to an African diasporic world of resistant practices in tension with "a teleology in which," according to Walter Johnson, "'African' forms of resistance are seen as 'roadblocks' on the way to the elaboration of a properly revolutionary notion of slave revolt, one, that is, which recognized 'the individual' as the subject of history and the language of rights as the only acceptable idiom of revolution, a teleology, that is, which ultimately reproduces the idea of a liberal agent as the universal subject of history."[14] US maroons, like enslaved people in general, were never considered liberal agents in this sense and, as such, have never figured in mainstream, white Western conceptions of the universal subject of history, particularly as that subject pertains to the ideal of a right to revolution from a white perspective. Instead, maroons and marronage are distinctly African diasporic (and at times, it is important to acknowledge, indigenous—though that won't be a focus here because of the emphasis on Black literature) in nature, registering throughout the hemisphere and even in West Africa throughout the entire duration of the transatlantic slave trade as forces of multidimensional resistance, survival, self-determination, and autonomy.[15]

Blake reveals the ways in which marronage unsettles white supremacist logics and the underpinnings of the system of chattel slavery itself, not just because maroons pose a potentially violent threat to the white population but most especially because, as Neil Roberts observes, they represent "a total refusal of the enslaved condition,"[16] or a total refusal of the racial, social, economic, and political logics by which their enslavement is rendered ideologically coherent in the tradition of Enlightenment philosophy and nineteenth-century liberalism.[17] Over the course of part 1 of the text, marronage challenges the ideological and operational logics of pre–Civil War white supremacist dominance in at least three specific ways: it facilitates the creation and sustenance of networks of affective, material, and familial support among the enslaved across varying geographical distances; it demonstrates singular evidence of Black self-sufficiency and mobility while upending notions of slavery as a benevolent, paternalistic institution; and it reveals the existence of liminal spaces as part of the "Black" or "maroons' landscape" that exceed the market framework of 1850s expansionist capitalism, especially as it relates to enslavers' fantasies of expansion of the US slaveholding regime farther south into the Caribbean. For these reasons, *Blake* may be imagined as a text that itself works to theorize marronage and freedom through its representations of multiple configurations of the practice as they endured in and against the landscape of US slavery, lending further credence to Angela Davis's observation, which underpins the primary arguments of this book, that "the history of Black Literature provides . . . a much more illuminating account of the nature of freedom, its extent and limits, than all the philosophical discourses on this theme in the history of Western society."[18]

An analysis of *Blake* through the optic of marronage extends the increasingly rich critical tradition on the text that has hailed it since Floyd Miller's initial publication as an impassioned articulation of Black nationalism(s) and an expression of transnational and hemispheric pan-Africanist solidarity, and more recently as a sophisticated critique of the interlocking mechanisms of US imperialism and expansionist fantasy, among other things. *Blake*'s overlapping geographies, circuits of movement for bodies and/as property, and treatment of diasporic resistant practices have anticipated the turns in American literary studies toward the transnational, hemispheric, Atlantic, and Black Atlantic over the past three decades. While critics have not attended directly to marronage in *Blake*, some have emphasized features of the text that subtend an analytic of marronage and are worth discussing briefly to provide greater context for my own intervention. Rebecca Biggio has argued that it is the threat of "black community" rather than "black violence" that is most unsettling about *Blake*, suggesting that the text enacts Black community through "plotting, spreading, or protecting the knowledge of the black conspiracy, even and especially maintaining the illusion of conspiracy where there is none."[19] Jeffory Clymer privileges *Blake*'s fixation "with the political quandaries that arise as people and commodities move and are moved across borders," making movement and mobility—crucial to the success of acts of marronage—defining features of the way we interpret the landscape of slavery in the text.[20]

Additionally, Jean Cole has examined the ways in which the extraordinary mobility of the protagonists in *Blake* (and in "Theresa—A Haytien Tale") contrasts with the delimited notions of enslaved mobility that have arisen from the primacy of the slave narrative in considerations of pre–Civil War African American quests for freedom.[21] Following Jo-Ann Marx's earlier work on Black language as "a tool for ordering and giving meaning to a black world . . . and for affirming a vision of freedom and nationalism,"[22] Andy Doolen and Gregory Pierrot have demonstrated the ways in which *Blake* breaks from the ideological traditions of the American and Haitian Revolutions, respectively, in order to establish a distinct tradition of Black radicalism emerging out of the political developments of the 1850s.[23] Britt Rusert employs *Blake* in part to recover what she calls "fugitive science" as a genealogy of "practices and actors" with a "role in the construction of a critical imagination of black freedom."[24] Katy Chiles draws upon Delany's idea of a "nation within a nation" to argue that *Blake*'s seriality "performs the logic of the 'nation within a nation' as a textual phenomenon," insisting that Delany "presents a nation-state in which local, regional, national, and transnational figurations overlap and permeate each other."[25] Chiles's notion that *Blake* "explores how individuals could be positioned within and without the nation"[26] prefigures the unique subject position of the maroon, who in Henry Blake's case remains *within* slaveholding territory but spatially and ideologically *without* its regulatory mechanisms of control and domination, troubling the stability of white supremacist logics through which slavery was folded into the identity of the emergent US nation-state. More recently, Sharada Balachandran Orihuela has engaged piracy as an analytic to perform what she calls a "piratic reading" of *Blake*, contending that it "uses the liberal logic of attaching personhood to property to counter the US state's exclusions of slaves from citizenship and recognition."[27] Orihuela argues that Henry Blake's "fugitivity is . . . a piratic act because it contests both the private property of the slave owner as well as the state reliant on the slave trade,"[28] a claim that can be made also for Henry's marronage, whereby he liberates himself and proceeds to move freely about slaveholding territory and the geography of Atlantic slavery, participating in and initiating a series of subversive acts that undermine the slave system both directly and indirectly.[29] Judith Madera argues that Blake is "a sentinel for another kind of potentiality," one characterized by the power of deterritorialized Black populations to "mobilize local knowledges within national space."[30] The revelation of these knowledges and the contours of their contestation of that space is part of what this chapter attempts to elucidate and represents a stark demonstration of how Black thinking about freedom and marronage expands beyond Stowe's vision, as explored in the previous chapter.

My choice to deploy the analytic and vocabulary of marronage rather than that of, for example, fugitivity, and to privilege Henry Blake's mobility and illegibility rather than the fantasy of revolution or a protonationalistic "nation within a nation" formation, signals a departure from some previous scholarship chiefly because marronage represents a possibility for Black freedom that does not require white intervention in the realm of the material or white mediation in the realm of the discursive. Fugitives run *away* from slavery, while maroons run *toward* freedom, opening up along the way possibilities for alternative formations of freedom that can be foreclosed by the language of state-sanctioned criminalization of

Black people: "fugitive" or "outlaw." While fugitivity has been reclaimed convincingly by some scholars as a heuristic for conceptualizing enslaved movement and subject positionality, I submit that Black literary representations of marronage specifically can be understood as even more complicated. They reject the "stand still and see the salvation"[31] position that Henry criticizes for its reliance on the ostensible future benevolence of enslavers or the state and prioritize the horizons of possibility actuated by maroon-focused flight practices. Thus, I am not rejecting fugitivity as valid and relevant as a heuristic in its own way but rather attempting to reorient the way we imagine fugitivity versus marronage as it appears in the Black writing considered in this book. For the essence of Henry's plan for large-scale Black self-liberation is quite simple: It begins psychologically, with the enslaved rejecting their assigned (non)subject positions as chattel and recognizing their individual and collective potential for autonomy and self-determination. In this sense Henry—as a mouthpiece for Delany himself—offers a framework for understanding the quest for Black freedom that resonates closely with the self-reliance-based arguments made by Henry Highland Garnet in "An Address to the Slaves of the United States" (1843) and David Walker in *Walker's Appeal* (1830). Like Garnet, who implored the enslaved to "arise, arise! Strike for your lives and liberties. Now is the day and the hour. Let every slave throughout the land do this, and the days of slavery are numbered,"[32] Henry rejects Daddy Joe's advice to "Stan still an' see de salbation,"[33] instead declaring that the day is *now*, and "I'll 'stand still' no longer."[34] Movement—along with the ability to slip in and out of legibility, to exist in liminal psychic and material spaces, and to stand still only as part of his movement-based maneuvering—becomes the cornerstone of Henry's tactics as a maroon and elucidates alternative possibilities for freedom-making that will be discussed further in this chapter.

Into the Maroons' Landscape

The action in *Blake* opens with a discussion between two white characters, the Southern enslaver Colonel Stephen Franks and his cousin, the Northerner Mrs. Arabella Ballard, regarding the Compromise of 1850. I reproduce a segment of the conversation here because it acts as a framing device for the contested political geographies of freedom and unfreedom with which Delany is concerned in the text:

"Tell me, Madam Ballard, how will the North go in the present issue?" enquired Franks.

"Give yourself no concern about that, Colonel," replied Mrs. Ballard, "you will find the North true to the country."

"What you consider true, may be false—that is, it may be true to you, and false to us," continued he.

"You do not understand me, Colonel," she rejoined, "we can have no interests separate from yours; you know the time-honored motto, 'united we stand,' and so forth, must apply to the American people under every policy in every section of the Union."

"So it should, but amidst the general clamor in the contest for ascendancy, may you not lose sight of this important point?"

"How can we? You, I'm sure, Colonel, know very well that in our country commercial interests have taken precedence of all others, which is a sufficient guarantee of our fidelity to the South."

"That may be, madam, but we are still apprehensive."

"Well, sir, we certainly do not know what more to do to give you assurance of our sincerity. We have as a plight of faith yielded Boston, New York, and Philadelphia—the intelligence and wealth of the North—in carrying out the Compromise measures for the interests of the South; can we do more?"[35]

This exchange is significant because it establishes the idea of slavery as a national rather than a sectional or strictly Southern issue in the 1850s, and it makes clear the fact that "commercial interests" are the driving force behind national policy regarding slavery. These are not novel ideas now, but for Delany they were necessary to clarifying and reinforcing the nature of the climate in which his story's action takes place. The conversation reveals the sociopolitical reality of slavery's scope in the 1850s in contradistinction to the post–Civil War ideological narrative that would come to imagine the South as backward and morally bankrupt, clinging to the outdated institution of slavery while the progressive North sought to modernize, industrialize, and embody the democratic promise of the nation's founding. Even "Lost Cause" narratives of the Civil War that gained traction in the 1870s and '80s, and were exemplified in the turn-of-the-century fiction of Thomas Dixon, depended upon imagining the North and South as irreconcilably different and separate.[36] Madam

Ballard's assurances that the North would uphold its end of the bargain in regard to the Fugitive Slave Law, and her references to Boston, New York, and Philadelphia—high-profile cities where by 1852 (the first date explicitly mentioned in *Blake*) judges had upheld the law and remanded fugitive slaves to bondage—stage the geopolitical reality of the terrain Blake enters and inhabits once he leaves Colonel Franks's plantation, the place at which he and his family have been enslaved. That Blake will find no quarter in the supposedly more enlightened Northern states is the subject of the next section; for now, however, what is important is the nature of the quarter he *is* able to find, seemingly paradoxically, in the "huts of America" all over the slaveholding Southern states.

Blake, described by the book's narrator as "a pure Negro—handsome, manly, and intelligent . . . a man of good literary attainments—unknown to Colonel Franks, though he was aware he could read and write—having been educated in the West Indies," sets off to spread his insurrectionary plans.[37] We learn three critical facts about Henry here: He is a "pure Negro," he is highly literate, and he is originally from the West Indies. All of these were features commonly associated with rebellious enslaved people and those most likely to run away and lead violent uprisings during the pre–Civil War period. His vague West Indian origins are of especial import, as they connect him with Caribbean islands like Haiti, Jamaica, Santo Domingo (the Dominican Republic), and Cuba, on which marronage and insurrection had been ongoing phenomena throughout the eighteenth century and into the first half of the nineteenth. The importance of the connection to Haiti and the specter of the Haitian Revolution and long tradition of marronage on that island, as I will discuss more shortly, cannot be overstated. As Ifeoma Kiddoe Nwankwo has observed, "the revolution made a fear of uprising and, by extension, of transnationally oriented notions of Black community, into a continentwide obsession." This fear, she argues, "was not just of people of African descent in a particular location rising up and rebelling against the power structure in that location, but rather of people of African descent from and in a variety of locations connecting with each other and fomenting a massive revolution that might overturn the whole Atlantic slave system."[38] Such is the case with Blake, whose revolutionary plans span the US South and Cuba simultaneously. With regard to Henry's being from the "West Indies," such elusiveness of reference and nomenclature in the realm of representation mirrors maroons' elusiveness in the realm of the material. In this case, ambiguity and uncertainty are more unsettling than their opposites, just as with maroons, whose existence might be known, but uncertainty about their numbers, location, intentions, and activities is what makes them especially unsettling to enslavers' surveilling operations and conceptions of the ordering of space in the plantation context.

We do, however, eventually learn some specifics about Blake's origins: Notably, he was born a free man in Cuba named Henrico Blacus. Marronage in Cuba presents a singular case, according to Gabino La Rosa Corzo, whose *Runaway Slave Settlements in Cuba: Resistance and Repression* (2003) presents the most comprehensive and authoritative study of the phenomenon on this island.[39] La Rosa Corzo argues that in Cuba, a third class of maroons outside the *petit/grand* binary discussed earlier deserves its own designation, that of the "armed band of runaway slaves," or *caudrillas de cimarronajes*.[40] He describes them thus: "Each armed band of runaway slaves kept on the move through isolated areas, occasionally spending the night in a cave or temporary settlement of runaway slaves. These runaways did not engage in agriculture but lived by hunting, fishing, bartering, and—especially—stealing."[41] Previous generations of historians of US slavery suggested the prevalence of such groups of maroon "bandits" in the pre–Civil War United States, though more recent scholarship has shown that US maroons probably engaged in such behavior rarely, at least in a sustained or concerted way. In any event, however, Blake's association with Cuba and by extension Afro-Cuban forms of marronage linked directly to violence is an intriguing one, especially considering the fact that maroon-related conspiracies and slave rebellions in the Caribbean were reported in US antislavery publications in the pre–Civil War era with some frequency, something *Blake* draws specific reference to in its sections that take place in Cuba. Blake's experiences with marronage in Cuba relate to La Rosa Corzo's characterization in ways that are addressed later in this chapter. That *caudrillas de cimarronajes* also interacted with "temporary settlement[s] of runaway slaves"[42] is significant as well, as *Blake*'s Cuba section reveals the complex workings of the relationships between different varieties of maroons and marronage and the ways that they disrupt coherent senses of planter space and control. Their connectivity with surrounding plantations, Black spaces, and constant movement resonates with Blake's activities and with those of US maroons more generally.

Colonel Franks's (over)reaction to Henry's refusal to go riding with him at the beginning of the story and Henry's blunt statement that "I am not your slave, nor never was,"[43] prompting Franks to run inside for a revolver, thinking revolt is afoot, are worth a closer look. At first it does indeed seem like an exaggerated response, an overreaction that demonstrates how easily enslavers could become hysterical over even the slightest inkling of organized violence or revolt on the part of the enslaved. It also, however, functions as very early foreshadowing, especially when we remember the novel's original serialized format. Readers prior to 2017, to whom only Floyd Miller's 1970 version of the text was available, would know coming into the text, thanks to the summary blurb on the back cover, that Henry "is a West Indian slave who travels throughout the South advocating revolution, and later becomes the general of a black insurrectionary force in Cuba,"[44] and thus would recognize Delany's deliberate foreshadowing in this moment. So, is the takeaway, then, that slaveholders are right to be afraid, even here in what seems like an exaggerated circumstance? that they're right to be afraid but are ultimately powerless to stop someone like Henry—determined, willful, clever, educated, fearsome as he is—from carrying out such a plan once he has set his mind to it? that they're right to be afraid because any one of these "insubordinate" enslaved people could turn out to be the next Nat Turner, or, as I will suggest in a moment, the next Dutty Boukman? Any interpretation places agency ominously in the hands of the enslaved, its possibilities activated by marronage that the white gaze is incapable of perceiving as such if it continues attaching marronage to rebellion.

The scene also reveals a misunderstanding on Franks's part regarding how insurrection would begin—the divide between the enslavers' perspective and the enslaved perspective, as it were, and Franks's inability to see resistance beyond or outside the context of revolt. Franks exclaims that "he sees it plainly, he sees it," but in reality he does not see it at all—though he might be right, ultimately, about the rebellion, the plot, he is incapable of "seeing" how such a thing would be organized and ultimately come to pass. He is not privy to the shadow networks of communication and organization that structure the planning of such a plot, the lower frequencies and registers through which the enslaved mobilize collective action. His loud proclamations of discovery only further reinforce this point, as Delany makes apparent the gap between white and Black perceptions and understandings of the operational mechanisms of enslaved revolt and by extension enslaved resistive and maroon practices writ large. These points bring us to Dutty Boukman. Laurent Dubois calls Boukman "the most visible leader during the first days of the insurrection [in Saint-Domingue]," a former maroon "who had worked first as a driver and then as a coachman."[45] It became well known after the insurgency began that

Boukman had led a religious ceremony with organizers and participants from various neighboring plantations at a place known as Bois-Caiman either a week or two weeks prior to the beginning of the rebellion.[46] According to the only surviving firsthand account of this ceremony that was written soon after it actually took place, Boukman and his men "took an oath of secrecy and revenge, sealed by drinking the blood of a black pig sacrificed before them."[47] As Dubois and others such as Jean Fouchard and Carolyn Fick have noted, the sacrificial aspect of the ceremony was probably derived from West African traditions, which influence much of Blake's actions in the novel, including his marronage, as the flight and survival tactic originated on the African continent itself before arriving in the Caribbean and the Americas.[48]

Gregory Pierrot has observed that "the island nation [Haiti] goes almost unmentioned in the novel" but that its influence, with which Delany was intimately familiar, pervades and haunts the story.[49] He argues that this avoidance was in fact strategic on Delany's part, a way to "[define] his novel as a cultural intervention, a new narrative of black agency offering an alternative to the story of the Haitian Revolution, a renovated literary model for a coming nation of black readers."[50] I direct attention to Boukman's ceremony because Henry conducts a similar ceremony with his closest compatriots, the enslaved men Charles and Andy, when he imparts to them his scheme for insurrection in a previously agreed upon secret meeting place, a thicket in the woods near Franks's plantation. The meeting begins with a prayer, at Henry's request, which Andy offers, who "was a preacher of the Baptist pursuasion among his slave brethren."[51] Afterward, Henry shares with them the nature of his secret plan: "Clasping each other by the hand, standing in a band together, as a plight of their union and fidelity to each other, Henry said, 'I now impart to you the secret, it is this: I have laid a scheme, and matured a plan for a general insurrection of the slaves in every state, and the successful overthrow of slavery!' "[52] Charles and Andy are immediately on board with the plan but are desirous of understanding how it is to be organized and executed. Once again, though, Henry calls the group to prayer before sharing the details of his plot: " 'Well then, first to prayer, and then to the organization. Andy!' said Henry, nodding to him, when they again bowed low with their heads to the ground, whilst each breathed a silent prayer, which was ended with 'Amen' by Andy. Whilst yet upon their knees, Henry imparted to them the secrets of his organization."[53]

The two scenes are similar in their elements of secrecy, religiosity, and brotherhood, and in that they mark the beginning of a shared promise of collective, militant Black action against slavery with, to return to Patterson in this case, a maroon dimension, though one that while it seems tied to revolt will not be entirely. Delany calls upon the familiar history of Haiti during the pre–Civil War period in the United States in order to establish a sense of revolutionary, hemispheric import for the events that are about to unfold, even if the specific terms, figures, and mythologies of that revolutionary history will be revised to account for contingencies of time and place as the narrative progresses. Linking Blake and Boukman, and by extension Blake's plot and the Haitian Revolution, establishes a hemispheric episteme through which the unfolding action might be interpreted, and it reinforces marronage as a hemispheric resistive practice for enslaved Africans that evokes intercontinental and interoceanic diasporic subjectivity, once again further unsettling the United States as the geographic center for analysis of enslaved resistance even within its own borders. Marronage therefore becomes a fount of subaltern knowledge and strategy linking enslaved populations all over the Atlantic world. This maroon consciousness is not contained by the organizing logics of national space and time, and its possibilities cannot be understood through that hegemonic lens. Blake's planned revolt does indeed feature a maroon dimension, though the process of organizing the revolt reveals the ways marronage functions not only as necessarily constitutive of revolt but as its own reserve of resistive and freedom-seeking tactics.

Henry's marronage begins even before he actually takes flight from the Franks plantation in Mississippi. After learning that his wife was sold in his absence to a plantation owner in Cuba, Henry openly defies Colonel Franks's orders to take a morning ride alongside him, telling him, "You may do your mightiest, Colonel Franks. I'm not your slave, nor never was, and you know it! and but for my wife and her people, I never would have staid with you til now. I was decoyed away when young, and then became entangled in domestic relations as to induce me to remain with you; but now the tie is broken!"[54] This scene illustrates what Neil Roberts describes as the "imagined" dimension of flight or marronage and according to Roberts "bolsters a central maxim of the theory of marronage: Freedom is not a place; it is a state of being."[55] Upon Henry's defiance, Franks fears the worst, running into the house to grab a revolver, exclaiming to his wife that this must mean "a rebellion! a plot."[56] But where Franks sees a simplified, paranoid correspondence between verbal disobedience and violent revolt—where one must logically lead to the other—Henry's actions reveal a more nuanced understanding of enslaved resistance as a spectrum of interrelated behaviors, practices, and activities that can be both psychic and material in nature, and often both at once. Henry has taken the first step, making it clear that he considers himself psychologically emancipated from Colonel Franks. I do not mean to romanticize or suggest that psychic freedom resulted in material improvements in enslaved life, but that it can function in Roberts's terms as a kind of important precursor. This moment sets in motion the remainder of the narrative, in which Henry is continually on the move, making his way in almost fantastical maroon style between plantations and slave quarters, legible and illegible spaces, in every slaveholding state as well as across the Atlantic to Africa and farther south into Cuba.

Henry does, however, remain on the Franks plantation for several more days following his pronouncement of defiance, but at this point we can imagine him as a kind of maroon figure on the plantation itself, based on the way he himself conceptualizes his position. Psychologically emancipated and having declared that he will die before allowing himself to be whipped for disobedience, Henry embodies a means through which readers may be privy to what Rebecca Ginsburg calls "the black landscape," or "the system of paths, places, and rhythms that a community of enslaved people created as an alternative, often as a refuge, to the landscape systems of planters and other whites."[57] Ginsburg also emphasizes the idea that "enslaved workers knew the land through a different set of cognitive processes than did whites,"[58] which here may serve to deepen our understanding of what imagined freedom as marronage means for Henry Blake and might have meant for other maroons. Though physically present on the plantation, Henry moves about as he pleases, dictating his own activities and mobility without imposed prescriptions from outside or above. As a result, clandestine affective and material networks of sociality, communication, and planning emerge into focus, enabled by and acting in support of Henry's marronage.[59]

For example, learning that he has been covertly sold in a private transaction as punishment for his insubordination, Henry secretly convenes with the elderly Mammy Judy and Daddy Joe to ask if they will join him in ferrying his son Joe north to Canada. When they decline, Henry devises an alternate plan, announcing, "Then from this time hence I become a runaway. . . . When I leave the swamps, or where I'll go, will never be known to you. Should my boy suddenly be missed, and you find three notches cut in the bark of the big willow tree, on the side away from your hut, then give yourself no uneasiness."⁶⁰ While it is indeed true that Henry does henceforth become a runaway, his activities from this point forward are more suggestive of the behaviors of a maroon. Maroons simultaneously run away *and* refuse to leave. In the eyes of the slavocracy, they possess a sense of both unruly mobility and ominous stasis, as they have fled toward freedom from enslavement but continue to remain in slaveholding territory. They contest normativized geographies and imaginaries of control. It is at this point that Henry enters into the phase of his multidimensional resistant project that can best be described as resembling more "traditional" marronage, reminiscent in many ways of the historical maroons who sought freedom by and while remaining in the South. Here, Diouf's description of what she terms the "maroons' landscape" provides a useful framework through which we might apprehend the nature of the material and psychic world Henry navigates once he takes flight from the Franks plantation, initiating a maroon's life of constant, adaptable movement and secrecy in order to both escape detection and, in this case, spread the word about his insurrectionary designs. Moving into the maroons' landscape, Henry begins a sustained period of flight *away* from his own enslavement but also *toward* the freedom of himself and as many other enslaved people as possible. His marronage imparts agency that exceeds the circumscriptions of what is often understood to be possible through fugitivity, a subject position assigned by the state and inextricable from the logics of person as property. According to Diouf, the "maroons' landscape" was

> a place of exile whose settlers sought not only freedom but also self-determination. It was a dynamic site of empowerment, migrations, encounters, communication, exchange, solidarity, resistance, and entangled stories. It was also, of course, a contested terrain that slaveholders, overseers, drivers, slave hunters, dogs, militias, and patrollers strove to control and frequently invaded. Still, it was a space of movement, independence, and reinvention where new types of lives were created and evolved; where networks were built and solidified, and where solidarity expressed itself in concrete ways that rendered the maroons' alternative way of life possible.⁶¹

By imagining Henry Blake as a maroon and his activities as acts of marronage within and between the contours of such a contested landscape, and by considering the text as-is—with the revolt never actually begun—we arrive at a sense of a multifaceted, networked landscape of defiance and survival that is inclusive of but does not become overdetermined by the anticipated teleology of insurrection. Instead, it moves us beyond revolt to consider objectives that do not register within the white psyche and sensibility regarding the pursuit of freedom. The pursuit itself becomes the objective, as marronage does not pause for or adhere to the conventions of national space and time.

Henry's psychic marronage enables his entrance into the maroons' landscape, which serves as an illuminating optic through which to view the various settings, activities, and movements that make up the quest for freedom in part 1 of the text. At the same time, readers are granted access to a world of alternative freedoms, socialities, and networks that are generally illegible to outsiders. *Blake* engages with and challenges white notions of freedom to reveal the intricacies of Black versions, the possibilities that are obfuscated in the white consciousness. During the first of what will become many "seclusions," or secret meetings between Henry and trusted enslaved compatriots in every slave state, we witness Henry explaining to his friends Charles and Andy the means by which the plan for insurrection should be spread. That plan ultimately appears simple: activate the same maroon consciousness in others that Henry adopted after his wife was sold, thus preparing the enslaved population throughout the South to strike for material freedom on their own terms once psychological freedom has already been accomplished. In order to spread the plan, Henry instructs his friends as follows: "All you have to do, is find one good man or woman . . . on a single plantation, and hold a seclusion to impart the secret to them, and make them the organizers for their own plantation, and they in like manner impart it to some other next to them, and so on. In this way it will spread like smallpox among them."[62] The basis of the plan, then, hinges on the maroon's tactics of secrecy and movement: the clandestine movement of enslaved people between and among plantations, the movement of ideas from one person to another, and the movement of individual enslaved consciousness to collective self-liberated consciousness. All of these movements are encapsulated in what Neil Roberts suggests are the various "domains" of "flight" in his definition of marronage: "physical environment, embodied cognition, and/or the metaphysical."[63] Movement and the ability to limit or expand one's mobility at will thus become fundamental to Henry's resistant maroon project and structure the progression of the narrative itself, as we will soon see in more detail.

Henry's strategy for throwing Colonel Franks and other would-be pursuers off his tracks once he departs further engages with practices of marronage. He declares to Charles and Andy that "I now go as a runaway, and will be suspected of lurking about in the thickets, swamps, and caves," the solution for which is to ensure that those suspicions are, in fact, maintained. " 'To make the ruse complete,' " the two men are to periodically kill animals and steal foodstuffs from the plantation, always leaving evidence about to make the pilfering appear hasty and half-complete.[64] This way, Henry will be suspected as the culprit of the thefts, a suspicion which he instructs the men to contribute to by overtly placing blame on him: "Everything that is missed do not hesitate to lay it upon me, as a runaway, it will cause them to have the less suspicion of your having such a design."[65] The success of Henry's venture, then, depends upon the maroon's need for *illegibility*, which, as James C. Scott contends, "has been and remains, a reliable source for political autonomy."[66] Here Henry engages directly with white fears regarding maroons, specifically with borderland maroons (those who remained in close proximity to plantation society) and acts of *petit marronage*, in order to play those fears against slaveholders and by doing so maintain the illusion that he is engaged in *petit marronage* instead of the more ominous *grand marronage*, a variation of which is in fact the reality, as he intends to depart and traverse the slaveholding states spreading his plan. The language of "lurking about" in "thickets, swamps, and caves" aligns precisely with the terms deployed by enslavers to describe maroons and maroon activities, the terms of disavowal that associate them with the less threatening class of "runaways" who are imagined to simply be seeking personal freedom rather than escaping enslavement and plotting against the system from within the terrain of the maroon landscape as it overlaps with the plantation order. Not naming Henry as a maroon, his actions as acts of marronage, or his tactics as maroon tactics comports with Delany's rhetorical strategy and with maroons' own need for concealment and obfuscation as a means for survival. The fact that *petit marronage* can serve as a cover for what Henry is truly engaged in, something more akin to a form of *grand marronage* but still, importantly for my argument, outside that binary formulation, also suggests the extent to which enslavers were aware of various forms and practices of marronage in their communities but sought to obfuscate them in order to shore up their claims to power and control. It demonstrates as well the inadequacy of binary conceptions of marronage, ones that do not account for the protean fluidity that characterizes the practice in the first place.

Henry must remain not just hidden or unseen but illegible in the sense that he is unable to be deciphered, unable to be known or understood. Such a feat is accomplished through a combination of communication and deception that will allow Charles and Andy to act on their "design"—that is, their plan to keep all eyes on Henry while they go out and spread the word regarding the insurrection. If we operate under the assumption that "marronage was political action on the part of enslaved persons," then we are able to understand the acts of marronage *themselves* as political acts in the ongoing quest for Black freedom, not just as vehicles for bringing about large-scale political action via insurrection or revolution.[67] When the fantasy of insurrection is removed or at least deferred, as it is at the conclusion of *Blake*, the illegible becomes just slightly more legible if we know how to look at it, which *Blake* teaches us to do.

Such sustained illegibility defies Colonel Franks's claim to ownership of Henry in a profound way, and in its specifically maroon manifestation it undermines claims to slavery's paternalism. Within these liminal spaces of "untamed wilderness," places that Stephanie LeMenager has called "marginal landscapes," or "environmental features that defied all usages associated with property value in the antebellum United States,"[68] Henry in fact establishes contact with maroons, whom he calls "the much-dreaded runaways of the woods, a class of outlawed slaves."[69] Here, through the narrator, Delany plays upon fears similar to Colonel Franks's at the beginning of the text, wherein the paranoia of enslavers leads them to believe that violent revolt or vengeance is the aim of maroons rather than radical and novel modes of and possibilities for freedom, however they may come to materialize. Just as criticism on enslaved resistance has often elided marronage in the US context, Diouf argues that Southerners during slavery "reserved the terminology maroons for the people of Jamaica and Suriname . . . [and] were precursors to the denial of the American maroons' existence. They called the people in their midst outliers . . . or runaways and banditti."[70] Then, as now, the term *maroon* came loaded with connotations of freedom-seeking behaviors that enslavers not only did not *want* to assign to runaways but also could not fully imagine as possibilities for freedom-seeking behavior in the first place. When Linda Brent in *Incidents in the Life of a Slave Girl* (1861) goes missing for seven years and is holed up in the garret above her grandmother's shed, everyone believes her to have of course fled north, never to have remained in the South, defiantly claiming a version of maroon freedom by essentially hiding in plain sight. Ironically, Linda is safest when she is in the South, nearer those who wish to re-enslave her but benefitting from a network of familial, material, and affective resistant support that resembles maroon collectivity and transcends what, from the enslavers' point of view, is possible for enslaved people under enslavers' supposed complete control.

Henry's travels through Louisiana, the first place he heads after leaving Franks's plantation, conjure up a particularly significant history of maroon tactics and maroon communities. In 1853, the kidnapped free Black man Solomon Northup's narrative *Twelve Years a Slave* brought the issues of marronage, rebellion, and their intersections in the Red River region of Louisiana to the attention of the antislavery reading public in striking detail, though this aspect of the narrative is infrequently discussed as it connects to marronage, presenting yet another opportunity to explore this dimension in African American literature. The region had also been represented previously in Harriet Beecher Stowe's *Uncle Tom's Cabin* (1852), as it was the location of Simon Legree's plantation, the place where the bestselling novel's titular protagonist made his fateful last stand. These texts, along with *Blake*, suggest that slavery is especially brutal in the Deep South recesses of rural Louisiana, but Henry believes he can turn this fact to his advantage: "The river is narrow, the water red as if colored by iron rust, the channel winding. Beyond this river lie his hopes, the broad plains of Louisiana with a hundred thousand bondsmen seeming anxiously to await him."[71] Northup notes a similar situation, where, despite the fact that capture is always imminent, "the woods and swamps are, nevertheless, continually filled with runaways."[72] Of the prospect of armed revolt in the area, he writes: "Such an idea as insurrection . . . is not new among the enslaved population of Bayou Boeuf. More than once I have joined in serious consultation, when the subject has been discussed, and there have been times when a word from me would have placed hundreds of my fellow-bondsmen in an attitude of defiance."[73] Northup proceeds to relate his knowledge of the enslaved man Lew Cheney's militant liberatory scheme from 1837, a year before he had arrived in the area:

> The year before my arrival in the country there was a concerted movement among a number of slaves on Bayou Boeuf, that terminated tragically indeed. . . . It has become a subject of general and unfailing interest in every slave-hut on the

> bayou, and will doubtless go down to succeeding generations as their chief tradition. Lew Cheney, with whom I became acquainted—a shrewd, cunning negro, more intelligent than the generality of his race, but unscrupulous and full of treachery—conceived the project of organizing a company sufficiently strong to fight their way against all opposition, to the neighboring territory of Mexico. A remote spot, far within the depths of the swamp, back of Hawkins' plantation, was selected as the rallying point. Lew flitted from one plantation to another in the dead of night, preaching a crusade to Mexico, and, like Peter the Hermit, creating a furor of excitement wherever he appeared. At length a large number of runaways were assembled; stolen mules, and corn gathered from the fields, and bacon escaped from smoke-houses, had been conveyed into the woods.[74]

Cheney's covert movements between plantations "in the dead of night," spreading his plan, very much resemble Henry's, and the meeting of assembled runaways in the swamps is evocative of Dutty Boukman's prior to the uprising of the enslaved in Saint-Domingue. But, according to Northup, the expedition's hiding place was discovered before the plan could be executed, at which point Cheney turned on his followers and "proclaimed among the planters the number collected in the swamp, and, instead of stating truly the object they had in view, asserted their intention was to emerge from their seclusion the first favorable opportunity, and murder every white person along the bayou,"[75] an objective resonant with the outcome of Nat Turner's revolt only six years prior. Unsurprisingly, "such an announcement," Northup writes, "filled the whole country with terror," and mass, indiscriminate hangings followed that were only stopped when "a regiment of soldiers . . . arrived from some fort on the Texan frontier, demolished the gallows, and opened the doors of the Alexandria prison."[76] While they would not name the participants as maroons, Southern officials acted swiftly and brutally to suppress what were clearly threatening maroon operations.

Blake continues to draw marronage into association with larger-scale resistance during Henry's visit to New Orleans, "the portentous city,"[77] and to complicate that relationship. He arrives during the Mardi Gras festivities, when the Black population, free and enslaved, was allowed significantly greater privileges of movement and congregation than usual, and he uses all of this to his advantage. Traveling through Arkansas, Blake had been counseled to "keep in de thicket, chile, as da patrolas feahd to go in de woods, da feahd runaway ketch 'em! Keep in da woods, chile, an' da ain' goin' dah bit! Da talk big, and sen' der dog, but da ain' goin' honey!,"[78] suggesting a robust maroon presence in the area, or at least the perception of one among the enslavers and their patrols. Blake's interlocutor suggests a world gone topsy-turvy, where enslavers fear capture by runaway enslaved people rather than the other way around. Such a conception of this relationship imparts significant power to the runaways or maroons, suggesting that they wield much more considerable local political power than might be otherwise imagined. In another "seclusion" reminiscent of Boukman's and of Blake's previous ones, Blake meets under the guise of the Mardi Gras celebration with likeminded Black leaders from fifteen plantations in a rented house. One of the enslaved men, Tib, becomes convinced that now is the time to strike, to put Blake's plan into effect, and leaves the house exclaiming "Insurrection! Insurrection! Death to every white!"[79] Panic quickly ensues, as "intelligence soon reached all parts of the city, that an extensive plot for rebellion of the slaves had been timely detected. The place was at once thrown into a state of intense excitement, the military called into requisition, dragoons flying in every direction, cannon from the old fort sending forth hourly through the night."[80] Thus, *Blake* opens up the possibility for large-scale rebellion even as it suggests ways in which it might be foreclosed, providing us time to consider marronage without also necessarily considering it as tied to revolt. Since revolt is what enslavers fear most, they are prepared at all times to squash it, especially after Nat Turner. But they are unprepared to reckon with the complex realities of marronage. The text remains open to any and all possibilities for freedom and freedom-seeking, delineating the connections between those possibilities rather than enforcing only one.

In what follows, the imagined insurrection initiates a hypothetical reversal of the normative spatial order: "The inquisition held in the case of the betrayer Tib developed fearful antecedents of extensive arrangements for the destruction of the city by fire and water, thereby compelling the white inhabitants to take refuge in the swamps, whilst the blacks marched up the coast, sweeping the plantations as they went."[81] Such an event has historical precedent in the New Orleans area. In January of 1811, somewhere between sixty and 130 enslaved people (though other estimates put this number at between two hundred and over five hundred) in the German Coast region of Louisiana, along the east bank of the Mississippi River in what are now St. John the Baptist and St. Charles Parishes, rose up, armed themselves with farming tools, and marched around twenty miles toward New Orleans, burning plantation houses, sugar houses, and crops along the way.[82] Reports indicated that the rebels' numbers increased as they moved through plantations recruiting other enslaved people to their cause, and rumors circulated that maroons—known to populate the area's many swamps—were involved, a fact that is likely true in this particular case. While only two whites were killed in the uprising, its bloody aftermath left nearly one hundred Black people dead. The man who came to be recognized as the leader of the uprising, the enslaved man Charles Deslondes, had been born into slavery in Saint-Domingue and brought by his enslaver to the Orleans Territory as a result of the outbreak of the Haitian Revolution, linking him and his actions to hemispheric acts of marronage and rebellion, and further entrenching white fears of enslaved people from the Caribbean.

That Lew Cheney's objective was to flee south, to Mexico, rather than north to the free states or Canada, is significant. Part of this has to do with the near impossibility of trekking that far north from the Deep South state of Louisiana—certainly Mexico is much nearer, and it is without a Fugitive Slave Law that would see runaways returned to enslavers if captured as fugitives in any Northern state. Again, we see how the altered geography of freedom and unfreedom initiated by the passage of the Fugitive Slave Law heightened representations of marronage and of escape west, or south, or outside the country entirely. As one possibility is closed, another opens, and the maroon's illegibility shifts forms. In *South to Freedom: Runaway Slaves to Mexico and the Road to the Civil War*, Alice Baumgartner writes, "The freedom that Mexico promised would threaten slavery not just in the nearby states of Texas and Louisiana, but at the very heart of the Union."[83] Baumgartner argues that Mexico, rather than Canada, presented opportunities for seeking freedom that appeared eminently more possible to enslaved people in the Deep South—but these flights did nothing to bolster the political and moralistic standing of Northeastern abolitionist elites, did not comport with the imagined geography of freedom associated with the Underground Railroad, and ultimately put the lie to the benevolence of US liberal democracy in discomfiting ways—as Baumgartner says, to the heart of the Union itself. These southerly movements have not been considered in depth in the scholarship on US slavery and resistance until recently, having run up against adherence to

US-centrism and the Underground Railroad paradigm in historical and literary study of African American life.

During Henry's sojourns between states, and particularly between and within those like "haughty South Carolina," where "the most relentless hatred appears to exist against the negro,"[84] he employs survival strategies consistent with what Diouf, Sayers, and Nevius have identified regarding US maroons and maroon communities. He conceals himself inside of fallen logs, sleeps out of sight in high tree branches, dexterously fends off wild creatures and slave catchers' dogs alike, and utilizes the inhospitable landscapes of swamps and marshes, all in service of his project of heading farther south and in horizontal movements from plantation to plantation, from slave quarters to woodland seclusions, extending the networks of his plan and elucidating alternate versions of freedom within the slaveholding South. These interactions and exchanges expand what we are to imagine, if Charles and Andy have followed the plan as well, is an ever-increasing, weblike network of maroon consciousness and resistant Black solidarity across cities, counties, and states. Even if the insurrection never comes to pass, as it indeed does not in the text, Henry's marronage—and, in turn, Charles's and Andy's as they sneak away to visit other plantations—enables affective support and solidarity that is crucial to the survival of the enslaved and potential maroon. The psychological marronage or maroon consciousness and acts of short-term marronage necessary to ensure its dissemination thus work to form a constellation of self-, community-, and life-affirming practices in the face of a system of white supremacist authority designed to stamp out just such things. They also provide hope for the future. Through the liminal woodland and swamp spaces traveled during acts of marronage, the systems and rhythms of Ginsburg's "black landscape" pulsate with greater life, infused with the energy of psychic emancipation and offering radical visions of freedoms that exceed a liberal framework.

When Henry does make it to the Dismal Swamp in North Carolina—a famed retreat for US maroons for as long as slavery existed on the continent—he encounters an actual maroon community where "a number of the old confederates of the noted Nat Turner were met with. . . . Many of these are still long-suffering, hard-laboring slaves on the plantations; and some bold, courageous, and fearless adventurers, denizens of the mystical, antiquated, and almost fabulous Dismal Swamp, where for many years they have defied the approach of their pursuers."[85] Considering marronage via the Caribbean model, we might see similarities here in the sense that the High Conjurers' Dismal Swamp community contains many members, is largely self-sufficient, and is prepared to defend itself from attack. It contains "secluded hut[s], underground room[s], and cave[s]"[86] like those Diouf describes in her research on US maroon communities. However, considering the community simply as a band of refugees from a failed attempt at large-scale revolt obscures the multidimensional axes of resistance and survival that are ongoing among this group. Most significantly, the men live in the liminal spaces of the maroons' landscape, having achieved a sense of freedom, autonomy, and safety even as that freedom defies the hegemonic spatial ordering of the plantocracy. They have formed a mutual aid network that sustains both psychic and material Black life. Gamby Gholar, one of the noted high conjurers among the maroons, is said to have been "more than thirty years secluded in the Swamp,"[87] thus arriving even before Nat Turner's Southampton Revolt in 1831. These maroons have staked a claim to freedom in a way that has not been sufficiently analyzed or understood in the United States, whereas marronage has featured in dialectical conceptions of freedom in places like Haiti, Jamaica, Suriname, and Brazil for hundreds of years. These undertheorized, alternative versions of freedom in the interstices of plantation society and the maroons' landscape enable, even as they are also the result of, Henry's multidimensional resistant project.

The elderly men of the maroon council have a significant role to play in expanding Henry's plan, propagating his ideas, and enlarging the berth of maroon consciousness among those already imbricated in practices of marronage in the world contained within and adjacent to the Dismal Swamp. As the high conjurers note, their maroon world is not one entirely disconnected from the plantation landscape that abuts and often invades it. But here, proximity to the enslaved population functions positively for the maroons and for the still-enslaved, as it provides the maroons opportunities to go out as "ambassadors from the Swamp" to "create new conjurers, lay charms, take off 'spells' that could not be reached by Low Conjurers, and renew the art of all conjurers of seven years existence."[88] Their marronage enables other forms and acts of marronage that radiate outward from the autonomous swamp encampment they have established. In this sense, freedom too radiates outward from this marginal, liminal space of the swamp. This freedom is embodied as well as psychic and metaphysical, and it defies the notion of freedom defined as legal emancipation, or freedom granted by external (white, state) actors. By extension, it once again also defies the unfreedom of chattel slavery as the codifed legal opposite of freedom. Here, following Neil Roberts, marronage as freedom can be understood variously as movements, speech acts, thoughts, and complex resistant behaviors initiated by the enslaved themselves. In the case of maroons and marronage, existence is resistance, but it is also solidarity and survival, psychic and material. Marronage thus continues to trouble totalizing conceptions of both freedom and unfreedom, drawing attention to the ambiguous realm of what possibilities lie between.

It's important to note that, while Henry locates the maroons in this community as useful to him insofar as they are willing to perpetuate his plan for insurrection and have valuable contacts and influence among the nearby enslaved populations, he speaks somewhat condescendingly and dismissively of them in the narration. They regale him with tales of past exploits as part of rebellions like Nat Turner's and Gabriel's Rebellion in Virginia in 1800, and one man claims to have fought in the American Revolution. Henry humors them and grants them what he sees as the fantasy of their own triumphant remembrances. He finds their elaborate ceremonies amusing, and even more so the fact that they insist upon anointing him as "a priest of the order of High Conjurers"[89] before he sets off on his journey once more. The men view Henry as a kind of savior figure upon his arrival, "hail[ing] the daring runaway as the harbinger of better days."[90] This aligns with the way Blake often conceives of himself, which is perpetuated by the narrator throughout the text. Blake, like Dred as well as historical figures like Nat Turner, advocates a version of Christianity in which, contrary to what enslavers often selectively preached to enslaved populations, slavery is fundamentally anti-Christian, and they imagine a vengeful Old Testament God whose destruction will be wrought on enslavers for violating the sacred rights of all human beings.

It's not particularly surprising, then, that Blake's attachment to Christianity puts him at odds with the conjuring practices and what he sees as superstitions among the elderly men of the swamp community. But, ever pragmatic and committed to furthering his plan by any means possible, he humors them and shows respect and gratitude while in their presence. Through these scenes in the Dismal Swamp, Delany as author and political thinker largely dismisses the men as relics of a bygone era, of thwarted small-scale revolts, who have lapsed into romantic nostalgia about their past. But this is because the kind of communal formation they have established does not fit conveniently into the Black nationalist project to which Blake (and Delany) was committed. In Blake's and Delany's estimation, the men are not successful in the terms they believe offer the best chance at collective Black liberation, as they have not succeeded in forging a separate political entity, even if one that is a nation within a nation. Even so, when placed into the expanded context of liberatory practices undertaken and explored throughout the rest of the novel, the point remains clear that, superstitious and nostalgic or not, the men live independently from white control, out from under the grasp of slavery, and in accordance with their own beliefs and social order. This social order is one staunchly at odds with what US liberal democracy has to offer and contests the general principles of liberalism that undergird the United States specifically.

Expanding the Maroon Landscape: Henry Blake in the North

Historians and literary scholars working on African American studies and the political geographies of freedom and unfreedom in the pre–Civil War period have recently begun to explore in earnest the commonalities between maroon communities in the South and purportedly free Black communities in both the North and the South. Steven Hahn argues that settlements of Black folks in the North resembled maroon communities for several reasons, not the least of which was because they very often contained numerous fugitives from slavery, who after (but also before) the 1850 Fugitive Slave Law were living in a situation of extreme precariousness.[91] He suggests that "the northern settlements and enclaves of fugitives and freed blacks—like maroons—everywhere shared a fundamental political orientation to the world around them. They were 'under siege.'"[92] "Northern blacks lived in constant fear," he continues, "whatever their legal status, and, like maroons in the southern states or in other parts of the hemisphere, they and their communities had to be perpetually alert, perpetually on guard, perpetually self-protective."[93] Similarly, Ted Maris-Wolf has recently challenged scholars to think beyond conventional ideas about maroon communities in the United States by looking at fugitive Black laborers in the Great Dismal Swamp. He argues that we should imagine communities of these fugitive laborers as maroon communities "hidden in plain sight," existing right at the "center of large-scale industrial operations."[94] We must, therefore, understand and acknowledge the ways in which slavery's scope and the ubiquity of federalized, legislative, and institutional white supremacy flattened national space and defied sectional considerations in its regulation and oppression of pre-Civil War African Americans—free, enslaved, fugitive, or maroon. And we must also maintain an expansive conception of what a maroon or a maroon community could be in the context of the social, political, economic, cultural, historical, and geographical contingencies of the United States.

Upon returning to Mississippi, and after a clandestine meeting with Charles and Andy in "the forest, two and a half miles from the city,"[95] Henry returns to Colonel Franks's Natchez plantation to find that Franks has been threatening to sell the elderly Mammy Judy and Daddy Joe to slave traders. But Henry, always at least one step ahead, has already established a plan to escort all of them to safety and freedom in Canada. That very night, they leave and meet Henry at a designated spot, "the old burnt sycamore stump above the ferry,"[96] at two o'clock in the morning. The boatman, a white man, is also already in on the plan and loudly asks Henry for a pass "as a ruse, lest he might be watched by a concealed party."[97] Coming upon another river, the Arkansas, Henry is forced this time to deal with a boatman whom he has not already co-opted as part of his grand scheme. The man is resistant at first, telling Henry, "I want none of yer nigger passes . . . They ain't none uv 'em good 'or nothin', no how!,"[98] but Henry quickly convinces him by "presenting the unmistaking evidence of a shining gold eagle, at the sight of which emblem of his country's liberty, the skiffman's patriotism was at once awakened, and their right to pass as American freemen indisputable."[99] Such instances illustrate the ways in which people and forces at odds with the runaways' enterprise are themselves part of the maroon landscape where Henry operates and can be made to serve the runaways' ends with, in this case, bribery. The old burnt sycamore stump, meaningless through the planters' gaze, is pregnant with meaning and possibility through that of the enslaved person and maroon. It draws attention to minor aspects of the physical landscape that do not figure into larger geographical analyses but are crucial to maroon survival.

At the Ohio River crossing, the ferryman the group meets makes it clear, despite his confusion, that the Fugitive Slave Law has made the North unwelcoming of and inhospitable to fugitives from slavery: "This are a law made by the Newnited States of Ameriky," he explains to Henry, "an' I be 'bliged to fulfill it by ketchin' every fugitive that goes to cross this way, or I mus' pay a thousand dollars, and go to jail till the black folks is got, if that be's never."[100] Henry is able to convince him otherwise with yet another bribe, but the stage has been set for the troubles the group will face once they cross into the Northern states and land on the shores of nominally free Illinois. The group proceeds in this way, producing gold in lieu of papers as necessary, until they reach "a village in the center of northern Indiana."[101] "Supposing their proximity to the British Provinces made them safe," the narrator relates, "with an imprudence not before committed by the discreet runaways, when nearing a blacksmith's shop a mile and a half from the village," Andy breaks out into song. He sings of being on the way to Canada, having "now resolved to strike the blow, / For Freedom or the grave," and all unite in the chorus: "O, righteous Father / Wilt thou not pity me; / And aid me on to Canada, / Where fugitives are free? / I heard old England plainly say, / If we would all forsake, / Our native land of Slavery, / And come across the lake."[102] The song suggests that the runaways fully understand that the North is unsafe and that Canada offers a safer haven, outside the purview of United States law. But this episode leads to disaster. They are sold out by a seemingly friendly blacksmith and his wife, who offer them a brief respite from their journey. In the blacksmith's shop, Henry discovers a handbill "fully descriptive of himself and comrades, having been issued in the town of St. Genevieve, offering a heavy reward" in the blacksmith's possession.[103] Having made it out of the slaveholding South without major incident, it is ironically in the North that the clutches of slavery come closest to re-ensnaring them. The complicity of the elderly Black couple, foils to Mammy Judy and Daddy Joe, who claim to have both once been enslaved themselves, in the group's capture is also worth noting. Delany makes clear by this example that no one in the North was to be trusted, that even formerly enslaved people and former fugitives from slavery could not be counted on as allies. Networks of solidarity are more precarious in the North, somewhat ironically, than they are in the slaveholding South, where the maroon finds possibility amid the most repressive of social regimes. The "Canada" Henry and his compatriots seek is not actually in Canada at all but is instead an idea. It is actually a place that Henry must will into existence, imbue with possibility, and activate *within* the heart of the slaveholding states.

Although they do make it to Windsor, Essex County, in Canada West without further incident, Delany begins the penultimate chapter of part 1 not with exultations of freedom but with a lengthy description of the discrimination faced by those of African descent in Canada:

> Poor fellow! he [Andy] little knew the unnatural feelings and course pursued toward his race by many Canadians. . . . He little knew that while according to fundamental British Law and constitutional rights, all persons are equal in the realm, yet by a systematic course of policy and artifice, his race with few exceptions in some parts . . . is excluded from the enjoyment and exercise of every right, except mere suffrage-voting—even to those of sitting on a jury as its own peer, and the exercise of military duty. He little knew the facts, and as little expected to find such a state of things in the long-talked of and much-loved Canada by the slaves. It had never entered the mind of poor Andy, that in going to Canada in search of freedom, he was then in a country where privileges were denied him which are common to the slave in every Southern state.[104]

While the narrator does admit, "But Andy was free—being on British soil—from the bribes of slaveholding influences; where the unhallowed foot of the slavecatcher dare not tread; where no decrees of an American Congress sanctioned by a president born and bred in a free state . . . could reach,"[105] this catalog of injustices remains striking nonetheless. It does, however, align with the sense of strategic, subaltern geography that Delany articulates throughout *Blake*. The Northern, so-called "free" states have been compromised by the Fugitive Slave Law, and Canada, while allowing Black residents legal freedom, harbors racial prejudices that are reflected in its societal and institutional structures. Harriet Jacobs, too, spends a great deal of time describing the means by which racial subjugation and oppression are enacted in the North after she makes her escape there and arrives in Philadelphia and eventually New York. Hopes for freedom on a grand scale cannot be rooted in Canada, the text suggests, as the perils of this one journey north reveal the impossibility of mass escape to that place. It is in the heart of the South, where the enslaved population is concentrated on large plantations, that he must place such hopes and possibilities. And it will be through maroon tactics that some alternative versions of freedom will be attained for the enslaved, not through a mass exodus to some outside landscape but through a concerted reconfiguration of existing landscapes.

All of Henry's movements between and through the slaveholding states of the US South, along with the networks of support and resistance brought into focus because of those peregrinations, expand our sense of maroons and especially of marronage, making it appear as an interrelated spectrum of behaviors, activities, and processes constellated around flight and the indefatigable desire for freedom on the part of the enslaved. Marronage works to center the relative agency of the enslaved and to position freedom as something for which they strike out rather than something they may be granted from the outside. In other words, marronage centers Black self-determination and by extension decenters and delegitimizes the white supremacist structures that make marronage necessary in the first place. In this sense, reading *Blake* through the lens of marronage contributes to our understanding of the text as a Black nationalist project while expanding our sense of what Black nationalism(s) in the form of Black self-reliance and self-determination might have meant for Martin Delany. Writing in a letter to the editor of *The New York Review of Books* in 1970, Floyd Miller emphasized that Delany "serves as the 'father' of *several* black nationalisms,"[106] a point worth remembering when Delany is still often invoked as a Black nationalist writer without clarification of the intricacies of that nationalism, which grew, transformed, and expanded over the course of his writing career. What emerges from an examination of Henry Blake as a maroon and of practices of marronage in *Blake* is a sense of a multifaceted resistant project wherein freedom, as opposed to emancipation, is the uniting feature. Considered this way, we may still identify significant connections between US and Caribbean marronage and freedom-seeking practices throughout the hemisphere without problematically collapsing their important distinctions or privileging one form over another.

Ultimately, we can imagine *Blake* as a literary text that performs considerable work to theorize marronage as freedom and freedom as marronage in ways that were and mostly remain illegible in the genealogy of liberal thought on freedom from the 1850s into our present moment. These theorizations of freedom via marronage, considered alongside interdisciplinary critical interventions on the subject, offer scholars of *Blake* as well as of African American literature more broadly a means of thinking about freedom that is dislocated from the teleology of revolutionary fulfillment and the hindrances of deferred action perceived as stasis. Henry Blake's marronage asks us to consider the social and political potentialities of radical forms of freedom and of interstitial subject positions that defy the hegemonic geospatial imaginary of nineteenth-century US liberal democracy, in the process revealing forms and methods of freedom-seeking that assume no recourse to the state or its institutions.

Cuban Links

As noted previously, *Blake* does not take place only in the United States. Henry makes a trip to the West African coast aboard a slave ship, and he travels to Cuba, his place of birth as the free Black man Henrico Blacus, after his wife has been sold there by his former enslaver in Mississippi. *Blake* takes us on a journey that decentralizes the United States in the hemispheric geography of freedom and unfreedom. The story suggests possibilities for freedom-seeking that dislodge the US as a beacon of freedom and possibility for African Americans in the nineteenth century, especially post–Fugitive Slave Law. Blake puts no faith in traditional liberalism or even an aspirational liberalism that can enact large-scale emancipation and secure rights and state-granted freedoms for African Americans. Instead, he depends on the exercise of enslaved agency through marronage, enacting radical collectivity and socialities among the enslaved and fostering a community consciousness of resistive practices and tactics. His plan requires no recourse to the state, as he plans to institute a radical state of his group's own collective making where slavery is consummately outlawed and freedom is the backbone of the newly envisioned societal structure.

Cuba represents a singular location for Blake's further pursuits of freedom. Spanish colonial law regarding slavery differed immensely from that present in the United States. In Cuba, enslaved people did have recourse to the law when seeking official manumission granted by the state. Fernanda Bretones Lane, discussing methods for freedom-seeking among Caribbean maroons, observes that "countless . . . maritime maroons had indeed achieved legal freedom in Spanish colonies after escaping from Spain's rivals and converting to Catholicism."[107] *Maritime marronage* refers to the practice as carried out by enslaved people who took flight via sea, usually by absconding aboard ships moving throughout the Caribbean islands, often operating according to intelligence circulated by what Julius Scott has called the "common wind" of Black communicative networks that were indecipherable to enslavers.[108] Because slave laws varied from island to island depending on the colonial powers in charge, maritime maroons frequently sought out Cuba because of the opportunities its laws allowed for negotiating one's own freedom outside self-purchase, which was nearly impossible for most enslaved people given the exorbitant amounts of money required.

Conversion to Catholicism presented perhaps the most common example for enslaved people in Spanish-controlled colonies, as Spain extended its proselytizing efforts to fugitives from slavery, granting them free status on the island regardless of where they had come from, largely as a method of shoring up colonial and religious power in the Caribbean. This was always a dangerous game for enslavers, as I have been arguing in this book that enslavers frequently lacked the imaginative capacity to envision the kinds of freedoms sought and enabled by nonliberal ideologies and practices of marronage. Such a form of religious sanctuary was unique to Cuba, in stark contrast to the systems of British and French law in their colonies as well as in the United States. Enslaved people in Cuba were also allowed to petition secular and ecclesiastical courts regarding claims of extreme abuse, instances of familial separation, and refusal by enslavers to accept payment for manumission. Such procedures functioned as a system of control and domination, providing a safety valve designed to stave off violent rebellion and marronage, but the enslaved found various ways to use them to their advantage, often in ways that did not register with how the slavocracy understood the logics of freedom and unfreedom as have been elaborated in this chapter. Henry overhears a conversation regarding these laws between two enslavers, who explain that "the law in its wisdom supposes it better to lose our property than our lives; better to let the negro have his liberty at his own expense at a price fixed by the law, than have him take his liberty and the Island by violence at the expense of our blood."[109] The fear is always present and animates the particularities of law across time and space during the era of Black chattel slavery. Whereas enslavers preferred to imagine freedom as something they held the power to grant on their own terms, the enslaved worked inside, outside, and within the interstices of the system to negotiate forms of freedom and create them on their own terms.

There is an especial radicalness and fount of possibility, therefore, to Blake's strategic choices as he continues to organize his insurrection in Cuba. While he does locate his wife and purchase her freedom once there, that is the end of his recourse to the state and colonial laws and procedures. His careful saving of money over a long period of time enables this transaction and reunification of family. The freedom he seeks is collective and communal and is not one resulting from officialized manumission or emancipation but rather a freedom that is taken on his terms, not given from outside by powers he does not recognize as legitimate in the first place. He has little interest in negotiation, preferring instead to assemble his own Black and antislavery governmental structure after the planned takeover of the island by the enslaved and sympathetic free Black populations. Though Henry's insurrection never comes to pass, the final lines of the text are distinctly foreboding. Gopher Gondolier, the cook whose always-sharpened, enormous knife he had ominous designs for other than cooking, leaves us with a final incantation: "Woe be unto those devils of whites, I say!"[110] Woe to be sure, though not the woe, at least in what survives of the text, of mass insurrection and overthrow of the colonial regime. But, as I hope has been made apparent in this chapter, considering Delany's work with attention to marronage rather than the ever-looming teleology of revolt allows us to better understand the contours and complexities of freedom as understood by those continually in search of it, negotiating the varying landscapes of freedom and unfreedom as they maroon themselves and engage in practices of marronage throughout the United States and Western Hemisphere. This decentering of revolt is also crucial to understanding Harriet Beecher Stowe's work in relation to marronage as textual and literary-historical disruption in *Dred*. Just as Delany's novel is likely unfinished, or at the very least feels that way, our feeling of being left wondering in a small way mirrors the uncertainty of enslavers regarding the intentions of the enslaved. Delany writes toward possibility, toward liberatory action, refusing to allow white, liberal understandings of freedom and modes of freedom-seeking to determine the course of his hero's journey. In the end, *Blake* leaves us free as readers from the constraints of the liberal imagination, further attuned to the possibilities that lie outside of, in between, and beyond it for freedom-seeking African Americans in the pre–Civil War era.

Chapter Three

Toward Stillness

> Five hundred years of flights from captivity, into communal and conceptual wilderness, created the maroon philosophers' natural habitat at the boundary of democracy. Such outside terrain superficially appears as a reservation or cell; yet it is in part a trajectory into freedom.
>
> —Joy James, "Afrarealism and the Black Matrix"

> the swamp is speaking, so she nods her branches in reply,
> introduces herself, a blooming idiosyncrasy.
>
> —Irène Mathieu, "maron (circa 1735)"

On July 25, 1853, the *New York Tribune* published a letter to the editor entitled "Cruelty to Slaves," signed by a pseudonymous writer known only as "A FUGITIVE":

> SIR: Having seen an article, a few days ago, that was going the rounds in some of the daily papers, denying the truth of an advertisement wherein Slaves were outlawed in North Carolina. I wish to reply to it through your columns. I was born in that good old State, and less than 20 years since I left it, and it is not that length of time since I witnessed there a sight which I can never forget. It was a slave that been a runaway from his master twelvemonths. After that time a white man is justified in shooting a slave, as he is considered an outlaw. This slave man was brought to the wharf, placed in a small boat, by two

white men, early in the morning, with his *head* severed from his body, and remained there in an August sun until noon, before an inquest was held. Then he was buried, and not a word of murder or of arrest was heard. He was a negro and a runaway slave, and it was all right. It mattered not who murdered him—if he was a white man he was sure of the reward, and the name of being a brave fellow, truly[.] The writer of that article has said, the people of North Carolina have hearts and souls like our own. Surely, many of them have. The poor slave, however, who had his head severed from his body was owned by a merchant in New-York.

—A FUGITIVE.[1]

The letter is remarkable for many reasons. It is the second piece of writing published by Harriet Ann Jacobs, one of three letters to the editor of the *Tribune* that she would publish prior to the work for which she is celebrated today: *Incidents in the Life of a Slave Girl* (1861).[2] Jacobs intends to set the record straight about the practice of outlawing enslaved people in North Carolina, a legal means by which an enslaved person who had been a runaway for a certain period of time could be killed by any white person without repercussion—in fact, with the knowledge that doing so would bring financial reward.[3] The enslaved man in question in her grisly example had been a runaway for twelve months and was caught after that time not far from the place from which he had fled, meaning in all likelihood that he had been living as a maroon in the dense nearby swamps.

Also worth noting is the fact that Jacobs signed the letter "A FUGITIVE" when she had been legally emancipated in 1852. This, as well as her point that the enslaved man in her anecdote was "owned by a merchant in New-York," anticipate her treatment of the North in *Incidents in the Life of a Slave Girl*, wherein she is unabashedly critical of Northern racism and what she views as its capitulation to enslavers' interests through the Compromise of 1850 and its new, draconian Fugitive Slave Law. The letter intimates Jacobs's knowledge of and interest in maroons and practices of marronage in the area of Edenton, North Carolina, where she was born in 1813 and would remain enslaved—and famously concealed in the garret, the tiny attic-like crawl space above her grandmother's shed—until her escape north in 1842. Moreover, it suggests that Jacobs, who had been a fugitive from slavery for seven years in North Carolina and for another ten years once she reached the North, still felt as if she inhabited that imperiled, interstitial unfree subject position even after she had been officially emancipated and was living in the home of Nathaniel Parker Willis and his family in Cornwall, New York—the secluded country estate where, in the attic's servants' quarters, in secret and at night by candlelight, she would pen her letters to the editor and eventually begin writing the manuscript that would become *Incidents in the Life of a Slave Girl*.[4]

This chapter asks what happens if we imagine Harriet Jacobs—or Linda Brent, her pseudonym in *Incidents*—as a maroon during her seven years concealed in the garret and in the events leading up to that concealment. It argues that doing so is both accurate and generative while illustrating that *Incidents* is pervaded by representations of all kinds of maroons and practices of marronage.[5] I demonstrate how Jacobs even further complicates more traditional understandings of maroons, expanding in particular on the ways Black women played a role in enabling and sustaining marronage, especially forms of short-term marronage wherein maroons remained in close proximity to the places of enslavement they had fled. Through careful, deliberate attention to marronage in *Incidents*, I identify a constellation of alternative tactics and forms of nonliberal freedom and locate these within the broader discourse on freedom and unfreedom throughout early and pre–Civil War African American literature with which this book has thus far been concerned.

During her time in the garret (and nearby), Brent is hiding in places in the juridical purview of the slave system, within the homes and outdoor locales of Edenton. Her condition, her maroon subject position, though one of extreme hardship, still affirms enslaved Black women's subjectivity, community, and affective kinship relations in the face of systemic and de jure white supremacy vis-à-vis chattel slavery. It is a total denial of slavery from within slavery's borders, from within the borders of the plantation landscape itself, and a realization of de facto freedom. *Incidents* suggests that spaces of marronage are imbued with nonmaterial resources like the hopes, fears, aspirations, memories, desires, and epistemes of enslaved people—particularly of enslaved women. From these spaces of marronage, from the maroons who created and inhabited them, and from Jacobs's representation of them, there arise ways of being and knowing that are overlooked when critical focus remains attached to an imagined political and geographical trajectory that locates unfreedom in the South and freedom in the North or Canada. In approaching Jacobs's text in this way, we come to realize that *Incidents* is not a text that exceptionalizes the individual experiences of its narrator (and author), but rather one that links those experiences with(in) a network of maroon activities and subject positions oriented toward alternative possibilities for freedom.

Carolyn Sorisio has argued that *Incidents* "participates in heated philosophical debates over the *nature of identity* that were prevalent during her [Jacobs's] time."[6] This chapter builds on that idea and explores also the ways that the narrative participates in debates about the *nature of freedom* in opposition to traditional liberal conceptions centering on civil rights and officialized state recognition. In not only identifying but especially by remapping and reconfiguring the terrains of marronage, *Incidents* anticipates recent critical interventions by Diouf, Sayers, Roberts, and Nevius that have sought to do the same in the US context.[7] Perhaps most importantly, I understand *Incidents* as a text that foregrounds the maroon experiences, perspectives, and activities of enslaved Black women in particular, building on and expanding in a new direction the foundational tradition of scholarship that analyzes the workings of gender, power, and the possibilities for freedom in Jacobs's narrative.[8] Similarly, Jacobs expands on Delany's work in *Blake* by foregrounding the roles of women in marronage rather than focusing primarily on men. Rather than imposing an analytical optic from above or outside, I am concerned here with what happens when we allow Jacobs, via Brent, via *Incidents*, to theorize marronage as part of the larger dialectic of freedom and unfreedom for enslaved people in the United States. What if we consider Jacobs as one of Joy James's "maroon philosophers," hiding out in the South in "what superficially appears as a reservation or cell"[9] but is in fact a locus of certain assemblages of underrecognized, alternative freedoms?

Marronage in *Incidents* foregrounds two features of the phenomenon that have yet to be discussed in detail by critics studying the narrative: namely, the primacy of short-term flight, and the roles played by women in enabling, executing, and sustaining that flight, a form of flight characterized by what at first might seem paradoxically to be stillness. Writing about the role of marronage in the Haitian Revolution, Julius Scott observes that "the activities of Saint-Domingue's maroon societies focused greater planter concern, but the tradition of short-term individual desertion was arguably of more consequence in the day-to-day functioning of plantations and among the slaves themselves."[10] His assessment is applicable as well to the United States context, where large, long-standing, organized maroon communities like those found in Haiti, Jamaica, and Suriname did not exist and did not emerge as challenges to the entirety of the colonial order.

Stephanie Camp has noted that, in the United States, "women appear to have considered permanent escape to be even more difficult than did many men."[11] *Incidents* thus invites us to sit with instances of individual short-term flight as marronage in the form of stillness and to focus on women, who have often been elided or written over in discussions of US marronage.

Most historical scholarship focuses on marronage as a form of resistance carried out primarily by men, the major exception being Queen Nanny of the Maroons, the famed Jamaican maroon leader who led an eighteenth-century military campaign against British colonial rule. Camp, in illuminating what she calls forms of "everyday resistance" carried out by enslaved women, observes that they were "imbricated in dense social relations"[12] and maintained "ties to and roles within the family" that "bound them more tightly to plantation life."[13] These things did not prevent women from engaging in short-term marronage but instead resulted in tactics that differed from men's. Women's marronage defied easy categorization by enslavers in its time and has defied easy identification and analysis by scholars since. However, we can read *Incidents* as an archive of maroon tactics that, while influenced by the editorial hand of white abolitionist publisher Lydia Maria Child, is not compromised by the epistemic violence that, as Marisa Fuentes argues, has reduced enslaved women's archival presence to "the manner in which they lived: spectacularly violated, objectified, disposable, hypersexualized, and silenced."[14] Instead, Jacobs writes and restores agency and subjectivity into herself and to the other maroon women in her narrative.

Maroons and Marronage in Harriet Jacobs's World

Historically, maroons and acts of marronage were a ubiquitous feature of the interdependent Black and white worlds of Chowan County, North Carolina, where Jacobs was born in the town of Edenton in 1813. In her landmark biography, *Harriet Jacobs: A Life*, Jean Fagan Yellin describes reports of maroon-related activity in Chowan County during the years Jacobs was growing up there.[15] Following closely on the heels of Gabriel's Rebellion in Virginia in the summer of 1800, a vast insurrectionary conspiracy was uncovered in neighboring North Carolina in 1802. Scores of counties near the Great Dismal Swamp in southeastern Virginia and northeastern North Carolina were gripped in a state of panic as letters ostensibly written by the conspirators surfaced containing details about the plan, which included "kill[ing] the whites, taking their weapons, and burn[ing] down their houses," with the intent of then, like Gabriel two years earlier, marching on Richmond.[16] Letters indicate that participants in the rebellion were coming from as far as Edenton, North Carolina, and Norfolk, Virginia.

Although the rebellion never came to pass, the backlash against the free and enslaved Black populations in both states was swift and brutal: "searches, arrests, interrogations, whippings, ear cropping, and hangings followed."[17] The alleged leader of the conspiracy was one Tom Copper, who was said to have lived in the swamps on and off as a maroon for some years. Interestingly, Tom Copper had been enslaved on Andrew Knox's plantation in Nixonton, North Carolina, the same plantation on which Jacobs's father, the skilled carpenter Elijah Knox, was also held in bondage. Knox's plantation was worked by approximately thirty enslaved people, so in all likelihood Tom and Elijah knew each other.[18] There is no indication that Elijah had any role in Copper's machinations, but one wonders what kinds of stories about the infamous swamp maroon and his conspiracy might have been shared among Elijah's family, and in earshot of his daughter Harriet, who was thirteen when her father died suddenly in 1826.

During the last decade of the eighteenth century and the first decade of the nineteenth, another threat posed itself to residents of Southern cities all along the Eastern Seaboard, and specifically, for my purposes, to residents of Edenton, a small but bustling port city located along the Albemarle Sound in Chowan County. This threat came in the form of refugees fleeing the enslaved-uprising-turned-revolution on the French colonial island of Saint-Domingue, today's Haiti.[19] Enslavers fearing for the safety of themselves and their families fled in droves, landing in places from New Orleans to Charleston to Philadelphia to Edenton—and many brought the people they enslaved with them. No event in the history of slavery and colonialism in the Western Hemisphere caused greater terror for enslavers than the Haitian Revolution. The French-speaking refugees fleeing the violence on the island imported that terror to Edenton, increasing the already pervasive fears about the enslaved population outnumbering that of white people in many parts of the US South. This terror was embodied in the refugees who fled, but even more tangibly in the enslaved people they brought with them, who Southern slaveholders feared had been infected with the contagion of liberty, exposed as they were to enslaved revolt and the successful overthrow of the French colonial regime by the formerly enslaved on the island. In addition, the role of maroons in the Haitian Revolution has been documented by historians at great length.

In 1808, Edenton imposed an official curfew on enslaved and free Black people to stop what townspeople believed were "nighttime thefts by fugitives hiding in the woods and swamps."[20] The *Edenton Gazette*, the town's newpaper of record, printed accounts of maroons and maroon communities being rooted out around this time. In March 1811, the paper reported that "a party of men, in scouring . . . Cabarrus's Pocosin, came across a Negro Camp, which contained 5 runaway Negroes, 2 wenches and 3 fellows, who were armed."[21] Cabarrus's Pocosin, located just southwest of Edenton, is the actual name of what Jacobs calls the Snaky Swamp in *Incidents*. It is, as this chapter will later examine, the place in which Brent spends two nights as a maroon while her Uncle Phillip prepares the garret for habitation.

Reports of maroon activity in the area continued through Jacobs's childhood. In 1816, when Jacobs was three years old, "Chowan County court empowered the sheriff to raise a troop to capture eleven 'runaway Negroes,' ordering that if they did not surrender, 'any person or persons may kill and destroy the said Slaves . . . by such means as he or they may think proper . . . without incurring any penalty.'"[22] Thirty-seven years later, Jacobs would publish the editorial that begins this chapter, wherein she explains and decries the practice of outlawing enslaved people, precisely what is being communicated in this decree. In February 1819, the *Edenton Gazette* reported on "an armed raid on a fugitives' camp in the swamp" that "resulted in the capture of an outlaw . . . called 'Dilworth,' known as 'General Jackson.'"[23] The article claimed that this man was "the noted ringleader of the band of runaway Negroes, who have for a long time been depredating upon the property of the good citizens of this Town and Country."[24] The same issue of the *Gazette* reported a gunfight between "a number of gentlemen" and "another gang of . . . desperadoes."[25] The persistent fear that maroons were plotting violence and revolt motivated decisive action against them by enslavers, but marronage remained a feature of the landscape of slavery and freedom that simply could not be stopped, taking on shifting and alternating forms, disappearing and reappearing from the gaze of enslavers whose inability to perceive the possibilities of marronage was crucial to the practice's successes.

In May of 1819, the year in which Jacobs's mother died, the *Gazette* reported that "on Tuesday evening last Negro *Shadrach*, formerly the property of Dr. Norcom, who had been a runaway for near two years, was shot near this town, and expired next morning."[26] Dr. Norcom, known as Dr. Flint in *Incidents*, was the enslaver to whom Jacobs was sold in 1825 as an attendant to his daughter. The article continues, "He [Shadrach] had long been depredating upon the property of the inhabitants of this town, and country; and was discovered lurking around the house of a widow lady."[27] Panic once again struck North Carolinians in several counties in the southern part of the state during the summer of 1821, when fears of an insurrection led by "a number of outlawed and runaway slaves and free negroes" reached a fever pitch.[28] Diouf argues that the rise in overt, "increased," and "predatory" maroon activity that summer was probably just the result of several different maroon groups raiding storehouses stocked with foodstuffs from previous harvests of corn, rice, and potatoes.[29] However, more than six hundred militiamen from five North Carolina counties were raised to scour the local woods and swamps in search of the suspected maroons, sending locals throughout the area into a sustained state of alarm. Ultimately, only two men were detained in connection with the supposed "insurrection"; neither man was convicted, which suggests that when the dust settled it became apparent that the threat had been considerably overblown.[30] But once again we see the term "outlawed slaves" appear as an identificatory juridical term for maroons. Reconsidering them as maroons begins to repair some of the epistemic violence done by interpreting them through the grammar of the state.

In 1830, when Jacobs was seventeen, evidence of a supposed conspiracy among the enslaved surfaced in connection with David Walker's *Appeal in Four Articles*, published the same year. North Carolina Governor John Owen had received several letters from local officials and prominent enslavers indicating that rumors of an uprising had been circulating among enslaved people in several counties. The trail led to an elusive man named Moses, who "had been a maroon for years, 'lurking' in Jones and Onslow counties" and was "well acquainted with all the haunts of the neighborhood of the runaways."[31] Moses was ultimately captured and jailed, at which time he produced a lengthy confession detailing the alleged plot. Diouf's phrase "neighborhood of the runaways" is a striking one, as it foregrounds the sociality, mutuality, and collectivity that characterize maroon communities and the social networks of which they are a part. "Neighborhood" suggests both physical closeness and collective interest in not only surviving but thriving. Such a neighborhood is not physically circumscribed or delimited but rather is characterized by an assemblage of locations within a geographic area that support and catalyze alternative freedom-making. The maroon neighborhood is not a fixed one; it shifts and transforms as certain places become unsafe, new places become temporarily safe, new routes are discovered, and old ones discarded. It is comprised of both adjacent and distant spaces, some characterized by movement and others by stillness. It disregards conventional geographical understandings of what a neighborhood looks like, reconfiguring both space and time in ways that are nonnormative and possibilistic. That an entire "neighborhood" of maroons could exist in and between the Black and white, enslaved and free overlapping worlds of the plantation landscape is an extraordinary feat, and one that the following section of this chapter will explore in more detail.

These newspaper snippets offer a glimpse from enslavers' perspectives into the landscapes and rhythms of maroon life and into the fear their uncontrollable movements and activities engendered in the white planter population. They also perform the work of establishing the enslavers' vocabulary for describing maroons and marronage, one that criminalizes them as breakers of the law, as outlaws, as illegally fleeing subjection rather than also seeking alternative freedoms through a revised subjectivity. When, following Saidiya Hartman, the "slave's property in the self is defined . . . by appropriation and theft," we limit ourselves to perceiving only one side of the story, the negating side of the enslaver rather than the possibilistic side of the maroon.[32]

Marronge in *Incidents*

Maroons and the myriad freedom-seeking tactics of marronage would, as we have now seen, have been quite familiar to Jacobs as she grew up enslaved on Dr. Norcom's plantation. *Incidents* demonstrates her interest in and knowledge of maroons and introduces the idea that marronage may take on forms and methods that expand our sense of what maroons and marronage look like, pushing back against simplifying binaries and conceptions that too often leave women out of the picture entirely, or relegate them to supporting roles rather than leading ones. To be sure, enslaved and free Black women did play supporting roles in marronage that were unique to their social positions, but, as Jacobs delineates, these "domestic" roles were not the only ones, though marronage did often look different for women than it did for men. There is tactical overlap, but, as we will see, the picture is an extremely complicated one that has yet to receive adequate recognition. Indeed, Jacobs has been teaching us about women's marronage for over 150 years, though we have yet to see or understand it as such, to recognize the possibilities it offers for alternative versions of freedom.

Jacobs, as Linda Brent in the narrative, relates the story, for instance, of an enslaved man named James's flight "to the woods" after suffering "a severe whipping, to save himself from further infliction of the lash."[33] This vignette appears in the "Sketches of Neighboring Slaveholders" chapter as one of several designed to familiarize readers with the landscape of slavery, freedom, and unfreedom in the area, and it is an example of the kind of short-term marronage described in both our contemporary scholarship on the subject and the local newspaper during Jacobs's time. In another example, an enslaved man named Harry finds that his previous enslaver has deceived him and that while his wife has been given her freedom, his children remain enslaved. Here, marronage becomes a means of protesting the particular cruelty of forced familial separation: "The unhappy father swore that nobody should take his children from him. He concealed them in the woods for some days; but they were discovered and taken. The father was put in jail, and the two oldest boys sold to Georgia."[34] These examples from Jacobs do not result in permanent or state-granted freedom for maroons, but they do work to complicate the US geographical imaginary by showing that the South offered spaces of freedom—even if temporary and treacherous—that could be accessed, created, and willed into existence by the enslaved. They are evidence of enslaved subjectivity and agency as manifested in mobility, concealment, stillness, and space-making practices, whereby a version of what Yuko Miki calls "insurgent geographies" begins to arise.[35]

Brent continues to describe situations depicting maroons and marronage that have not been previously discussed as such but when recognized that way illuminate women's maroon tactics and their relationship with contemporaneous events. In another striking portrait of short-term marronage that challenges slavery's spatial supremacy, Brent describes what sounds like a common practice among Black women—enslaved and free—during the muster she refers to in the "Fear of Insurrection" chapter: "Many women hid themselves in woods and swamps, to keep out of their [the poor whites and country bullies'] way."[36] The show of force organized by enslavers but carried out by poor, nonslaveholding whites occurred in reaction to news of Nat Turner's revolt in Southampton, Virginia, in 1831, which sent panic throughout Virginia and neighboring states like North Carolina, both of which share a portion of the Great Dismal Swamp's vast territory. Turner himself had lived as a maroon during his time on the run after the revolt, making use of swamps and forests for concealment and using survival strategies, such as manipulations of the physical landscape and subaltern geographical networks, common to US maroons. Thomas R. Gray's *Confessions of Nat Turner* (1831) includes description of how Turner had once "scratched a hole under a pile of fence rails in a field, where [he] concealed himself for six weeks," and again established refuge during his time as a maroon "in a little hole [he] had dug out with [his] sword, for the purpose of concealment, under the top of a fallen tree."[37] Here, a weapon used previously for violence is repurposed in order to actuate marronage. Eventually, Turner was discovered by authorities there. Print coverage of Turner's revolt in its immediate aftermath often gestured toward the Great Dismal Swamp as a potential site of planning and refuge after the attack, citing it as a place from which Black and maroon self-emancipatory schemes and desires might dangerously emanate.

More to the point, however, in Jacobs's reference to Black women's collective short-term marronage we find solidarity, community, and sociality among enslaved and free Black women. Whereas Turner is imagined and represented as a lone male figure, as maroons have so often been, Jacobs introduces dimensions that have gone unnoticed but likely represent the tactics employed by many more maroons. Jacobs's description of the Black women's marronage in nearby woods and swamps illustrates the possibility that Hortense Spillers characterizes as the necessity of women "gaining the *insurgent* ground as female social subject."[38] While this example of marronage is again one that is, by design, temporary, we should not imagine it as simply reactive, in the sense that the women fled concerted imposition on their space and safety by enslavers. It is reactive, in one sense, but it is simultaneously true that this act was proactive, defiant, and insurgent in that it was not just an act of negation or refusal of slavery but one of Black women's solidarity in and against the landscape of the slave system and across official statuses of freedom. This freedom-seeking act of temporary flight enables the women to maintain a sense, even if provisional, of their humanity, individuality, and collectivity within the physical geography of slavery as a social and legal institution that otherwise attempts to undefine and disavow their lives, humanity, and subjectivity. Through this example, Jacobs locates a gendered network of solidarity, resistance, and avowal of continued life within the official geography of slavery, one that supersedes the events of the immediate moment. It is a glimpse at and into the hidden networks of survival and autonomy that provided iterations of freedom that do not comport neatly with an overdetermined sectional geography that locates freedom in the North or Canada and unfreedom via slavery in the South and do not emphasize the role of men in resisting slavery and expanding the horizons for alternative freedoms. The women who "hid themselves in the woods and swamps" have taken agency over their bodies and their movements, acting and moving in ways that enslavers do not expect and cannot comprehend as possibilistic.[39]

Jacobs's is not simply an African American story or a North American slave narrative but a story that, once we decenter the emphasis on the slave narrative genre's teleological progression from South to North, from slavery to freedom, from voiceless to heard, is actually doing the work of theorizing alternative, transitory, interstitial forms of African diasporic freedoms with hemispheric valences. We must imagine Jacobs's representations of maroons and marronage as always in implicit conversation with the discourses and practices of marronage in places like Haiti, Jamaica, Suriname, Brazil, Mexico, Venezuela, and others. The official geography of slavery, crafted and weaponized through the state, is rendered through cartographic imagination, but first and foremost through language. When we use the language of the enslavers and their written records—particularly *truant, outlier, runaway, bandit,* and *fugitive*—to describe what the women in this example were, or were doing, we inadvertently reinforce the material and discursive violence enacted upon enslaved people by official stories and official cartographies.

Incidents reveals a Black maroon world that is at once a part of and apart from the ordered, imposed geography of the slave system. Its specific contours are drawn into even greater focus as the narrative introduces Brent's own experiences of marronage. After initially running away, refusing Dr. Flint's underhanded offer of a personal cabin that she knows would become yet another site of sexual violence, Brent spends time hiding—finding refuge in stillness—in nearby homes of sympathetic Black and white women. While at first she plans to flee north, she soon recognizes the likely futility of this pursuit and comes to rely on the affective and material support network of her friends and family, free and enslaved, as was the mode of survival of the maroon. Prior to holing up in the garret for what will become an agonizing seven years, Brent endures some of the perils more conventionally associated with escaping slavery and also with experiences of marronage.

The first of these maroon experiences occurs when Brent runs away and takes refuge with her friend Sally, a free Black woman who lives in a room in Brent's grandmother's house. Here, she quickly comes to believe she has already been found out. She flees this site of temporary refuge for another maroon-like space of concealment in the dense thickets outside Sally's room. Her brief experience comes to serve as a preview of the greater challenges to come once she takes to the swamp and ultimately the garret. In a "thicket of bushes" outside, Brent hides in the darkness for two hours, enduring a venomous snake bite and eventually returning inside, where Sally prepares a "poultice of warm ashes and vinegar" for the wound.[40] Brent explains that "the dread of being disabled was greater than the physical pain I endured," a gesture toward not only the mobility generally required of maroons but also, significantly, the necessity of sometimes being able to remain in place—to embrace moving toward a radical stillness.[41] If one of the requirements of successful marronage is the ability to, like Henry Blake, be constantly on the move, another is the ability to remain—in what at first might appear paradoxical—concealed and still, and spaces of marronage are, as the narrative suggests here, often prohibitive, but this very feature is also what makes them available for catalzying marronage in the first place. While flight is expected by enslavers and white people in general as a possible act of freedom-seeking by the enslaved, the possibilities associated with stillness remain largely unseen.

Brent's subsequent experiences with flight continue to expand our sense of what spaces of marronage might be and how they might be conceived and supported by Black women. These spaces are not just swamps and forests but also homes, rooms, thickets, and concealed interior areas associated with the domestic world of women in the nineteenth century and in the tradition of sentimental literature from which *Incidents* borrows. They offer freedom in ways that are provisional and contingent. Marronage is not exclusively the domain of lone men in wilderness landscapes; it is, as *Incidents* shows, imbricated in the various landscapes of Black life, where versions of alternative freedoms might unexpectedly arise against a landscape dominated by unfreedom.

Marronage is not exclusively a faraway thing, characterized by runaways lurking in the shadows at the margins of plantation life. Even more ominously, it happens almost in plain sight, if one only knows, as Rebecca Ginsburg argues, the shifting rhythms and possibilities of the "black landscape" through which enslaved people reordered and repurposed their physical surroundings to enable resistance.[42] Brent's experiences here reveal that freedom via marronage may actually arise within the very heart of a slaveowning town, though unrecognized or unnamed as such by enslavers. The overlapping nature of Black and white worlds in Edenton's slave society becomes even clearer when Brent leaves Sally's and is concealed by a white woman in "a small room over her own sleeping apartment" that was used to "store away things that are out of use."[43] In this maroon space, in this maroon state, Brent is no longer reduced to a "thing," to a piece of property to be owned and used by enslavers. She takes herself "out of use" by those who would abuse and brutalize her. Instead, her marronage enables an escape from the subject position of a thing, emerging instead as an agential subject whose radical stillness renders her invisible through the eyes of the enslaver. Similarities between this small room and the garret Brent will soon inhabit abound: they are both tiny and not intended as human dwelling places; they are both dark, stifling, and cramped; they are both attic-like spaces intended for the storage of unused things; and they both contain means by which Brent is able to secretly observe goings-on outside. Both evince that nearly any concealed space can be transformed into a maroon space—even those seemingly innocuous spaces where domestic work is performed by women. *Incidents* thus illustrates that maroon spaces and alternative possibilities for freedom are not static but are part of a process of being and becoming initiated by women's ingenuity. Brent, a "thing" herself according to slave law, turns that very "thingness" into a mode of resisting the disavowal of her subjectivity as a human being inside a space where *actual* things, inanimate objects, are stored away when out of use. She stores herself away, refusing to be used as a thing by Dr. Flint and thus avowing her humanity and agency through temporary marronage.

If maroon spaces are protean and fluid, so too are the networks of people who enable marronage. They are not necessarily Black or white, enslaved or free, male or female; they are some of these things, all of these things in different times and places. Their existence resists normative conceptions of both time and space as dictated and understood by white society. The white woman in the previous example is an enslaver who knows her husband would never approve of her hiding Brent. When Brent again fears exposure, Betty, an enslaved woman who works in the home, quickly moves her into yet another hiding place under a plank in the kitchen of her quarters—another hidden, repurposed, domestic space where we might not expect to see a version of freedom as stillness manifested. From the attic of a white woman enslaver to the crawl space of an enslaved Black woman, Brent moves, and is moved, without detection. What was previously an empty, concealed space becomes a maroon space, if only temporarily, and becomes a part of the Black and maroon landscapes, the ever-expanding and contracting elements of a geography that complicates the official and political one and incorporates itself as well into the realms of the personal and domestic, where stillness rather than movement reigns as a tactic for survival.

After this variegated series of experiences with marronage, it becomes apparent that frequent movement within the small town of Edenton will eventually give Brent away, and thus is introduced a form of marronage that depends almost entirely upon stillness rather than flight and mobility. Before she enters the garret, she is brought by her Aunt Nancy's husband, Peter, to the Snaky Swamp to hide out while her Uncle Phillip prepares the garret as best he can for long-term habitation. This act of marronage is conceived of and enabled, yet again, by a Black woman. Brent's detailed description of this marronage is worth reproducing at length:

> About four o'clock, we were again seated in the boat, and rowed three miles to the swamp. My fear of snakes had been increased by the venomous bite I had received, and I dreaded to enter this hiding-place. . . .
>
> Peter landed first, and with a large knife cut a path through bamboos and briers of all descriptions. He came back, took me in his arms, and carried me to a seat made among the bamboos. Before we reached it, we were covered with hundreds of mosquitos. In an hour's time they had so poisoned my flesh that I was a pitiful sight to behold. As the light increased, I saw snake after snake crawling round us. I had been accustomed to the sight of snakes all my life, but these were larger than any I had ever seen. To this day I shudder when I remember that morning. As evening approached, the number of snakes increased so much that we were continually obliged to thrash them with sticks to keep them from crawling over us. The bamboos were so high and so thick that it was impossible to see beyond a very short distance. Just before dark we procured a seat nearer to the entrance of the swamp, being fearful of losing our way back to the boat. . . . I passed a wretched night; for the heat of the swamp, the mosquitos, and the constant terror of snakes, had brought on a burning fever.[44]

This account of short-term marronage illustrates William Tynes Cowan's observation that "the fear of the swamp . . . may have led to the assumption that the region acted primarily to keep slaves at home" but that "from the beginning African Americans were able to assert a utilitarian proprietorship over the swamps of the South, claiming those spaces as their own."[45] The swamp is an unequivocally inhospitable place, but, thanks to Nancy's idea and Peter's knowledge, skills, and local geographical intelligence, the two of them are able to pass not only one but two nights in this feature of the maroon landscape that is only three miles from the grip of the slavocracy but sounds and feels like a place entirely foreign. One also gets the distinct sense, as a reader, that this is not the first time the swamp has been used by Edenton's Black residents for such purposes, and we know this to be true based on historical evidence. It is a place that superficially appears "obsolescent, nonproductive, or generally removed from the scenes on which real modern action is believed to transpire,"[46] part of what Stephanie LeMenager calls "marginal landscapes" but actually a nodal point of concealment, survival, affiliation, and affirmation of life within the Black, maroon landscapes of the narrative.[47] While parts of larger swamps like the Great Dismal had been being used for decades by land companies for things like logging, smaller, isolated swamp spaces served as an impediment to rather than a source of capitalist expansion, accumulation, and production. Thus, their maroon inhabitants constituted a threat to the way in which a liberal, capitalist nation imagined itself as the omniscient settler-colonial organizer of its spatial and geographical domain.

The second night in the swamp further elucidates its dangers as well as its safety as a space outside the immediate reach of slavery. Brent explains, "Peter took a quantity of tobacco to burn, to keep off the mosquitos. It produced the desired effect on them, but gave me nausea and severe headache. At dark we returned to the vessel. I had been so sick during the day, that Peter declared I should go home that night, if the devil himself was on patrol."[48] The swamp sits ominously, mocking enslavers and thwarting their desire for ultimate control over enslaved people, free Black people, and the towns and cities they reign over. But Jacobs constantly reminds us of its ephemerality. One problem's solution creates yet another problem to be solved, another setback to be considered and overcome. Still, the swamp space serves its purpose for Brent, buying her just enough time to be able to get back into town and effectively disappear into thin air as a maroon.

Later on in the narrative, when Brent is at last making her escape north, the captain of the boat she has taken remarks upon passing by and pointing toward the Snaky Swamp, "There is a slave territory that defies all the laws."[49] Brent is reminded of the "terrible days [she] had spent there, and though it was not called the Dismal Swamp, it made [her] feel very dismal as [she] looked at it."[50] This white boatman reveals the complex relationship that enslavers and white Southerners in general had with maroons and with the knowledge that marronage was constantly occurring all around them, most often not geographically distant from the ordered, official geography of the plantation landscape. This uneasy knowledge also illustrates Michelle Burnham's point that "concealment is thus both what slavery demands and what it fears; concealment produces a reservoir of secrecy that perpetuates slavery but also unsettles it from within."[51] Concealment, secrecy, and stillness will, of course, become the defining and most imperative features of Brent's life once she leaves the swamp and enters the garret.

A Maroon in the Garret

A major focal point of the large body of scholarship on *Incidents* has, of course, been Brent's time spent in the garret. I am not the first to suggest that the garret—and Brent's time in it—is representative of, or evocative of, or a metaphor for something else. Critics have taken up the meaning of the garret space as a site of confinement, resistance, and freedom in various ways since Yellin first authenticated Jacobs's narrative in 1981.[52] Caleb Smith, Douglas Taylor, and Keith Michael Green have situated the narrative within emergent discourses on penology in the United States, fruitfully illuminating Caleb Smith's notion that slavery and imprisonment are "mutually constitutive institutions."[53] Georgia Kreiger has argued that Brent's time in the garret is a metaphor for social death, that she is "playing dead" in the garret, "an extended entombment before her escape and 'resurrection' in the North."[54] Most critics agree that the garret is in some way a space of empowerment for Brent despite the nature of its physical and psychological confinement, while taking care to avoid idealizing or romanticizing it. Additionally, Gloria Randle points to Brent's "ability creatively to construct sites of temporary refuge where none exist; to discover space where there is no space,"[55] and Katherine McKittrick concludes that "the garret makes available a place for Brent to articulate her lived experiences and emancipatory desires, without losing sight of the dehumanizing forces of slavery."[56] Miranda Green-Barteet has engaged with the discourse of architecture to argue that the garret is an "interstitial space" or "a border space, one that exists betwixt and between other more clearly defined spaces."[57] I suggest that these analyses of the garret space also point to its qualities as a maroon space, a locus of embodied and philosophical freedom-making in the world of the text and beyond it that arises specifically from the epistemes of the enslaved Black woman. In this way, my focus on marronage in *Incidents* works to contest the "epistemic violence"[58] that Fuentes finds enacted against enslaved Black women through the archive. For Brent, marronage is not a metaphor and the maroon space of the garret is not metaphorical; it is a real, physical site of embodied contestation and resistance.

Having painstakingly detailed the odious nature of the Snaky Swamp and of her time as a maroon within it, Brent at last establishes herself in the garret, of which she says, despite its small space and many discomforts, "Yet there was no place, where slavery existed, that could have afforded me so good a place of concealment."[59] As I have previously noted, concealment, especially of a sustained nature, lies at the heart of the condition of marronage and of the conditions of possibility and success for static maroon spaces. Concealment remains paramount because detection would obviate all other concerns and set the maroon from stillness into flight like Blake's once more. Thus, the garret does indeed appear to be Brent's best place of concealment in slaveholding territory, preferable to swamp marronage for a variety of reasons made clear during her time in the Snaky Swamp. Seven years of stillness will atrophy both her muscles and her mind, but it is that stillness that allows her to remain physically safe and able to coordinate her continued concealment with family and friends. She is able to eke out tiny and fleeting forms of freedom from within the garret, sustaining her mind and body as best as she can and still keeping her children and relatives close. Marronage thus enables freedom as familial contact, something so frequently stolen from enslaved people and threatened as punishment for resistive actions. Dr. Flint doesn't threaten Brent with forced familial separation because he believes that she has fled north, and thus marronage provides continued unification through her dissembling enabled by that same family.

At the same time, the language Brent uses to describe the garret and her time within it, along with the actual material conditions she faces as its inhabitant, constellates her unique experiences with those of the maroons who did in fact dwell for variable lengths of time among the wild beasts in the Snaky Swamp, Great Dismal Swamp, and swamps throughout the US South. Once Brent enters the garret, she begins an extended period of hiding or concealment while, like a maroon, still within slaveholding territory. With movement removed as a possibility, Brent then enters that interstitial ontological state that defines the existence of the maroon somewhere, as Neil Roberts has written, as antithetical to a "polarized, static conception of slavery and freedom with no attention to the liminal spaces between these states and the relational nature of freedom."[60] As the narrative makes clear, maroons inhabit an in-between status that is at once physical and metaphysical, material and discursive, not clearly enslaved or free, but something else (perhaps intentionally) not yet defined or even definable at all.

Immediately, the language Brent uses to describe the garret suggests a deliberate affinity with spaces of marronage and with the potentialities for alternative freedoms, autonomy, and self-determination that these spaces create in the ways I've been describing. For example, upon entering it for the very first time, she refers to the garret as "a dismal hole" in which "the air was stifling; the darkness total."[61] She refers to the garret as a "hole" four times and as a "den" nine times throughout the narrative. These words, along with her use of the descriptor "dismal," employed a total of five times, evoke the idea that the garret is just barely able to support human life. It's worth noting that, according to the *Merriam-Webster Dictionary* as well as the *Oxford English Dictionary*, "the noun *dismal*, meaning 'swamp,' goes back to the 1700s when the marshy region in Virginia and North Carolina was named the Great Dismal Swamp."[62] Much like a maroon space, the garret is, in other words, a liminal space that blends elements of the public and the private, the domestic and the wild, the safe and the unsafe, the free and the unfree, sometimes beyond recognition. Brent is not fully protected from either the elements or the unwanted intrusions of insects and rodents. While she is safe from predators like the much-feared venomous snakes and other reptiles of the Snaky Swamp, she remains "tormented" "for weeks" "by hundreds of little red insects, fine as a needle's point, that pierced through [her] skin, and produced an intolerable burning."[63] In addition, she is subjected to the seasonal changes and their attendant drops and rises in temperature, which severely inhibit her relative comfort as well as her movement and even faculty for speech. During the first winter, despite her grandmother's "bed-clothes and warm drinks," Brent's "shoulders and feet were frostbitten."[64] These descriptions reinforce the idea that the garret is not a fully domestic or indoor space and that it in fact shares certain unavoidable qualities, in a painfully corporeal sense, with maroon dens, holes, and caves.

More to the point, words like "hole" and especially "den" had specific and significant connotations related to maroons. Diouf establishes that "The borderland maroons' most emblematic lodging . . . was neither a tree, nor a cabin, nor a cavern, but a cave," and "these caves, also called dens, were dugouts, underground houses: the ultimate man-made invisible shelters. Once they entered them, maroons literally disappeared from the face of the earth."[65] Diouf provides extensive archival evidence of maroon cave dwellings from the antebellum period located in North Carolina, South Carolina, Virginia, Georgia, Mississippi, Louisiana, and Alabama. In addition, formerly enslaved people interviewed as part of a Works Project Administration (WPA) initiative in the late 1930s predominantly use the term *den* over *cave* to describe maroon habitations they had either seen, heard of, or lived in themselves.[66] To use this language is not simply a way to make her garret experience more vivid to readers through descriptions that are suggestive of the inhuman or unhuman nature of her living conditions. Rather, it is evocative of the contemporaneous print public discourse surrounding maroons and marronage as they relate to fears of enslaved violence and insurrection, and it is one significant way at the textual level that Jacobs intimates a parallel between the space she inhabits and her subject position vis-à-vis notions of freedom and enslavement and those of maroons. In particular, Jacobs introduces and reinforces the notion that an alternative form of freedom may be accessed standing still rather than on the move.

Several other aspects of Brent's position and condition in the garret liken her circumstances to those of a more conventional maroon. For one thing, if her hiding place was to remain a secret—inconspicuous to slave hunters, patrols, militias, musters, and the accidental passerby—then it must have a concealed entrance, the same being a necessity for maroons living in the swamps or forests of Chowan County. In this vein, Diouf writes of the maroon Goober Jack of South Carolina, for example, who dug out a cave in the forest with a trap-door entrance made from "an old plank window shutter ingeniously constructed into a suitable cap for a ventilator shaft," where he had "bored holes in it with an augur."[67] Like most cave-dwelling maroons, Jack would have swept leaves, dirt, and underbrush over the top of the shutter to conceal it within the forest landscape.

Previous work on *Incidents* has extensively analyzed the ways Brent creatively transforms and finds agency in the garret space, using her relative privileges to monitor her surroundings and account for the safety of her children, but it has not done so from the standpoint that Brent is a maroon in the garret. Brent explains that "my Uncle Phillip, who was a carpenter, had very skillfully made a concealed trap-door, which communicated with the storeroom [from the garret above]."[68] Though bereft of light for some time in the garret, Brent eventually stumbles upon a gimlet left behind by her uncle when he was preparing the space. Ever resourceful, and in the tradition of maroons like Goober Jack, she bores out three small holes to serve as apertures through which she might covertly observe and listen to the goings-on outside in the nearby street. Thanks to this improvement, Brent clandestinely eavesdrops on conversations "not intended to meet her ears," some of which pertain directly to herself and her potential whereabouts.[69] Given her unique position as a maroon—simultaneously inside a domestic space but outside an actual habitation, and therefore treading the boundary between public and private and surveillable, governable spaces—Brent is able to overhear conversations that would be unlikely to occur within known earshot of enslaved people or their living quarters. Enslavers' control over the space and movement of enslaved people is challenged here, and the enslavers do not even know it. Marronage is reorganizing and reconfiguring the logics of racialized space and control right before their eyes, though its possibilities remain shrouded in illegibility. No one suspects the presence of a maroon in the garret, listening in and gathering information and intelligence about slave hunts and speculative gossip about where she might be hiding. This vigilance and access to information is key to Brent's survival and to the livelihood of those networked enslaved people and complicit parties who enable her marronage. Her marronage enables a form of countersurveillance that is itself a kind of freedom and contributes to the continuation of others previously discussed.

The tiny apertures she made allow Brent to subvert and resist her condition as both enslaved person and fugitive from the law by virtue of the insight she gains into local happenings, but they also provide her with much-needed illumination, by which she "contrived to read and sew."[70] Perhaps most noteworthy is Brent's ability to sew, to produce new clothes for her children and contribute to their welfare despite—but also in some ways because of—her marronage. This production exists outside the domain of accumulative capitalism, in a subaltern network of Black production and accumulation that sustains life and enables relative comforts. She remains, in effect, productive and proactive as a mother protecting her children rather than simply reactively hiding from enslavement, therefore "claim[ing] the insurgent ground of her social identity and formulat[ing] her resistance to human bondage."[71] Rather than occupying the subject position of a fugitive—one assigned to runaway enslaved people by the slave state and suggestive of haphazard and unplanned flight—Brent emerges into the subject position of a maroon, one that is idiosyncratic and shifting, one feared and unspoken by enslavers because of its evocation of agency and autonomy. Like a maroon, she remains networked within the alternative geographies of freedom created and sustained by enslaved people and maroons in the South. Her sewing also has the effect of further supporting the idea that she has escaped to the North, which Dr. Flint assumes is the case in part because he cannot seem to imagine a woman engaging in marronage. It is sewing as resistance. Physical labor that is chosen rather than forced; domestic labor the means and production of which cannot be stolen by enslavers. Like so many white characters in other works that have been analyzed so far, Flint cannot see possibilities in the same way Black people do in the narrative. In her maroon condition of seemingly paradoxical absent presence, Brent continues to indirectly provide care for her children and, like the most successful of the US maroons, retain an affective support network of friends and family. In this case, marronage is enabled by and enables freedoms attached to woman- and motherhood, taking on forms and possibilities that further contribute to our understanding of the spectra of behavior associated with marronage.

Living as a maroon in close proximity to plantation life meant certain risks, but, like Linda Brent, many maroons decided that the advantages like those described above outweighed the potential dangers. Another advantage to having a line of communication with enslaved people still on nearby plantations was that maroons could collect information about fugitive slave notices advertising rewards for their capture and gossip about the potential selling of loved ones or anything else pertinent to their safety or the well-being of their family and friends. Brent, too, enjoyed this small opportunity by virtue of her place in the garret. She was able to overhear conversations between Dr. Flint and others in the street, some of which regarded Flint's plans for tracking her down and returning her to slavery. Playing on the common ideas that enslaved people fled north and that women were unlikely to engage in marronage, Brent is able to trick Flint and subvert his expectations about the unilateral South-to-North geographic route to freedom for enslaved people. Brent turns the tables on Flint and demonstrates the unique advantages of inhabiting the maroon space that is the garret. Again, it is her subject position as a maroon that facilitates all of this activity through which she maintains her concealment and supports her children affectively and materially as a woman, mother, and hidden community member.

Alternative Freedom-Making in *Incidents*

Almost forty years ago, Angela Davis wrote that "the black woman was assigned the mission of promoting the consciousness and practice of resistance. A great deal has been said about the black *man* and resistance, but very little about the unique relationship black women bore to the resistance struggles during slavery."[72] The goal of this chapter has been in part to continue to heed Davis's call to read African American literature as an archive of philosophy on freedom, doing so specifically by using *Incidents* to illuminate the role that enslaved Black women played in "promoting the consciousness and practice of resistance" through marronage. If Jacobs is, as I suggest, exploring and expanding the nature of freedom in *Incidents*, further complicating what we think we know about oversimplified South-to-North understandings of the possibilities for freedom, revealing a landscape of marronage hidden in plain sight in her text and in the world it represents and positioning herself as a kind of maroon in the garret, how, then, does this reshape our understanding of the narrative? Such a reading recasts the landscape of freedom, slavery, and unfreedom as one fundamentally attuned to the palimpsestic contours and variations of the maroon world as a set of alternative geographies and perspectives contesting the official geography of the slavocracy from within. With this, *Incidents* anticipates recent critical interventions that have sought to broaden our understandings of maroons and the landscapes and geographies of slavery and freedom in the US South. Acting as both an archive for and theorization of forms of temporary, mobile, fleeting freedoms-in-process and freedom-seeking tactics and actions, *Incidents* offers an intervention into debates over the nature of freedom, especially as it relates to notions of freedom within a nation whose philosophical underpinnings and juridical systems enshrine slavery as the absolute antithesis of freedom for the liberal subject of history. Thus, *Incidents* effectively expands ideas about who maroons could be and what marronage could look like in the ways this chapter has elucidated, giving us insight into how free and enslaved Black women coordinated and located alternative freedoms within the very heart of slavery.

Although *Incidents* concludes with Brent's successful arrival in Philadelphia, and ultimately New York, into the relative security of states where slavery had been illegal, we cannot ignore the text's sustained focus on alternative geographies and tactics of freedom as marronage in the South if we want to more fully understand its interest in marronage and in maroons as historical actors who should be considered participants in the antislavery and ultimately abolitionist movements of the antebellum period. Joy James's "boundary of democracy"[73] in *Incidents* is not stationary or stable but constantly shifting under the feet and in the psyches of maroons who both took flight from slavery and concealed themselves within the very epicenter of its clearly nonuniversal ability to control the mobility and disavow the agency, subjectivity, and humanity of enslaved people. And these borders and contours of democracy and freedom radiate outward into the hemisphere: into the hemispheric, diasporic, overlapping Black landscapes, seascapes, and competing geographies that constituted a decidedly always Black Atlantic world characterized by enslaved mobility, resistance, and especially diasporic marronage. *Incidents* identifies and reconfigures what Carol E. Henderson has called "those 'stories' overlooked and underseen in the literary imaginary, those stories crucial to understanding the essence of black life as it existed in the nineteenth century."[74] Ultimately, then, *Incidents* offers us an idiosyncratic story of maroon women in nineteenth-century African American literature.

Chapter Four

Emancipation, Interrupted

If kindness were the rule, we should not see advertisements filling the columns of almost every southern newspaper, offering large rewards for fugitive slaves, and describing them as being branded with irons, loaded with chains, and scarred by the whip. One of the most telling testimonies against the pretended kindness of slaveholders, is the fact that uncounted numbers of fugitives are now inhabiting the Dismal Swamp, preferring the untamed wilderness to their cultivated homes—choosing rather to encounter hunger and thirst, and to roam with the wild beasts of the forest, running the hazard of being hunted and shot down, than to submit to the authority of kind masters.

—Frederick Douglass, "Inhumanity of Slavery"

I have no end to serve, no creed to uphold, no government to defend; and as to nation, I belong to none.

—Frederick Douglass to
William Lloyd Garrison (January 1, 1846)

Douglass's only work of published fiction, *The Heroic Slave* imagines the story of the real historical figure Madison Washington, an enslaved man from Virginia who flees north to Ohio, finds safe passage to Canada, returns to Virginia to attempt to free his wife, and is recaptured and sold to a slave trader to be brought to the New Orleans market.[1] Once aboard the ship *Creole*, Washington leads a revolt that ends with the enslaved killing the captain, taking control, and sailing the ship to the

British-controlled Bahamas, at which point the rebels are held captive but the other enslaved are set free, as Britain had outlawed the slave trade in 1807. Though Douglass's story ends here, a long real-life trial ensued after the events depicted in the story, the focus of which became a diplomatic flashpoint for US relations with Britain in the context of the trade in enslaved Africans and global economic supremacy.

In the story, Washington is aided on several occasions by a Mr. Listwell, who first covertly observes Washington in the Virginia forest, then coincidentally owns the home in Ohio Washington stops at on his way north, helps Washington get to Canada, and then encounters him again once he's been recaptured in Virginia, slipping him some files to help him escape his shackles. The actual story of the revolt is narrated by another white character, the former first mate of the *Creole*, who is relating it to a fellow sailor in Richmond, the port from which the *Creole* sailed south.[2] This heavy-handed and at times double mediation of Black experience and thought through a white prism of interpretation is one way, from the outset, that Douglass draws attention to the fictiveness of the story's construction. That the story opens with a dramatic soliloquy marks a startling departure from Douglass's more familiar rhetorical style in his other published works and speeches.

Robert Levine has summarized (though ultimately as a means to challenge) an uninterrupted ideological progression of Douglass's antislavery thought as "shift[ing] from Garrison's moral suasionism to political abolitionism to Republican reconstructionism," a path clearly charted, deliberately documented, and promoted and repeated in Douglass's writing and speeches, and a trajectory to which scholarship framing Douglass as a "representative man" of, ultimately, the political Republicanism for which he is most remembered still sometimes remains attached.[3] Levine pushed back against the idea of Douglass as strictly representative of any political ideology, illustrating instead the uneven path his thought took to the form we often associate with it today. With Levine's reconfiguration in mind, that Douglass chooses, prior to Stowe's *Dred* and following his break from Garrison, to include an episode of marronage, and more that may be considered through a lens attuned to marronage, is worthy of closer attention because of the ways it complicates such a characterization of Douglass's evolving thought and introduces a relatively early rupture in his commitment to civil rights and faith in Republicanism as the path to African American liberation. Douglass chose to write in the genre of fiction at this one time in his long career, permitting himself space to make more speculative gestures than he could in his essays and speeches. Marronage by nature is a speculative endeavor, always reaching for what is not quite yet there, always without a decisive end, a process rather than a stable event, and reflective of evolving thought rather than established ideological program. In *The Heroic Slave*, we see Douglass speculate beyond commonplace and what, under popular liberalism, appeared to be commonsense conceptions of what freedom could look like and how and where it could be achieved.

While scholarship on *The Heroic Slave* oftentimes focuses on what Krista Walter has called the "trappings of nationalism," suggesting that "Douglass, like so many of his contemporaries, was finally unable to resist the powerful ideological and rhetorical appeal of nationalism,"[4] my argument departs from an insistence on that connection. In their introduction to the 2015 edition of *The Heroic Slave*, Levine and his colleagues observe that "though Douglass invokes American Revolutionary ideals, his novella displays no overarching or unconditional loyalty to the United States; it is an uncompromising critique of American society and liberal (that is, white male) democracy."[5] Working from that premise, this chapter reads *The Heroic Slave* for fissures in the text's otherwise overt emphasis on Madison Washington's revolutionary Black exceptionalism to argue that its representations of marronage unsettle the possibility of Black freedom via emancipation and integration within the United States and ultimately disrupt the coherence of liberalism as an organizing sociopolitical logic. The story poses a direct challenge to the notion that African Americans could depend upon recourse to the state for emancipation, instead offering possibilities that ignore or contest official, juridical, state-sponsored means of achieving freedom. These possibilities cohere around speculative explorations of freedom as marronage.

The liberatory practices of marronage in the text offer insight into freedom-making that interrupts narratives of liberal freedom that frame Black history and literary history as linear and attached to pivotal moments in US law and politics. *The Heroic Slave* sometimes appears to present episodes of marronage as waypoints on the path toward violent revolt rather than as themselves moments of possibility that might be explored on their own terms, but these episodes can be generatively paused at to explore how they function within a greater landscape of insurgent and resistive freedom-seeking practices. These episodes serve as interruptions and irruptions worth stopping at for a glimpse into alternative freedom-seeking tactics, and they reveal how attention to marronage in the archive of African American literature illuminates novel possibilities for resistance, survival, and freedom-making unbound from and unlicensed by liberalist thought. I want to suggest that fiction as a generic mode provides a way for Douglass to both permit and deny access to Madison Washington's interior life as an enslaved person. Thomas Koenigs has argued that "Douglass emphasizes his fiction's speculative nature in order to confront . . . readers with their ability to ever know" the real inner depths of an enslaved person's life.[6] Washington's unnarrated and inaccessible five-year period of marronage presents a stark example of such a denial on Douglass's part. No white person like Listwell is there to observe and report on these events for us as readers. It doesn't matter how well he listens if the thing to listen to is on a frequency he cannot hear, is concealed from his ways of knowing and organizing a sense of what is possible in the realm of Black life. While Listwell is there to observe a more predictable, if highly dramatized, moment when Washington speaks in the forest of the oppressiveness of enslavement and his desire to be free, no such access to the ambiguous ontology of marronage is made available. Thus, my point is that even while *The Heroic Slave* offers readers a way to imagine Washington as participating in a tradition of righteous rebellion likened to the spirit of 1776, it also belies the possibility of a one-to-one correspondence because of the ways enslaved people were denied access to the logics of liberal personhood required to be subsumed into American democracy as political project and social order. Reading for marronage uncovers the possibilities outside that correspondence with which Douglass experiments in the story and which are often at odds with the aspirational liberalism to which his enormous body of nonfiction frequently subscribes. By deploying fictional conventions familiar to nineteenth-century readers and common in Black writing like slave narratives from the time period, Douglass invites them into Washington's world, but only into the parts they already think they understand.[7]

At times, Douglass's fictionalization of Madison Washington's life and his rebellion aboard the *Creole* breaks from the symbolic, allegorical, and ideological unity that otherwise appears to organize the story through direct, associative engagements with the mythology of the American Revolution and founding fathers, Enlightenment-based natural rights philosophy and theories of liberal personhood, and the Byronic heroic tradition. What results is ruptures in a story that links—narratively, aesthetically, and ideologically—the unmitigated, violent imperatives of individual sovereignty within a collective, prenationalistic framework underwriting the American Revolution with those underwriting diasporic African resistance. Washington's marronage interrupts the forward march of a story otherwise seemingly embedded in a familiar teleology, one in which the enslaved African, after a series of trials and obstacles, sheds their (in this case) chains and achieves a state of "freedom" by escaping slavery in the South and striking out for the Northern states or Canada. Even if that freedom is provisional, and marked still by racial prejudice and discrimination, and often, especially after the 1850 Fugitive Slave Act, a pervasive insecurity, it is still, the logic goes, obviously preferable to chattel slavery and legible as slavery's dialectical opposite. The geography associated with this teleology is also a familiar one—a simultaneously moral, political, oversimplified abolitionist and sectionalist geography defined by what is imagined to be a strict boundary between slavery and freedom at the Mason-Dixon line.[8] Within this teleology and attendant geography, directionality of movement is also normativized such that we expect the enslaved-turned-fugitive to follow a linear trajectory from south to north, most commonly along the coordinates of the Underground Railroad, which is often imagined as a set of known, fixed, stable locations—ahistorical, abstracted, and somehow at once real and mythological.[9] When we attend more closely to what I am suggesting can be understood as marronage in the story, we can better see how Douglass works within that framework even as he simultaneously subverts it.

The long tradition of the racial uplift story, initiated by the slave narrative genre and the development of scholarship on it, is frequently thought of on the most literal level as a movement "up," as in northward. "Up from slavery" represents an elevation in one's condition from chattel to free person that most often necessitates first a movement upward from a southern location to a northern one, whether it be the northern United States, Canada, or even England. Even in the case of Booker T. Washington's autobiography *Up from Slavery* (1901), so strong is the association of freedom with the North and slavery with the South that the metaphor holds even if Washington's postemancipation work occurs in the geographical realm of the Southern states.[10] In a profoundly subversive gesture, maroons stake an insurgent claim to land and, following Monique Allewaert, to ecology and nonhuman life—to physical space that, despite its peripheral status outside the plantation zone and domain of market value, is nevertheless denied them in both theory and practice by virtue of their status as chattel, as fugitive, as runaway, as maroon, as Black. Maroons represent an encroachment on the foundational pillars of white liberal democratic citizenship and on the complex set of social, political, and economic relations that constitute the system of chattel slavery in the pre–Civil War United States. In *The Heroic Slave*, Madison Washington will ultimately find his freedom not in the North or the South but *way* south, outside the conventional geography of US freedom and its state apparatuses for emancipation, in the British Bahamas. In the end, Madison Washington arguably abandons the project of US liberal democracy altogether as Douglass demonstrates a notion of freedom incompatible with its means for Black emancipation.

Douglass knew his audience: Whether subscribers to the *North Star* for *The Heroic Slave*'s first serialized run in 1852 or recipients of Julia Griffiths's antislavery gift book *Autographs for Freedom*, where the story appeared in novella form in 1853, he knew that a certain predisposition toward abolitionist feeling would incline them toward the message of his story and the ideological link it attempted to make, its suggestion that the impulses behind slave insurrection were as fundamentally "American" as those behind the Revolution, the spirit of 1776.[11] In this way, we might imagine *The Heroic Slave* as adjacent to Martha Schoolman's idea of the 1850s as the "Maroon's Moment" in abolitionist literature, as Douglass takes to experimenting with routes to freedom that are distinctly revolutionary in nature and feature singular Black radical figures. Douglass also knew abolitionist support for the real-life *Creole* rebels led by Madison Washington in 1841 had been widespread and almost universal in the US presses. It is the rupture points brought on by representations of marronage, however, that I wish to consider because of the ways they reveal a politics of identification/disidentification and displacement/deferral inherent in the seams of the comparative work to which Douglass puts the story.

The Literary-Historical Madison Washington

The real historical figure Madison Washington, like so many of the enslaved people in the United States, named and anonymous, is a kind of maroon in the historical archive itself, presenting mere "glimpses" and "snapshots," a figure whose illegibility for most of his life, until the *Creole* incident and the massive textual production it occasioned in the courts afterward, is reenacted in his illegibility in the archive. James B. Haile III argues that "in his historical fiction, Douglass tackles the fact that the enslaved had no record, no official account of themselves, and the fact that the official record contradicted the fact of their own existence."[12]

Haile continues,

> "The Heroic Slave" is the introduction of an alternate and parallel history and the introduction of an altered reality. *This is why it had to be written as fiction.* Yet Douglass did not write it as fantasy—that is, a reconstruction of the past to give meaning and value to the present—but was teaching us of an already existing alternate world where enslaved persons dwelled, one that does not exist within the contemporaneous timeline of enslavement but that presents a parallel timeline in which he can and does account for the existence of the enslaved as more than just chattel.[13]

Haile's points about "an already existing world" that "does not exist within the contemporaneous timeline of enslavement" resonate strongly with the ways I have been attempting to position maroons as people out of time and out of place in normative, national imaginaries. Even as Douglass anchors his story using real times, places, and people in *The Heroic Slave*, I aim to show how elements of marronage unsettle the stability of that version of historical reality. As Haile insists, this is why Douglass had to write the story as fiction, and also, I think, along with Koenigs, why he repeatedly draws attention to that fictionality. We must, therefore, take Douglass seriously as a writer of fiction and *The Heroic Slave* seriously as a work of fiction in order to really grasp the complexity engendered by his rhetorical decisions.

What little is known about Madison Washington, historically, comes from the actual trial records of the *Creole* affair, written about him from the perspective of the state. Others who wrote about Washington after Douglass—including William Wells Brown, Lydia Maria Child, and Pauline Hopkins, among others—borrowed liberally from Douglass's fictionalization of Washington's life in their own accounts. But they all include reference to Washington's period of marronage, aided by his wife, an invention of Douglass's that does not appear in the historical documents. Douglass's story has Washington living as a maroon for "five long years," while this time period is altered by other authors who wrote about him. Douglass used the genre of fiction to create flourishes and imagine beyond the confines of slavery and restrictions on Black life in general, and also to experiment with alternative and often nonliberal forms of freedom as marronage.

In *The Black Man, His Antecedents, His Genius, and His Achievements* (1863), William Wells Brown included a chapter devoted to Madison

Washington, drawing much of his inspiration for it from *The Heroic Slave*'s fictionalized biographical details along with what had become known of the man through the court proceedings following the *Creole* affair, which dragged on for over a dozen years after the incident itself occurred in 1841. It still had not been resolved when *The Heroic Slave* went to press in 1853 and was only just finally wrapping up when Douglass published the second version of his autobiography, *My Bondage and My Freedom*, in 1855. Brown's book—which also notably includes chapters on Nat Turner, the Afro-Cuban poet Placido (featured as part of Henry Blake's insurrectionary plot in Delany's *Blake*), Joseph Cinque, Denmark Vesey, Martin Delany, and Frederick Douglass—reproduces but recasts Douglass's fictionalization of Washington's marronage in its chapter devoted to him. Brown describes Washington's failed attempt to go north, clandestine meeting with his wife, and decision to become a maroon thusly:

> I took her to my bosom as my wife, and then resolved to make the attempt. But unfortunately my plans were discovered, and to save myself from being caught and sold off to the far south I escaped to the woods, where I remained during many weary months. As I could not bring my wife away, I would not come without her. Another reason for remaining was, that I hoped to got up an insurrection of the slaves, and thereby be the means of their liberation. In this, too, I failed. At last it was agreed between my wife and me that I should escape to Canada, get employment, save my money, and with it purchase her freedom. With the hope of attaining this end I came into your service. I am now satisfied that, with the wages I can command here, it will take me not less than five years to obtain by my labor the amount sufficient to purchase the liberty of my dear Susan. Five years will be too long for me to wait, for she may die or be sold away ere I can raise the money. This, sir, makes me feel low-spirited, and I have come to the rash determination to return to Virginia for my wife.[14]

Most notably in Brown's version, Washington had planned to incite an insurrection while engaged in his life of marronage, in hopes of being the "means of the liberation" of his people. Writing a decade after *The Heroic Slave* was published, and in the midst of civil war, Brown draws upon long-held associations between marronage and revolt in the enslavers' imagination—the same kinds of impulses Stowe drew on in *Dred*. Even if Washington was unable to organize the insurrection he hoped to while living as a maroon, we might take the speculative liberty of imagining that any such planning and preparation could have become useful in the event of the insurrection at sea on the *Creole*. The physical and psychic space opened through marronage and its affordances of freedom allow Washington the ability to think and consider his means for survival outside the realm of the slavocracy. During his period of marronage he is, to return to Haile, in many ways a man out of time. Brown's version of events is further suggestive of the idea that Washington's marronage serves as a kind of staging ground, a material and psychic incubator of revolutionary fervor and potential, which necessarily precedes his rebellion aboard the *Creole*. By locating Washington's militancy in this earlier moment, Brown contributes to the same kind of teleological drive as Douglass, suggesting a sense of inevitability in Washington's ultimate act of rebellion. Both writers use this technique of "great men" history writing that already permeated the literature on the founding fathers, so often imagined after the fact as always having been destined for the great deeds they carried out as members of the revolutionary generation, and the Revolution itself was a historical event frequently narrated retroactively as inevitable in the development of the American democratic national project.

In 1865, Lydia Maria Child edited and published *The Freedmen's Book*, an anthology containing writing by, among others, Harriet Beecher Stowe, John Greenleaf Whittier (who authored a poem about marronage), Harriet Jacobs, and Frederick Douglass himself. Child contributed a biographical portrait of Madison Washington to the book, which, like William Wells Brown's, borrows heavily from *The Heroic Slave* in order to flesh out Washington's life story prior to the *Creole* affair. Child relies heavily on the sentimentalism afforded by Washington's relationship with his wife, and she uses it to simultaneously evoke Washington's capacity for tender affection and also his unwavering commitment to freedom: "Perhaps he [Washington] would have attempted to escape sooner than he did, had he not become in love with a beautiful octoroon slave named Susan."[15] In Child's version, however, unlike Douglass's, Washington's term of marronage lasts only several months:

> If he had hated Slavery before, he naturally hated it worse after he had married Susan; for a handsome woman, who is a slave, is constantly liable to insult and wrong, from which an enslaved

husband has no power to protect her. They laid plans to escape; but unfortunately their intention was discovered before they could carry it into effect. To avoid being sold to the far South, where he could have no hopes of ever rejoining his beloved Susan, he ran to the woods, where he remained concealed several months, suffering much from privation and anxiety. His wife knew where he was, and succeeded in conveying some messages to him, without being detected. She persuaded him not to wait for a chance to take her with him, but to go to Canada and earn money enough to buy her freedom, and then she would go to him.[16]

Both Brown's and Child's accounts differ from Douglass's in their description of the duration of Washington's marronage: in Douglass's it lasts "five long years," whereas in theirs it lasts instead "many weary months" and "several months," respectively. Part of the reason for Douglass's singular choice could be the timeline in his story: Mr. Listwell first encounters Washington in "the spring of 1835, on a Sabbath morning," so in order for the *Creole* revolt to take place in November of 1841 (as it did according to the historical record), five years of marronage were necessary to fill in the bulk of the intervening years.[17] But there is potentially more at work here. Why such a long period of time? And why gloss over five years in one paragraph? It is an aesthetic gesture that acknowledges, by not acknowledging any specifics, the fact that secrecy and concealment were crucial to real-life maroons' survival. As has been noted previously, a preponderance of historical and archaeological evidence exists indicating maroons inhabited the swamps and forests of Virginia, among many other places, up through the culmination of the Civil War.[18]

One way to understand the purposeful omission of any details regarding how Washington actually survived as a maroon could be the same way we understand Douglass's omission of the details surrounding his escape from slavery in his 1845 *Narrative* as he described them himself: these survival strategies were not for public consumption while slavery remained the law of the land. They must be protected, a form of knowledge and fount of possibility that could not be textualized.[19] This resonates again with Koenigs's and Haile's assessments of what is made legible and illegible in the text and why. In this moment we can see how Douglass navigated writing for various readerships at once, deploying the imaginative strategies of fiction to move beyond Black writing as merely testimony about experiences with enslavement. But Douglass also has Madison Washington suggest, "I had partly become contented with my mode of life, and had made up my mind to spend my days there; but the wilderness that sheltered me thus long took fire, and refused longer to be my hiding-place."[20] The possibilities of marronage for freedom-making are thus gestured toward but pivoted away from as the narrative moves forward—space is opened, though, and through further engagement with narrative in the story, it is never entirely closed. In this reading, maroons like Washington know something about possibility, but readers are left knowing only that such possibility exists, not what those possibilities might actually be. The interiority of marronage stays ambiguous, if not entirely concealed. Should Washington have remained in his forest retreat, concealed from capture and assisted by the provisions and support of his wife, he may have found a way to survive in an interstitial physical location and subject position, within but apart from the apparatuses of slavery and state control, free in a way that does not register within the context of freedom understood through the prism of liberalism. Even though this is not how things ultimately unfold, the possibility is raised, introducing a survival strategy via marronage that disrupts and interrupts confidence in the state's willingness or ability to grant freedom through emancipation and in Douglass's own seeming commitment to that possibility throughout his other nonfiction work.

Writing in a post–1850 Fugitive Slave Law context, despite the fact that the story's events take place prior to the law's passage, Douglass felt viscerally the increased paranoia and danger occasioned by the law's federal redistricting of the political geography of freedom for African Americans in the United States. He continued, in fact, to refer to himself as a fugitive (like Harriet Jacobs did, as well) after his escape from enslavement. To suggest, therefore, that Washington "had partly become contended with [his] mode of life" as a maroon in a Virginia swamp is a radical move, and one that can be understood as amplified in its urgency at the particular political moment of *The Heroic Slave*'s publication among the increasingly radical abolitionist discourse of the 1850s, which often foregrounded revolutionary Black counternationalist figures. Having been unable to make it north the first time, Washington's experience resonates with Douglass's own thoughts in *My Bondage and My Freedom*, wherein he writes, "We [slaves] all had vague and indistinct notions of the geography of the country," and "I knew something of theology, but nothing of geography."[21] But Madison Washington does know something of geography, of the ways in which alternative geographies of marronage and potentials for freedom outside the United States are available. In the case of Washington's first attempt to escape north, the Underground Railroad never factors into the equation because he finds himself unable to navigate the labyrinthine geography of Virginia's dense swamps and forests. Though his second attempt is successful, he determines to return south to free his wife, as well. More to the point, however, is the fact that this moment also deeply unsettles the familiar association of freedom with the North and enslavement/unfreedom with the South, as Washington eventually returns south to free his wife and must navigate living in concealment in that landscape, learning by necessity and experience that labyrinthine geography outside of state surveillance and knowledges. While the traditional figuration of north as free and south as unfree does exist here, and appeals to white-abolitionist sentiments about Northerner benevolence and heteronormative coupling, the second register, in which freedom is sought in the South through marronage, interrupts the neatness of that traditional geographic trajectory into freedom.

"Marks, Traces, Possibles, and Probabilities"

The story of *The Heroic Slave* begins thus: When Mr. Listwell, an Ohioan traveling in Virginia, happens upon Madison Washington soliloquizing on his plight in the clearing of the dense pine forest, which, we will learn, is his habitual retreat, the narrator describes Washington in the vein of an enigmatic fugitive or maroon figure, one hovering along the peripheral landscapes that intersect with but are not fully enclosed by the plantation zone's regulatory mechanisms of control, surveillance, and domination. The narrator, inviting readers to glimpse Washington as Mr. Listwell soon will, concealed "by the side of a huge fallen tree" "near the edge of a dark pine forest,"[22] explains, "Glimpses of this great character are all that can now be presented. He is brought to view only by a few transient incidents, and these afford but partial satisfaction. Like a guiding star on a stormy night, he is seen through the parted clouds and the howling tempests; or, like the gray peak of a menacing rock on a perilous coast, he is seen by the quivering flash of angry lightning, and he again disappears covered with mystery."[23] Along with cultivating a sense of foreboding around Washington with this series of comparisons involving a "menacing rock," "perilous coast," and "flash of angry lightning," there is an element of voyeurism in the dynamic of the scene. The narrator continues: "Curiously, earnestly, anxiously we peer into the dark, and wish even for the blinding flash, or the light of northern skies to reveal him. But alas! he is still enveloped in darkness, and we return from the pursuit like a wearied and disheartened mother, (after a tedious and unsuccessful search for a lost child,) who returns weighed down with disappointment and sorrow. Speaking of marks, traces, possibles, and probabilities, we come before our readers."[24] The fantasy being activated here is one in which white readers may imagine for themselves an encounter with a runaway slave, a one-on-one intellectual and embodied reckoning with the institution of slavery, though one in which that reader is a passive observer, not asked to interact with the enslaved man but simply to listen well (i.e., "List-well"). The Northern, white character Mr. Listwell serves as a mediator and buffer for Douglass's imagined (largely white, Northern) readers, a safe and convenient means by which they who may never have traveled through the South might encounter a fugitive slave in the comfort of their own homes. Douglass appeals here to white curiosity about the enslaved experience but also to an underlying curiosity—one marked by a combination of fear and a complex set of desires, which are reflected in Listwell's descriptions of Washington—regarding the simultaneously threatening and desirable Black male body. It's worth pausing, as well, at Douglass's invocation of a wish for "the light of *northern* skies to reveal him [Washington]" (my emphasis).[25] The light of northern skies does not and cannot illuminate this nebulous figure. Attempting to understand or interpret him through a normative white geographical lens in this way is not viable in a story that ultimately upends, in part through gestures to marronage, a stable geography locating freedom in the US North and slavery in the South. Washington will find no satisfying freedom in the North; its skies and stars do not guide his way, as he gets turned around in the swamps and must remain concealed but within the geography of Southern slavery. Though he does make a brief successful escape to Canada, he is ultimately pulled back south in hopes of freeing his wife to join him, where his capture necessitates a new form of escape and strategy for freedom-seeking interwoven with tactics and strategies of marronage. Looking at the story this way thwarts readers' desires to imagine themselves as part of a benevolent geography, a material and ideological place from which they want to believe freedom for African Americans emanates. Listwell's encounter with Washington registers the idea that there are levels of interiority to Black life and resistive strategies coursing along frequencies unheard and indecipherable in a liberal white context.

Through a disembodied narrative voice—though one that readers have come to understand since the story's opening paragraph as an agent of progressive historical revisionism, one dedicated to elevating Madison Washington from "the chattel records of his native State [Virginia]" to his proper place alongside the likes of Patrick Henry, Thomas Jefferson, and "he who led all the armies of the American colonies through the great war for freedom and independence"[26]—we are introduced to Washington for the first time in his forest retreat. He is described as being "black, but comely," "of manly form. Tall, symmetrical, round, and strong," with the apparent "strength of a lion," and "arms like polished iron," a man whose "whole appearance betokened Herculean strength."[27] But the narrator quickly qualifies these traits, telling us, "Yet there was nothing savage or forbidding in his aspect. A child might play in his arms, or dance on his shoulders. A giant's strength, but not a giant's heart was in him. His broad mouth and nose spoke only of good nature and kindness."[28] Washington is, in the narrator's final estimation, "just the man you would choose when hardships were to be endured, or danger to be encountered,—intelligent and brave. He had the head to conceive, and the hand to execute. In a word, he was one to be sought as a friend, but to be dreaded as an enemy."[29] So begins a careful balancing act that Douglass will employ throughout the text, simultaneously humanizing and romanticizing Washington as part of the extraordinary task of, as a Black writer, making a slave-ship revolt leader palatable and sympathetic to a mostly white reading public.

Listwell overhears Washington first decry his mean position in life under slavery and then declare his determination to be free, whatever the cost. Washington bemoans the freedom he lacks compared to that even of simple creatures like birds, which "fly where they list by day, and retire to freedom at night."[30] He goes on to compare himself to a snake, a comparison that resonates with his later marronage episode and also with Douglass's thoughts on swamp-dwelling fugitives in the chapter epigraph from "Inhumanity of Slavery": "How mean a thing am I. That accursed and crawling snake, that miserable reptile, that has just glided into its slimy home, is freer and better off than I."[31] But, as Washington thinks aloud, free temporarily in this forest space to consider his circumstances without the ever-present threat of violence in a slave society, he begins to convince himself that he is not a coward for submitting to enslavement for as long as he has:

> *Liberty* I will have, or die in the attempt to gain it. This working that others may live in idleness! This cringing submission to insolence and curses! This living under the constant dread and apprehension of being sold and transferred, like a mere brute, is *too* much for me. I will stand it no longer. What others have done, I will do. These trusty legs, or these sinewy arms shall place me among the free. Tom escaped; so can I. The North Star will not be less kind to me than to him. I will follow it. I will at least make the trial. I have nothing to lose. If I am caught, I shall only be a slave. If I am shot, I shall only lose a life which is a burden and a curse. If I get clear, (as something tells me I shall,) liberty, the inalienable birth-right of every man, precious and priceless, will be mine. My resolution is fixed. *I shall be free.*[32]

The narrator explains that after Washington uttered these words, "a smile of satisfaction rippled upon his expressive countenance, like that which plays upon the face of one who has but just solved a difficult problem, or vanquished a malignant foe; for at that moment he was free, at least in spirit. The future gleamed brightly before him, and his fetters lay broken at his feet."[33]

Washington's words in this space are performative: he speaks the space and his intentions and their end result into being, and they will be so, engaging with the oral tradition so often associated with African American culture and in defiance of the logics of property ownership and land claims under the settler capitalist state. But on the page itself, Douglass as the Black, formerly enslaved author also writes this space and these intentions, preordained and inevitable as they come to seem, into being, much like—and we might imagine Douglass had such a comparison in mind—the Declaration of Independence virtually wrote into being the existence of a United States of America, and the Constitution further codified the existence of that entity from thought, to word, to material reality. In this sense, Douglass via Washington is speaking and writing into the dominant "structure of feeling" radical Black spaces—what I am arguing are in fact maroon spaces—within both the physical landscape of US slavery and the discursive landscape of the Northeastern, white-dominated abolitionist print public sphere, which by the early 1850s Douglass knew so well.[34] These are maroon spaces precisely because of their positionality and relationality vis-à-vis dominant, hegemonic white spaces. They are apart but within. The nature of their radicalness lies in their apart/within–ness and their frustration of national time. They are spaces of autonomy, self-determination, and provisional freedom physically located within slaveholding territory but outside the purview of the plantocracy. For these reasons, we can imagine Washington's forest retreat as the first maroon space introduced in the story and the first place where Douglass speculates toward freedoms that contradict a commitment to aspirational liberalism that could bring Black people into its fold, a place of possibility from which further possibilities for nonliberal freedom and self-liberation will ultimately emerge.

Washington's forest retreat comes to serve as an antecedent and precursor to the other maroon spaces that he will speak and act—and Douglass will write—into existence over the course of the rest of the story, namely his swamp hideout and the ship he will eventually take over, and into the port space at Nassau. While the forest setting is certainly significant to my overall argument regarding marronage, which is most often associated with forest and swamp landscapes, perhaps even more important are the cognitive-psychological and metaphysical dimensions of the production of a maroon space in this particular example.[35] Through processes of embodied cognition, Washington thinks, believes, speaks, and realizes into existence the autonomous space of refuge in the woodland clearing, one that simultaneously offers and denies access into the interiority from which that realization manifests. Such an act is a crucial component of the formation of maroon spaces and of the acting out of marronage, both of which rely upon physical, material places as well as cognitive projections of provisional freedom and self-determination. Here I am thinking alongside Carolyn Cooper, who argues that maroonage is the "tradition of resistance science that establishes an alternative psychic space both within and beyond the evolving boundaries of the plantation," and Greg Thomas, who suggests that "maroonage can be mobile or urban; hydro or maritime; folkloric, cosmological, metaphysical, or supernatural; spiritual or religious as well as territorial and psychological."[36] The precedent established is that maroon spaces are embodied and have the potential to be mobile; they are not preexisting in the world but are rather enacted via processes of human agency, an agency that is often downplayed or denied to the enslaved as historical actors otherwise bound up in the logics of the US sociopolitical order.

Madison Washington's final ruminations in this maroon space regard his wife, whom he does not want to leave within the plantation regime but fears he cannot do anything for if he himself remains enslaved. He determines, therefore, to make a break for the North, hoping to achieve freedom for himself, whereafter, "[his] arms [his] own," he "might devise the means to rescue her."[37] In part 2 of the story, Washington coincidentally seeks refuge at the Listwells' home in Ohio on his way north to Canada (another overtly fictive gesture), at which time Mr. Listwell recognizes him and prompts Washington to tell him all that has happened since their last "meeting" in the Virginia forest. Washington explains in detail the circumstances that had led to his appearance in the pine forest and the occasion of Listwell overhearing his ruminations:

> I had, on the previous Saturday, suffered a cruel lashing; had been tied up to the limb of a tree, with my feet chained together, and a heavy iron bar placed between my ankles. Thus suspended, I received on my naked back forty stripes, and was kept in this distressing position three or four hours, and was then let down, only to have my torture increased; for my bleeding back, gashed by the cow-skin, was washed by the overseer with old brine, partly to augment my suffering, and partly, as he said, to prevent inflammation. My crime was that I had stayed longer at the mill, the day previous, than it was thought I ought to have done, which, I assured my master and the overseer, was no fault of mine; but no excuses were allowed. . . . I could do nothing but submit to the agonizing infliction. Smarting still from the wounds, as well as from the consciousness of being whipt for no cause, I took advantage of the absence of my master, who had gone to church, to spend the time in the woods, and brood over my wretched lot.[38]

As many commentators such as Herbert Aptheker have argued, this kind of marronage, whether referred to as *petit marronage* or "lying out" (the phrase more commonly used in the United States), was quite common throughout slaveholding societies all over the hemisphere and even in Western and coastal Africa as the slave trade took formal shape.[39] Enslaved men and women might frequently abscond as a form of protest after a vicious beating or whipping, particularly one perceived to have been without provocation or to have exceeded in severity the act of wrongdoing. Taking advantage of an enslaver's absence, too, as Washington does, was a common strategy for those enslaved people wishing to abscond temporarily—usually, but not always, with the intent to return on their own. Such practices were, as Richard Price suggests was true throughout the hemisphere,[40] sometimes tolerated by enslavers because they imagined that allowing for periodic acts of protest in the form of temporary truancy might act as a kind of safety valve and stave off actual flight with the intent not to return at all or to instigate some kind of imagined collective revolt.[41] These small, individual acts distort the imagined coherence of the slave system and open up novel possibilities for locating and defining freedom. They confer agency upon the enslaved, which becomes the basis of these further possibilities that Douglass will explore.

Madison Washington explains that before making the decision to live as a maroon, he had made a prior aborted attempt to flee north, following the trajectory and logic of the Underground Railroad:

> I will try to tell you, said Madison. Just four weeks after that Sabbath morning, I gathered up the few rags of clothing I had, and started, as I supposed, for the North and for freedom. I must not stop to describe my feelings on taking this step. It seemed like taking a leap into the dark. The thought of leaving my poor wife and two little children caused me indescribable anguish; but consoling myself with the reflection that once free, I could, possibly, devise ways and means to gain their freedom also, I nerved myself up to make the attempt. I started, but ill-luck attended me; for after being out a whole week, strange to say, I still found myself on my master's grounds; the third night after being out, a season of clouds and rain set in, wholly preventing me from seeing the North Star, which I had trusted as my guide, not dreaming that clouds might intervene between us. . . . This circumstance was fatal to my project, for in losing my star, I lost my way; so when I supposed I was far towards the North, and had almost gained my freedom, I discovered myself at the very point from which I had started. It was a severe trial, for I arrived at home in great destitution; my feet were sore, and in travelling in the dark, I had dashed my foot against a stump, and started a nail, and lamed myself. I was

wet and cold; one week had exhausted all my stores; and when I landed on my master's plantation, with all my work to do over again,—hungry, tired, lame, and bewildered,—I almost cursed the day that I was born.[42]

This failed attempt at navigating north is worth further examination. The Underground Railroad paradigm maintains strong currency as a means for understanding and interpreting enslaved escape in the popular imagination and, to a lesser extent, the scholarly outside of African American and Black literary and historical studies. This has led to often-reflexive, seemingly commonsense thinking that the majority of enslaved people who fled from bondage in the South set out knowingly and deliberately for the North—to the free states or Canada. But this is simply not so. As John Hope Franklin and Loren Schweninger write in the preface to their documentary historical study *Runaway Slaves: Rebels on the Plantation*, "Indeed, most runaways remained in the South, few were aided by abolitionists or anyone else, and many fled with a sense of terrible urgency."[43] Included among "aspects of the history of slavery" that "even today . . . remain shrouded in myth and legend," they include the ideas that "slaves were generally content, that racial violence on the plantation was an aberration, and that *the few who ran away struck out for the Promised Land in the North or Canada*" (my emphasis).[44] There are, of course, many reasons why these myths exist and often persist. For one thing, the abolitionist presses were located almost exclusively in the Northeast. Those comparatively few runaways who made it successfully to the North were or became literate—or in some cases, like Harriet Tubman's, shared their stories with a white writer—and entered abolitionist circles, through which narratives of their lives, hinging on the daring escape from slavery in the South to "freedom" in the North, were ultimately published, promoted, and then distributed by people with a vested interest in painting themselves and by extension their section of the nation as morally superior to the degraded condition of the slaveholding South.[45] Many, though not all, white abolitionist writers often struggled to imagine possibilities for freedom outside the structuring logics of the Underground Railroad. It is to African American writing like Douglass's, Jacobs's, and Delany's that we must turn for insight into and elaboration of these alternative possibilities.

Sylviane Diouf has argued that abolitionist ideological aims had little use for maroons, who, rather than integrating or assimilating into white society, sought refuge in a "clandestine life outside white-controlled spaces."[46] "Abolitionists had no use for them [maroons]," she writes, "except to paint them as lost souls living among and like wild beasts, so as to underscore the cruelty of slavery."[47] I would further expand on her claim to suggest that abolitionists also had little use for maroons because maroons contested the idea of freedom as manumission or emancipation via white patrons, therefore complicating the paternalistic, state-sanctioned mode of freedom upon which the proslavery/antislavery dialectic depended for ideological coherence in ways that undermined the position of Northern abolitionists invested in a moral-political geography defined against the backwardness they identified with the slaveholding South.

Maroons constitute themselves as free rather than being endowed with freedom by others. By their actions and resistive psychic manifestations, they disavow the endowment of freedom by others. Marronage as freedom shifts agency from white abolitionists to enslaved and formerly enslaved people, thus shifting moral currency away from Northern abolitionists who relied upon that currency as political-ideological fuel as sectional tensions in the 1850s increased. Ultimately, that the North American fugitive slave narratives, the experiences and escapes they relate, and the formerly enslaved people who wrote them have largely been taken to be representative—to exist, as Carla Peterson has noted of Frederick Douglass's *Narrative* and Harriet Jacobs's *Incidents in the Life of a Slave Girl*, as "the metonym for nineteenth-century African-American literary production"[48]—has contributed to the longevity of an interpretive paradigm that often forecloses, for example, the experiences of maroons, free African Americans in the South and North, those who fled west or to Indian nations, those who fled to Mexico or Spanish Florida, and those who left the United States altogether, often by sea, as Washington does at the end of *The Heroic Slave*. Such a fact also obscures the true provisionality, instability, and complexity of meanings of freedom for African Americans—possibilities that do not depend upon white, state intervention in the context of liberalism as a governing paradigm. These facts force a reckoning with how African American literary development and history have been conceived, upsetting neat generic, temporal, and geographical narratives.

After explaining to Mr. Listwell his aborted attempt to flee north, Madison Washington tells of the alternative he devised: marronage, living in a cave in a "dismal swamp."[49] Washington describes returning, weary and exasperated, to the plantation from which he had fled, where his wife remained as an enslaved house-servant in the kitchen. They meet briefly in secret, and she agrees to join him at the clearing in the pine forest where

Mr. Listwell had first encountered Washington, a place she "knew . . . well, as one of [his] melancholy resorts, and could easily find . . . though the night was dark."⁵⁰ This description reinforces the idea that Washington has absconded to this place with some frequency in the past, has made a habit of engaging in acts of *petit marronage* as a form of personal resistance against his unjust condition as chattel, and that the landscape of slavery includes liminal maroon spaces, which are known to and employed by the enslaved but are illegible as such through the planter gaze. The spaces themselves might be perceptible, but it is their potentiality, their "possibles, and probabilities," the alternate purposes to which they might be put that remain obscured in the planter imaginary.⁵¹ These spaces are illegible through the planter gaze, visible only as possibilities with no sense of what those possibilities may actually look like and create.

Washington's experience of this midnight meeting with his wife and the subsequent decision to engage in prolonged marronage are described as follows:

> I hastened away, therefore, and concealed myself, to await the arrival of my good angel. As I lay there among the leaves, I was strongly tempted to return again to the house of my master and give myself up; but remembering my solemn pledge on that memorable Sunday morning, I was able to linger out the two long hours between ten and midnight. I may well call them long hours. I have endured much hardship; I have encountered many perils; but the anxiety of those two hours, was the bitterest I ever experienced. True to her word, my wife came laden with provisions, and we sat down on the side of a log, at that dark and lonesome hour of the night. I cannot say we talked; our feelings were too great for that; yet we came to an understanding that I should make the woods my home, for if I gave myself up, I should be whipped and sold away; and if I started for the North, I should leave a wife doubly dear to me. We mutually determined, therefore, that I should remain in the vicinity. In the dismal swamps I lived, sir, five long years,—a cave for my home during the day. I wandered about at night with the wolf and the bear,—sustained by the promise that my good Susan would meet me in the pine woods at least once a week. This promise was redeemed, I assure you, to the letter, greatly to my relief. I had partly become contented with my

> mode of life, and had made up my mind to spend my days there; but the wilderness that sheltered me thus long took fire, and refused longer to be my hiding-place.[52]

At the most fundamental level, and as it relates to the progression of the narrative and the exposition of its main character, Washington's marronage functions as a means by which he might remain in the vicinity of his beloved wife, able to see her "at least once a week," while exercising some degree of autonomy and self-determination over his own life and circumstances. As Douglass well knew, punishments for running away, repeated truancy, and "lying out" often included being sold south or to a slave trader. In other cases, the returned runaways might be subjected to some of the most brutal, sadistic punishments meted out by slave owners, sometimes resulting in death. In *Incidents in the Life of a Slave Girl*, Harriet Jacobs describes the fate of a runaway named James, who fled the plantation, evaded capture for some weeks, but was eventually caught and fastened between the screws of the cotton gin for the same number of days he had been lying out. He was eaten alive by rats and vermin, his corpse picked at by insects.[53] Others might have been fastened with heavy metal collars affixed with bells, keeping them from being able to flee without being heard. Alternatively, a heavy log or piece of metal might be affixed by shackle to the enslaved person's leg, preventing future escapes, or at least making them significantly more challenging. At the very least, Washington could expect a whipping of the severest order, a branding of R for *runaway* on his face, or some such act of vengeful barbarism, all of which reveal the fear with which enslavers lived in the shadow of the Haitian Revolution and domestic incidents like Nat Turner's 1831 revolt, both of which have associations with marronage discussed earlier.

Engaging in the kind of marronage Washington undertakes was very often done for the purpose of being able to retain contact with a loved one or group of family members or friends.[54] The practice afforded this element of freedom, which was otherwise restricted by slaveholders' obsession with controlling the movement and whereabouts of enslaved people through judicial and extrajudicial means. While Washington's wife is the reason he becomes a maroon, she is also the reason he is *able to* become—and remain—a maroon at all. At their first meeting at the agreed-upon secret location in the woods, she arrives "laden with provisions," knowing that it will be nearly impossible for him to survive solely by hunting and gathering and without adequate protection from the elements.[55] Borderland maroons—those who stayed close to the plantation zone so as to retain contact with brethren still in bondage—almost always depended upon such a relationship in order to survive.[56] The enslaved people to whom their secret was entrusted often put themselves at great risk to aid the maroon in their vicinity, becoming complicit, as it were, in both the crime and the conspiracy to cover it up. But this marronage enables the retention of familial and social relations among the enslaved and maroon, a freedom to communicate, sustain, even build small semblances of community and collectivity in ways that subvert the coherence of the slave system.

Rather than privilege *grand marronage* (large-scale, organized community formation) because of the potential it held for enslaved populations to wield considerable political influence over or against colonial regimes—such as was the case in Jamaica, Suriname, Brazil, and elsewhere—Alvin Thompson has argued that, "like short-term *marronage*, individual *marronage* has historically been treated as a peripheral issue within the wider context of desertion, but perhaps this activity had much more significance than scholars have attributed in terms of the ideology of freedom."[57] Madison Washington's "solo" marronage plays into the masculinized, Romantic heroic tradition of the Byronic order, aligning Washington with Douglass and downplaying the role of others so as to highlight individual self-reliance, fortitude, and strength of character. Krista Walter has pointed out the fact that an element of chauvinism in *The Heroic Slave* contradicts Douglass's long-standing public support of women's suffrage. Perhaps, though, this is another reason for including the marronage episode in the first place. To survive for five years in a cave in a swamp is an extraordinary feat, even with occasional assistance. It certainly serves to increase our estimation of Washington's physical prowess, determination, persistence, and psychological fortitude described by Listwell earlier. But it also further elucidates the ways, following Thompson and others, that marronage figured into Black conceptions of nonliberal freedom-making that Douglass engages with in the story.

Washington does, however, hint at the existence of other maroons in the vicinity of his own abode when he is describing to Mr. Listwell the great fire that ultimately forced him from his place of refuge: "Many a poor wandering fugitive, who, like myself, had sought among wild beasts the mercy denied by our fellow men, saw, in helpless consternation, his dwelling-place and city of refuge reduced to ashes forever."[58] Douglass does not romanticize the difficult life of the maroon, but he does hint here at the possible existence of an unelaborated web or assemblage of maroon swamp inhabitants, a subaltern social formation quietly contesting domination by its mere existence, a community apart but within, provisionally free *within* slaveholding territory itself, free in a way that does not comport with the governing philosophy of liberalism. We do not learn anything of these other maroons in the swamps, but, as the epigraph to this chapter from Douglass's 1850 speech "Inhumanity of Slavery" suggests, their existence itself is a powerful testament to the cruelties of slavery, a living retort to those who would defend slavery as a paternalistic, benevolent institution, and a challenge to the idea that freedom could be found in the free states or through state-granted emancipation. Douglass's vague gesture toward these other maroons and potential maroons invokes possibility, again, outside the structuring logics of racial integration, a counter-refrain that begins to appear over and over in the text when looked at in this way.

The cave that Washington makes his home in the "dismal swamp" is typical of maroon habitations in the US South.[59] It serves both materially and psychologically in the story as a place of shelter and refuge, allowing him effective concealment during the daylight hours so that he may move about more freely under the cover of darkness at night. Here, he "wanders about at night with the wolf and the bear," hearkening back to the opening soliloquy in which he spoke of the freedom that wild animals like birds and snakes enjoy but he, as a man who is enslaved, cannot.[60] He eats what he wants, sleeps when he wants, hunts when he wants, free to make these choices for himself that under slavery would almost never be his to make, choices that remain limited for "free" Black persons as well. The ways slavery governs the temporality and rhythms of Black life and movement are unsettled here. We might imagine that his marronage becomes a kind of intermediate state between enslavement and freedom, wherein he inhabits a liminal, interstitial space and also occupies an interstitial subject position somewhere between the codified, reified poles of freedom and bondage. Here, he is not entirely free but not entirely enslaved, either. Writing in the context of Haitian marronage, Jean Fouchard has called maroons "*de facto* free persons," and Orlando Patterson has flatly called maroons "not slaves."[61] Of course, maroons were criminalized, often outlawed, and still considered fugitive/lost/stolen property by the state, but this does not negate the agency, autonomy, and degree of self-determination they demonstrated by virtue of engaging in acts of marronage, especially long-term ones like Washington's. He may remain a de jure bondsman or officially designated fugitive, but, as Fouchard suggests, in practice he is operating according to his own volition, not under direct, immediate control by outside forces, a peripheral actor ungoverned by state jurisdiction.

In this way, we may on one hand consider Washington's marronage as a staging ground for his later act of overt rebellion against his own condition as chattel and against the larger system of slavery—captivity, imprisonment, forced migration, trade and selling, physical and psychological violence—through which he and his fellow bondspeople aboard the *Creole* are held and maintained in racialized subjugation. As a maroon, he experiences a version of freedom—a freedom that he comes to appreciate so much that he only leaves his place of seclusion, as we are told, because of a great, almost biblical forest fire that forces him out. Douglass carefully stages these hints at alternative freedom and rebellion while Washington is in US territory but represents the actual revolt offstage, as it were, at sea and via double white-narrative mediation. Having experienced the kind of freedom, quite literally, that wild animals enjoy, and which he previously coveted, Washington becomes even further unable to bear the cruelties, violences, and degradations of enslavement once he is recaptured in the attempt to free his wife and sold to a slave trader to be brought to the New Orleans market. Thus, the seeds of his revolutionary consciousness have been sown as a result of his time as a maroon and his violent, abrupt return to slavery after five years as a de facto free person. At least, this is the reading suggested by the overall ideological alignment of Douglass's other writing and abolitionist philosophy more generally, but still we are repeatedly invited to consider how marronage connects to other resistive practices and gestures toward unsettling conceptions of Black-centered time and space. This is the invitation by Douglass that this chapter has and will continue to take seriously.

Marronage at Sea

> You may bind chains upon the limbs of your people if you will; you may place the yoke upon them if you will; you may brand them with irons, you may write out your statutes and preserve them in the archives of your nation if you will; but the moment they mount the surface of our unsteady waves, those statutes are obliterated, and the slave stands redeemed, disenthralled.
>
> —Frederick Douglass, "Slavery, the Slumbering Volcano"

Part 4 of *The Heroic Slave*, wherein the actual story of Madison Washington's revolt on board the *Creole* is related, begins with the narrator's scathing condemnation of the hypocrisy evidenced by the continued legality of an internal American slave trade even after the United States had officially outlawed the international slave trade via federal legislation that became effective on January 1, 1808. This condemnation contributes to Douglass's building idea that freedom may in fact be unavailable to Black people within the United States as place and idea.

> What a world of inconsistency, as well as of wickedness, is suggested by the smooth and gliding phrase, AMERICAN SLAVE TRADE; and how strange and perverse is that moral sentiment which loathes, execrates, and brands as piracy and as deserving of death the carrying away into captivity men, women, and children from the African coast; but which is neither shocked nor disturbed by a similar traffic, carried on with the same motives and purposes, and characterized by even more odious peculiarities on the coast of our MODEL REPUBLIC. We execrate and hang the wretch guilty of this crime on the coast of Guinea, while we respect and applaud the guilty participators in this murderous business on the enlightened shores of the Chesapeake.[62]

Such hypocrisy frames the spatial and geographical terms through which we are to understand Madison Washington's revolt in *The Heroic Slave*. By asserting the unjustness of the internal American slave trade, Douglass sets the stage for an understanding of Washington's revolt as just in the face of hypocritical and unjust conditions of continued systematic oppression and subjugation by the state and its apparatuses.

The story of the revolt aboard the *Creole* is highly mediated. We are invited, as readers, to overhear the story as told as a recollection by the ship's first mate, one Tom Grant, to a group of sailors at the Marine Coffee House in Richmond, Virginia. Grant is taunted by another sailor, Jack Williams, who knowingly goads him with the question, "I say, shipmate, you had rather rough weather on your late passage to Orleans?"[63] In what follows, Williams suggests with hubris that had he been on board the *Creole* when its human cargo rose in revolt under Madison Washington's leadership, the whole thing would have ended very differently. Grant sets the record straight by explaining in detail the events that occurred onboard that night. As with Listwell, Grant serves as a vehicle through which Douglass presents the interpretation of the events and their participants that he seems to want readers to embrace. The white character presents the reading of the events that Douglass wants to impart to his own readers. Just as Listwell earlier had an epiphany regarding slavery after seeing and hearing Washington in the pine forest, Grant explains that "I have resolved never to set my foot on the deck of a slave ship, either as officer, or common sailor, again."[64] He continues, "I'm resolved never to endanger my life again in a cause which my conscience does not approve. I dare say here what many men feel, but dare not speak, that this whole slave-trading business is a disgrace and scandal to Old Virginia."[65] At this, Williams replies derisively, "Hold! Hold on! Shipmate, I hardly thought you'd have shown your colors so soon. I'll be hanged if you're not as good an abolitionist as Garrison himself."[66]

Thus, we receive the story of the *Creole* revolt from another white character who has come, through personal experience, to decry slavery and the violences of the slave trade. In this case the conversion is even more resonant because Grant is a Southerner by birth and had long been a willing participant in the internal slave trade militated against by the narrator at the beginning of this section. Of Washington personally, Grant says, "I confess, gentlemen, I felt myself in the presence of a superior man; one who, had he been a white man, I would have followed willingly and gladly in any honorable enterprise. Our difference of color was the only ground for difference of action. It was not that his principles were wrong in the abstract; for they are the principles of 1776."[67] By drawing us into sympathy with Grant, we are, by extension, brought into sympathy with Madison Washington. These white interlocutors might be imagined as serving the same purpose as someone like William Lloyd Garrison, who in Douglass's earlier days on the abolitionist circuit would have Douglass tell his own story but would then step in to provide the "appropriate" interpretation of that story for white listeners. Again, Douglass demonstrates extraordinary awareness of his multiple audiences through this narrative technique. Here, however, given the nature of the story at hand, one of militant revolt of the enslaved with a hypermasculinized Black man at its helm, Douglass chooses to employ sophisticated techniques of narrative displacement and mediation afforded him by the textual genre in which the story is being told, that of fiction. Readers are asked to sympathize with Washington on an individual level via the white characters Listwell and Grant and on an ideological level via the principles of 1776 and the white founding fathers who espoused them. But, still, this does not elide or negate the competing possibilities for freedom and sustenance outside the liberal framework that the story repeatedly develops, and even while it reveals it continues to conceal any full conception of Washington's interiority as he leads and participates in these events.

The fact that Douglass—once again showing extraordinary awareness of his audience and of how to manipulate the narrative and aesthetic conventions of the genre—mediates the telling of the revolt through spatial, temporal, and narrative displacement should not cause us to underestimate the radical, incendiary, counternationalist nature of this episode. Rarely did abolitionist writers, especially Black ones, depict successful slave insurrections in literature of the time period—with the very notable exception of representations of the Haitian Revolution in the Black press. And in this case, the story is overtly arguing for the slaves' right to revolution in the context of the *Creole* affair, drawing all the while a direct parallel to the ideological origins and violent insurgency of the American Revolution. Arguing in the abstract for slaves' right to revolution, as a short piece by the reverend George W. Perkins entitled "Can Slaves Rightfully Resist and Fight?" does in *Autographs for Freedom*, where *The Heroic Slave* was printed, is quite different from depicting enslaved resistance and violence carried out against white Americans. Indeed, the author of this piece writes, in relation to the title, "I do not answer this question. But the following facts are submitted as containing the materials for an answer."[68]

The facts submitted are a brief account of the grievances expressed by the American colonists against the British government leading up to 1776, by which time "it was distinctly maintained . . . that men may rightfully fight for liberty, and resist the powers ordained of God, if those powers destroyed liberty."[69] These grievances are very similar to those raised by Washington when he considers the unjustness of his position in slavery. The writer does directly state, "I do not say that these positions were right, or that the men of 1776 acted right. But I do say, that if they were right, we are necessarily led to some startling conclusions. . . . If it was right in 1776 to resist, fight, and kill, to secure liberty,—it is right to do the same in 1852."[70] "If the reader is shocked by such inquiries and inferences," he continues, "and as directly and intentionally designed to encourage servile insurrection and civil war, he may be assured, that my aim is entirely different. It is my wish, to secure timely precautions against danger."[71] This is resonant with Stowe's aims in *Dred*. He also enumerates, in the style of the Declaration of Independence, the many legitimate grievances of the enslaved population against their oppressors in the United States but remains safely out of the territory of actually suggesting that the enslaved rise up in violent revolt, and he certainly does not depict the kind of insurrection that he argues the enslaved are entitled to based on a comparison to the grievances of 1776.

Another short piece from *Autographs for Freedom* by the reverend S. J. May, entitled "The Heroic Slave Woman," bears mentioning briefly because of its representation of enslaved heroism and resistance. The story relates an incident from 1834, in Connecticut, the author's home state, in which he and a fellow abolitionist visiting from England happen upon an enslaved woman accompanying her enslaver on a trip up from Mississippi. They speak with the enslaver, who acknowledges his belief that slavery is wrong in the abstract but that it had "become a necessary evil, necessary to the enslaved, no less than to the enslavers," and he gives them permission to attempt to convince the enslaved woman that she is legally free now that she has set foot on northern soil.[72] In what follows, they endeavor to persuade her to claim her natural right of freedom and remain in the North, but she flatly refuses on account of having made a promise to her mistress that she would return: "She had bound herself by a promise to her mistress, that she would not leave her; and that promise fastened upon her conscience an obligation, from which she could not be persuaded, that even her natural right to liberty could exonerate her."[73] The men become enamored with and deeply impressed by such probity and are "astonished, delighted at this instance of heroic virtue in a poor, ignorant slave."[74] We're left to wonder, however, what other possibilities exist for this woman back south, what kinships and collectivities may sustain her, what resistive activities she may be engaged in there that don't appear as such through the eyes of the enslaver or the sensibilities of the white Northern abolitionist. Her refusal to pursue freedom through official, legal state means is depicted as both absurd and admirable, as her white interlocutors are incapable of imagining freedom or liberation otherwise. That different forms of freedom may be available to her in the South, ones taken on her own terms and within the landscape of enslaved resistive and survivance tactics, is inconceivable in this account.

At one point, the men ask her, "Is it possible that you do not wish to be free?," to which she replies, "Was there ever a slave that did not wish to be free? I long for liberty. I will get out of slavery, if I can, the day after I have returned, but go back I must, because I promised that I would."[75] This story is of interest because its title is a clear allusion to *The Heroic Slave*, which represents heroism and resistance of quite a different sort. "Heroism" in this story is to be understood through a gendered prism wherein heroism for women really constitutes something more akin to heroic virtue, or at least virtue maintained in the face of great obstacles or temptations. This story is really about demonstrating the inherent morality and virtue of enslaved women, and by extension Black women, whose character had long been under attack thanks to enslavers and their wives wishing to invent Black women's promiscuity as a cover for their own lascivious behavior and rape of enslaved women, which often produced lighter-skinned children. In essence, the story suggests, enslaved Black women possess the same innate capacity for virtuousness as white women—a point which, significantly, Harriet Jacobs makes as well. But, again, while such a message is certainly radical for the time and representative of the multipronged approach to antislavery critique the volume espouses, it requires significantly less rhetorical and narrative finesse than does that of Douglass in actually depicting militant, violent resistance by the enslaved targeted at white bodies and white national imaginaries of freedom as part of a struggle against the system of slavery.

Returning to *The Heroic Slave*, the first mate of the *Creole*, Tom Grant, begins his telling of the revolt with a discussion of space—namely, the fundamental differences between practices of slaveholding on land and practices of slaveholding at sea: "It is quite easy to talk of flogging niggers here on land, where you have the sympathy of the community, and the whole physical force of the government, State and national, at your command; and where, if a negro shall lift his hand against a white man, the whole community, with one accord, are ready to unite in shooting him down."[76] On land, he suggests, an enslaver can be confident that his actions will have the physical and legal support of the government, authorities, and greater community and that he will be defended against reprisal from the enslaved by these same hegemonic forces. Once at sea, however, things are entirely different: "It is one thing," Grant explains, "to manage a company of slaves on a Virginia plantation, and quite another thing to quell an insurrection on the lonely billows of the Atlantic, where every breeze speaks of courage and liberty."[77] Through Grant, Douglass sets up the space of the ocean as one naturally associated with freedom, or at least alternative possibilities for freedom and for marronage, a space particularly conducive to what Hakim Bey has referred to as "Temporary Autonomous Zones" outside the imagined geographic bounds of the United States, a connection I explore further below.[78]

Indeed, as the epigraph to this section indicates, Douglass believed that on land the enslaved could be subjected to both physical and legal violences that kept them in subjugation, "but the moment they mount the surface of our unsteady waves, those statutes are obliterated, and the slave stands redeemed, disenthralled."[79] Here the slave-turned-maroon is, in Yannick Marshall's terms, "Sisyphus escaped." Following Kim Dovey, I am interested in considering the ontology of space as one of becoming rather than being, resisting essentialist formulations that depend upon a preexisting place within a space as an originary site for the formation of identity and subjectivity.[80] Such anti-essentialist and antinationalist notions of space, place, and subjectivity are also at the heart of Paul Gilroy's conception of the Black Atlantic, with its emphasis on the particular rhythms and possibilities of the ocean space and the lower frequencies of freedoms existent there.[81] Bey does not define the Temporary Autonomous Zone but rather "circle[s] around" it with gestures and examples that illuminate its both material and psychic dimensions across time and space—its potentialities and realities.[82] Bey's impulse aligns with my way of defining by not entirely defining marronage. Like the TAZ, maroons are hard to define as well, oscillating between various modes of being, subject positions, and possible spaces outside normative temporalities and logics of apprehension.

Some of Bey's examples of spaces and sites of social formation akin to or possessing elements of the TAZ are reminiscent of Homi Bhabha's and Edward Soja's conceptions of "third spaces": "camps of black tents under the desert stars, interzones, hidden fortified oases along secret caravan routes, 'liberated' bits of jungle and bad-land, no-go areas, black markets, and underground bazaars,"[83] and, indeed, Bey makes mention on several occasions of maroon communities from the West Indies to the Great Dismal Swamp, noting their "guerrilla ontolog[y]: strike and run away."[84] For my purposes, I'm interested in the way Washington's revolt aboard the *Creole* occasions the formation of a kind of TAZ as maroon space, one that, like most any slave-ship revolt—and not just a mutiny, as I will show—forces a near total reversal of the normativized spatiotemporal order of the ship, upsetting the delicate balance between slavery and emancipation as understood through the lens of the state and white abolitionism. In the case of the *Creole*, the TAZ possesses a mobility that is both real and imagined: the enslaved captives–turned–ship's crew steer the craft toward British Nassau, to a free port city that will come to act as an extension of the TAZ that they both fought and realized, cognitively, into existence. "The first step," Bey writes, "is somewhat akin to satori—the realization that the TAZ begins with a simple act of realization," recalling

Washington's own earlier realization in the forest and Blake's psychic liberation from slavery while still physically on the plantation.[85] The slave ship and the events that unfold on it act as a microcosmic representation of what could happen should the spatiotemporal order created and enforced by the slave system be upended.

Grant describes little of the actual revolt's unfolding because, just as he apprehended "the nineteen negroes . . . all on deck, with their broken fetters in their hands, rushing in all directions," "he put [his] hand quickly in [his] pocket to draw out [his] jack-knife" but was "knocked senseless to the deck" before he could do so.[86] When he came to "a few minutes later," the entire socio-spatial order of the ship had been upended: "there was not a white man on deck."[87] He had not been privy to the goings-on below deck, in the space of the enslaved, where Washington had freed himself and subsequently eighteen others of their shackles using a file given to him by Mr. Listwell when he last encountered Washington as a member of a slave coffle en route to the ship's port of sail in Richmond. The revolt occasions a disruption of normative space on the ship, as the enslaved rise from the depths of the holding area below deck and force most of the crew "aloft in the rigging," where "they dare not come down."[88] In this case it is the free white men who flee "northward," or up into the ship's riggings, to escape violence, desperate to evade the unimaginable consequences of such a reversal of power, of who is free and who isn't, and in what ways, and where. It also occasions a disruption to the normative temporal order of the ship. Captives aboard slave ships were intermittently allowed, at the crew's discretion and at specific times under heavy guard, to come on deck in gendered groups for forced exercise, often in the form of dancing, derided all the while by the crew, and to allow the crew to hose out the hold, or the captives themselves as they stood on deck.[89] The revolt, however, breaks with this enforced, regulatory temporal order, shifting control of time, as well as space, to the enslaved while once again obscuring the particulars and avoiding revealing details that might be used to surveil and control Black bodies at sea. The spatiotemporal cycle of power, control, and domination that rigidly structures life aboard a slave ship has been upended, creating a temporary autonomous zone, a floating maroon space, a site of marronage at sea where freedom has been forcibly produced and possibilities yet unknown but outside the US nation-state have emerged.

What does the slave ship become once its human cargo is at the helm in international waters outside US law, in control of its destination?

Its sole purpose—to transport captive bondspeople, to act as a floating conduit in a circuit of human exchange bound up in an Atlantic system of capital circulation and accumulation—has been foiled. It can have no static being; its ontology is one of becoming, its existence a continual process and possibility in the making rather than something concrete, identifiable. It is now a potential site of provisional, possibilistic freedom, or means toward achieving freedom, and it is marked by the autonomy, agency, and self-determination of the self-liberated enslaved people—who can no longer be neatly understood as slaves at all but are, to return to Fouchard's earlier phrase, "de facto free persons."[90] "The TAZ is like an uprising which does not engage directly with the State," writes Bey, "a guerilla operation which liberates an area (of land, of time, of imagination) and then dissolves itself to re-form elsewhere/elsewhen."[91] Maroon spaces like the one aboard the *Creole*—and to a certain extent that of the pine forest clearing, and the cave in the dismal swamp—may be understood as types of Temporary Autonomous Zones insofar as they constitute spatial, temporal, material, and psychic dimensions that both reveal and generate the conditions of possibility for a kind of provisional freedom—a freedom that is not the dialectical opposite of slavery, which can be understood as emancipation on a large scale and manumission on a smaller one, but that is representative of an interstitial, protean subject position existing somewhere between politically, legally, and philosophically codified notions of freedom and enslavement—or possibly outside of them all, as the state has no other way of recognizing this subjectivity as anything other than a criminal one.

In this case, the maroon space/TAZ of the liberated slave ship, its purpose and its ontology redefined, moves along and within former routes of the Atlantic slave trade to the port at Nassau in the British Bahamas, which is inflected by the ship's emancipatory potential and itself becomes implicated in the TAZ's rhizomatic web of influence.[92] In the story, Douglass has Grant describe another reversal of normative order at the port, wherein

> by order of the authorities, a company of black soldiers came on board, for the purpose, as they said, of protecting the property. These impudent rascals, when I called on them to assist me in keeping the slaves on board, sheltered themselves adroitly under their instructions only to protect property,—and said they did not recognize persons as property. I told them that by the laws of Virginia and the laws of the United States, the slaves

on board were as much property as the barrels of flour in the hold. At this the stupid blockheads showed their ivory, rolled up their white eyes in horror, as if the idea of putting men on a footing with merchandise were revolting to their humanity. When these instructions were understood among the negroes, it was impossible for us to keep them on board. They deliberately gathered up their baggage before our eyes, and, against our remonstrances, poured through the gangway,—formed themselves into a procession on the wharf,—bid farewell to all on board, and, uttering the wildest shouts of exultation, they marched, amidst the deafening cheers of a multitude of sympathizing spectators, under the triumphant leadership of their heroic chief and deliverer, MADISON WASHINGTON.[93]

Their disembarkation resembles the welcoming home of war heroes. The company of Black soldiers boarding the ship links the space of the emancipated slave ship to the space of the port landing through an insurgent maroon Blackness that is both embodied and, for Douglass, symbolic. The rebels are hailed as heroes by the cheering crowds of emancipated Black Bahamians who welcome them ashore after their victory aboard the *Creole*—a material victory for them and a symbolic victory for diasporic Black populations imbricated in the hemispheric praxis of captivity, subjugation, enslavement, circulation, and multifaceted forms of resistance. Ifeoma Kiddoe Nwankwo posits that the ending of the novella "reveals a pro-Black world stance" and that "By including the Bahamians, Douglass situates the rebels, whom he has set up as descendants of the patriots of the American Revolution, as also part of a Black world. The rebels are both heirs to the American Revolution and brethren to these Black Bahamians."[94] The port itself, then, and its Black inhabitants become an extension of a maroon consciousness as the self-emancipated African Americans aboard the *Creole* remake the ontology of place as process on the island, "realizing" another space into material liberation via embodied cognition and physical resistant practices and affirming a connection with diasporic resistant identity via marronage. What possibilities for freedom lie in this new space are left up to the imagination of the reader, but what's significant is that those possibilities have been raised, and they have nothing to do with the United States or its slave system. Ivy Wilson, agreeing with Nwankwo that transnationalism of place and geography does not capture what was happening in the connection between African

Americans and Black Bahamians, writes that " 'The Heroic Slave' ends not with a depiction of the United States as a 'trans-national America' . . . but with a displaced cadre of transnational blacks whose affiliations and affinities are determined less by their reference to the United States than by their relationship to other blacks in the diaspora."[95] In the end, Douglass represents the outcome of the *Creole* affair not as a fulfillment of promise but as a reaffirmation of a negative. The *Creole* eighteen, along with all of the enslaved on board, ultimately walk free, but for Douglass the possibility of their freedom in Nassau has the effect of reinforcing the current impossibility of their freedom in the United States.

Back to the Swamp

If we return to Madison Washington's period of marronage in the swamp considering what has been illuminated through attention to marronage in the story, it takes on new possibilistic resonances. If we pause at the narrative interruptions of marronage and sit with the five years that have gone unnarrated in the story, we begin to see with clearer focus the nonliberal and even anti-liberal elements that pervade the story's exploration of Black liberatory possibility. In *The Heroic Slave*, as in much of his other writing, Douglass conjures an aspirational liberalism, one with greater possibilities for freedom and equity than have previously existed in a liberalism afflicted with the blight of slavery. His strategy of appealing to the foundational principles of US liberal democracy, of appealing to its proponents to see it through to the point where African Americans are provided the same route to citizenship, civil rights, and state protections afforded to white people, is extraordinarily well developed and executed, but in the end he calls them dramatically into question when he locates freedom for Washington outside of the United States entirely.

Such a revised interpretation of *The Heroic Slave*—authored as it is by probably the most well-known and celebrated African American author in the nineteenth century—opens the greater archive of African American literature for examination with and through the lens of marronage, offering a means by which we might reimagine our reading practices to be attentive to how marronage generates possibilities for freedom that contest its understanding in the context of the politics and ideology of liberalism. Instead, marronage provides insight into how freedom might be accomplished through peripheral collectivities, assemblages, and social structures with no recourse to the state. Douglass's fictional story speculates toward and imagines counternationalist and antiliberal freedoms absent from his other and more studied work. That this occurs in work by Douglass, arguably the most celebrated Black abolitionist and canonical writer of the nineteenth century, gestures toward, in this book's argument, an entirely different way of reading and thinking the African American literary canon.

Coda

Maroon Pasts, Maroon Futures

On August 6, 2022, the Great Dismal Swamp Ancestors Day of Remembrance was held at the Hampton Roads Convention Center in Hampton, Virginia. It featured a guest speaker, Ambassador Lazarous Kapambwe of the Republic of Zambia to the United States, and was funded by a grant from the Virginia Tourism Corporation to Mubita LLC, the organization responsible, along with the Great Dismal Swamp National Wildlife Refuge, for bringing the event to fruition. Eric A. Sheppard, the president of Mubita LLC, explained that "the event purpose is to name the pier at Lake Drummond in recognition and honor of indigenous people, Moses Grandy [Sheppard's ancestor], the Underground Railroad Freedom Seekers and Maroons of the Great Dismal Swamp and promote the Great Dismal Swamp, nationally and internationally, as a heritage tourism destination."[1]

A plaque, the first of its kind in the United States, was erected at what has been named Reflection Pier; it reads, "This plaque recognizes the contributions of Indigenous people, Moses Grandy, the Underground Railroad Freedom Seekers, Maroons and supporters for their sacrifice and contributions to American history. Let this pier and lake forever be enjoyed by all people as a place of healing, reflection and hope, as it was for others seeking refuge before us."[2] Grandy's name on the plaque suggests an engagement with marronage that was lifelong but also extends backward to those who came before him and forward to those, like his ancestor Eric Sheppard, who fight to recover and remember the history, but also to make that history a part of the present and future.

In the *Narrative of the Life of Moses Grandy* (1843), Grandy shares that his first memory, after that of having "four sisters and four brothers," of which he was the youngest, was how "my mother often hid us in the woods, to prevent master selling us" (7). His narrative, and thus the way he represents his life, is irrevocably shaped by repeated acts of *petit marronage*, initiated and carried out by his mother for the sake of keeping safe and maintaining the integrity of his family through temporary refuge in wilderness spaces. Marronage is both an originary event and an ongoing one, a means and an end for creating temporary freedom in an attempt to ensure the long-term freedom to remain with her children. This was a freedom within unfreedom, within slavery, a freedom fought for without relent. Like many enslaved people before and after her, Grandy's mother used small acts of temporary marronage as a lever to negotiate the specific terms of her, and by extension her children's, unfreedom within the system of slavery. She fled with her children as a means to ensure her children's freedom from being sold in the short term and the continuance of her family unit in the long. She renegotiated the terms of her and her family's enslavement through flight, a form of flight that preoccupies African American writing from its beginnings through the American Civil War.

Those temporary, fleeting, dangerous moments of unstable freedom—acts of agency and self-determination—were characterized, as Grandy tells us, by creative methods of loving and care: "when we wanted water, she sought for it in any hole or puddle formed by falling trees or otherwise: it was often full of tadpoles and insects: she strained it, and gave it round to each of us in the hollow of her hand."[3] "For food," Grandy continues, "she gathered berries in the woods, got potatoes, raw corn, &c."[4] This suggests that she either gathered potatoes and corn before taking flight or returned surreptitiously to the plantation to do so. It suggests collective knowledge and networks of communal care on the part of enslaved people in the area. It is evidence of how enslaved people helped and cared for one another in the ways that they could, born out of circumstance and experience, of time and planning, of an unbroken desire to fight for their lives and livelihoods, to be human even as that humanity was continually denied and violated by enslavers. Grandy's life, like that of many enslaved people who lived and labored on the border zones of the swamp, was deeply inflected and influenced by its presence as a landscape and centuries-old ecology that white colonizers and enslavers could never quite "tame" or control. As they encroached upon it further, the ways enslaved people interacted with it changed. In it, and in the African American literature that engaged with and represented it, we find alternative rhythms, novel experimentations, and creative modes of freedom and freedom-seeking that are life giving and life sustaining in ways unregistered by conventional abolitionist thinking about Black freedom as emancipation.

Public recognition of maroons through an event like the Great Dismal Swamp Ancestors Day of Remembrance is unprecedented and a testament to the tireless work of activists like Mr. Sheppard and scholar-activist academics like Christy Hyman and many others. Part of what this book has tried to do, and hopes to do, is provide a way to recover some of the long history of maroons and marronage in the United States by drawing attention to representations of them by Black writers during the last decade of legalized chattel slavery. Where the historical archive falters, we can look to the ways Black literature, broadly defined, serves as an archive for remembering and for reconfiguring the ways we conceive of explorations of and experimentations with freedom in that literature. Twenty-five years ago, Saidiya Hartman wrote that "the complicity of slavery and freedom or, at the very least, the ways in which they assumed, presupposed, and mirrored one another . . . troubled, if not elided, any absolute and definitive marker between slavery and its aftermath."[5] *Beyond Emancipation* has asserted that pre–Civil War African American literature wrestling with the complexities of marronage suggests that the event of formal emancipation was, in Hartman's terms, also a "nonevent." Focusing on marronage in pre–Civil War Black literature reveals writers grappling with this (non)event before it happened, thereby contesting triumphalist narratives that retroactively mark legal emancipation and the American Civil War as a stable, definitive moment in both Black history and, in turn, habits of periodization of Black writing and thought. The ontology of marronage preemptively rejects legal emancipation without needing to know it would ever exist. Maroons couldn't and wouldn't depend upon it in the first place. Marronage ultimately refutes the conditions of possibility for its coherence and resists a futurity reliant upon its realization, disrupting normative and commonsense notions of time.

In the lower frequencies of Black life as evoked through explorations of marronage, we see an always already nonlinear and nonteleological temporality of Black life in relation to the state. What these writers illuminate, and what they illuminate for us via marronage, is that slavery would never quite be over once it had begun, that a true route to freedom within American liberalism would never exist in a place where freedom itself had only come to be defined—both in idea and law—in relation to and because of its opposite: chattel slavery. In other words, in

Hartman's figuration, Moses Grandy's mother would never quite be able to stop fleeing to those woods; this flight would only take on different forms and variations over time. Freedom would always be contingent, its true realization impossible when the truth of its possibility in those terms was born out of the yoke of slavery.

To privilege maroons and marronage in an analysis of African American literary history is, in some small measure, to work to restore Black agency, humanity, and subjectivity from the worlds of those texts. Doing so emphasizes Black action rather than reaction, centering Black tactics and strategies for creative resistance rather than centering white oppression as the catalyst for and defining feature of pre–Civil War Black writing. In the end, which is really only a humble beginning, I submit that *Beyond Emancipation* concludes where other scholars have already picked up in earnest, locating the legacies of slavery in events and cultural production through our contemporary moment, as Hartman argued would always be the case. What the maroons can teach us about the tangled legacies and possibilities of freedom and unfreedom remains ever-present and ongoing.

Notes

Introduction

1. James Redpath, *The Roving Editor; or, Talks with Slaves in the Southern States* (A. B. Burdick, 1859), 288.

2. Redpath, *Roving*, 288.

3. Quoted in Thomas Wentworth Higginson, *Travellers and Outlaws: Episodes in American History* (Lee and Shepard, 1888), 194. Brown's own plan following the raid on Harpers Ferry in 1859 included flight to the Allegheny Mountains in what is now West Virginia in order to establish a kind of guerilla maroon encampment from which further forays into the plantation landscape could be conducted for the purpose of liberating enslaved people. For an extremely comprehensive history of John Brown's raid and abolitionist activity, see David S. Reynolds, *John Brown, Abolitionist: The Man Who Killed Slavery, Sparked the Civil War, and Seeded Civil Rights* (Vintage, 2006).

4. Redpath, *Roving*, 288.

5. I borrow, adapt, and further this concept of "lower frequencies" from Paul Gilroy and Ralph Ellison. Paul Gilroy, *The Black Atlantic: Modernity and Double Consciousness* (Harvard University Press, 1993), 37. Gilroy borrows the phrase from the final line of Ellison's *Invisible Man* (1952): "Who knows but that, on the lower frequencies, I speak for you?" Ralph Ellison, *Invisible Man* (Vintage, 1995), 581.

6. See Sylviane A. Diouf, *Slavery's Exiles: The Story of the American Maroons* (NYU Press, 2014); Daniel O. Sayers, *A Desolate Place for a Defiant People: The Archaeology of Maroons, Indigenous Americans, and Enslaved Laborers in the Great Dismal Swamp* (University Press of Florida, 2014); Neil Roberts, *Freedom as Marronage* (University of Chicago Press, 2015); Marcus Nevius, *City of Refuge: Slavery and Petit Marronage in the Great Dismal Swamp, 1763-1856* (University of Georgia Press, 2020); J. Brent Morris, *Dismal Freedom: A History of the Maroons of the Great Dismal Swamp* (University of North Carolina Press, 2022); Richard

Bodek and Joseph Kelly, eds., *Maroons and the Marooned: Runaways and Castaways in the Americas* (University Press of Mississippi, 2020); Timothy James Lockley, ed., *Maroon Communities in South Carolina: A Documentary Record* (University of South Carolina Press, 2009); Martha Schoolman, *Abolitionist Geographies* (University of Minnesota Press, 2014), especially chapter 5; Kathyrn E. Golden, "Through the Muck and Mire: Marronage, Representation, and Memory in the Great Dismal Swamp" (PhD diss., University of California, Berkeley, 2018); William Tynes Cowan, *The Slave in the Swamp: Disrupting the Plantation Narrative* (Routledge, 2004); Hugo Prosper Leaming, *Hidden Americans: Maroons of Virginia and the Carolinas* (Garland Publishing, 1995); Justin Hosbey and J. T. Roane, "A Totally Different Form of Living: On the Legacies of Displacement and Marronage as Black Ecologies," *Southern Cultures* 27, no. 1 (2021): 68–73; Christy Hyman, "To Render a Landscape of Trauma: Deep Mapping a Historical Landscape of Domination—The Great Dismal Swamp," in *Expanding the Boundaries of Black Intellectual History*, ed. Leslie Alexander, Brandon Byrd, and Russell Rickford (Northwestern University Press, 2021); and Damian Alan Pargas, ed., *Fugitive Slaves and Spaces of Freedom in North America* (University Press of Florida, 2018).

    7. Richard Price, ed., *Maroon Societies: Rebel Slave Communities in the Americas* (Johns Hopkins University Press, 1979). It would be difficult to overstate the impact that Richard and Sally Price's anthropological and cultural work on maroons has had on the impact of maroon studies over the past several decades. While most of their work has focused on marronage outside the United States—particularly in Suriname, French Guiana, and the Caribbean—the influence of their methods and explorations has been and continues to be profound across fields of academic as well as more popular study.

    8. See Diouf, *Slavery's Exiles*, especially the introduction.

    9. For some collected works, see Higginson, *Travellers and Outlaws*; David Hunter Strother, *Virginia Illustrated: Containing a Visit to the Virginian Canaan, and the Adventures of Porte Crayon and His Cousins* (Harper & Brothers Publishers, 1857); and Frederick Law Olmsted, *A Journey in the Seaboard Slave States, with Remarks on Their Economy* (Dix and Edwards, 1856).

    10. Edmund Jackson, "The Virginia Maroons," *National Anti-Slavery Standard*, February 12, 1852, 152, *Slavery and Anti-Slavery: A Transnational Archive*, Gale.

    11. Moses Grandy, *Narrative of the Life of Moses Grandy; Late a Slave in the United States of America* (C. Gilpin, 1843).

    12. William Byrd II, *The Westover Manuscripts: Containing the History of the Dividing Line Betwixt Virginia and North Carolina; A Journey to the Land of Eden, A.D. 1733; and A Progress to the Mines. Written from 1728 to 1736, and Now First Published* (Edmund and Julian C. Ruffin, 1841), 20.

    13. See note 6 above.

    14. Cowan, *Slave in the Swamp*; Schoolman, *Abolitionist Geographies*; Bodek and Kelly, *Maroons and the Marooned*.

15. Christopher Taylor, *Empire of Neglect: The West Indies in the Wake of British Liberalism* (Duke University Press, 2018), 1.

16. Manisha Sinha, *The Slave's Cause: A History of Abolition* (Yale University Press, 2017), 1. This reading practice is partly informed by the work of David Kazanjian. See note 53.

17. For recent consideration of Douglass, Jacobs, and Delany as political philosophers, see Melvin L. Rogers and Jack Turner, eds., *African American Political Thought: A Collected History* (University of Chicago Press, 2021), particularly chapters 2–5.

18. Douglass moved his family to Rochester, New York, in 1847, from which he would launch the publication of the *North Star* a year later. He called Rochester "right over the way" from Canada, a location that allowed him to help ferry escapees from slavery to freedom, and also to ensure his own family's safety.

19. The rationale given by Chief Justice Roger Taney in the *Dred Scott v. Sandford* case states, "We think . . . that they [Black people] are not included, and were not intended to be included, under the word 'citizens' in the Constitution, and can therefore claim none of the rights and privileges which that instrument provides for and secures to citizens of the United States." This decision would ultimately be superseded only following the conclusion of the American Civil War by the passage of the Thirteenth and Fourteenth Amendments to the US Constitution, which abolished slavery and guaranteed citizenship to anyone born or naturalized in the United States, respectively. See Erwin Chemerinsky, *Constitutional Law: Principles and Policies*, 6th ed. (Walters Kluwer, 2015), 722.

20. See Robert S. Levine, *Martin Delany, Frederick Douglass, and the Politics of Representative Identity* (University of North Carolina Press, 1997); Levine, *Martin R. Delany: A Documentary Reader* (University of North Carolina Press, 2003); and Levine, *Dislocating Race and Nation: Episodes in Nineteenth-Century American Literary Nationalism* (University of North Carolina Press, 2008) as well as Robert S. Levine et al., introduction to *The Heroic Slave: A Cultural and Critical Edition*, by Frederick Douglass, edited by Levine et al. (Yale University Press, 2015).

21. Levine, *Dislocating*, 2, 13.

22. It's worth noting also that one side effect of this framing was to position the Northern states as sites of freedom, which led the Union Army to position itself as liberators of enslaved people during the American Civil War, further cementing an oversimplified sectionalist geography and ideology of freedom.

23. Ifeoma Kiddoe Nwankwo, *Black Cosmopolitanism: Racial Consciousness and Transnational Identity in the Nineteenth-Century Americas* (University of Pennsylvania Press, 2014), 10.

24. Nwankwo, *Black Cosmopolitanism*, 10.

25. Fred Moten, *In the Break: The Aesthetics of the Black Radical Tradition* (University of Minnesota Press, 2003), 1.

26. Kathryn B. Golden has done extensive work "utilizing the voices of descendants of the enslaved as central to the recovering and uncovering of the historical legacy of the Dismal Swamp maroons." See Golden, "Through the Muck and Mire," abstract. On the subject of maroon communities in national memories, see also Adam Bledsoe, "Marronage as a Past and Present Geography in the Americas," *Southeastern Geographer* 57, no. 1 (2017).

27. There is a very large body of scholarship studying the Jamaican maroons. A good starting point is Mavis Campbell, *The Maroons of Jamaica: A History of Resistance, Collaboration and Betrayal* (Bloomsbury, 1988).

28. Hosbey and Roane, "Totally Different Form of Living," 70.

29. Monique Allewaert, *Ariel's Ecology: Plantations, Personhood, and Colonialism in the American Tropics* (University of Minnesota Press, 2013), 31.

30. William Tynes Cowan argues that "an escaped slave generally signified a disruption to the plantation system, the maroon frequently disrupted the otherwise placid portrayal of the institution of slavery." Cowan, *The Slave in the Swamp*, 15.

31. Judith Madera, *Black Atlas: Geography and Flow in Nineteenth-Century African American Literature* (Duke University Press, 2015), 82.

32. Madera, *Black Atlas*, 73.

33. My organizational thinking here is informed by the way Levine carefully constructs his chapters in *Dislocating Race and Nation*: "one could read these chapters as they are presented, as 'episodes' in which linkages between discrete moments are not overly insisted upon, in which outcomes remain vague and unpredictable, and in which the authors themselves have no clear sense of connections between their contemporary present moments and possible pasts and futures" (13–14).

34. Celeste Winston, *How to Lose the Hounds: Maroon Geographies and a World Beyond Policing* (Duke University Press, 2023), 1.

35. Harriet Beecher Stowe, *Dred: A Tale of the Great Dismal Swamp*, ed. Robert S. Levine (University of North Carolina Press, 2006).

36. Eric Gardner, *Unexpected Places: Relocating Nineteenth-Century African American Literature* (University Press of Mississippi, 2009). Gardner elaborates on this title phrase in the book's introduction.

37. Roland Leander Williams, *Smooth Operating and Other Social Acts* (State University of New York Press, 2022), 4–5; see also 15–18.

38. Bledsoe, "Marronage," 30.

39. Christina Sharpe, *In the Wake: On Blackness and Being* (Duke University Press, 2016), 20.

40. Frederick Douglass, *The Heroic Slave*, in *Autographs for Freedom*, ed. Julia Griffiths (John P. Jewett, 1853).

41. Douglass, *Heroic Slave*, 194.

42. Harriet Jacobs, *Incidents in the Life of a Slave Girl* (Dover, 2001). The original version of the text was published in Boston, by the author, in 1861.

43. Jean Fagan Yellin, "Written by Herself: Harriet Jacobs' Slave Narrative," *American Literature* 53, vol. 3 (November 1981): 479–86, is the article in which Jacobs's narrative was first authenticated. See also Yellin's biography of Jacobs: *Harriet Jacobs: A Life* (Basic Books, 2004).

44. Martin R. Delany, *Blake; or, The Huts of America*, ed. Jerome McGann (Harvard University Press, 2017).

45. David Walker, *Walker's Appeal, in Four Articles; Together with a Preamble, to the Coloured Citizens of the World, but in Particular, and Very Expressly, to Those of the United States of America, Written in Boston, State of Massachusetts, September 28, 1829*, 3rd ed. (David Walker, 1830); Henry Highland Garnet, "An Address to the Slaves of the United States of America," in *A Memorial Discourse* (J. M. Wilson, 1865).

46. Harriet Beecher Stowe, *Uncle Tom's Cabin; or, Life Among the Lowly: Arranged for Young Readers* (Henry Altemus, 1900).

47. Stowe, *Uncle Tom's Cabin*, 256.

48. Stowe, *Uncle Tom's Cabin*, 256–57.

49. See Jennifer Rae Greeson, *Our South: Geographic Fantasy and the Rise of National Literature* (Harvard University Press, 2010). My chapter "Maroons and Marronage in Antebellum African American Literature," in Harilaos Stecopoulos, *A History of the Literature of the U.S. South* (Cambridge University Press, 2021), also explores this idea more specifically as it relates to African American literature in the pre–Civil War period. See also Michael P. Bibler, "Introduction: Smash the Mason-Dixon! or, Manifesting the Southern United States," *PMLA* 131, no. 1 (January 2016): 153–56.

50. My thinking beyond these foundational texts, and beyond the traditional ways they have been read, is informed by Eric Gardner's call to look for and at African American literature in "unexpected places" that exceed, complicate, expand traditional geographies and narratives about African American literary production. See Carla L. Peterson, *"Doers of the Word": African-American Women Speakers and Writers in the North* (Rutgers University Press, 1998); Gardner, *Unexpected Places* (University Press of Mississippi, 2009).

51. Vincent Carretta, *Unchained Voices: An Anthology of Black Authors in the English-Speaking World of the Eighteenth Century* (University of Kentucky Press, 2003).

52. See William L. Andrews, *To Tell a Free Story: The First Century of Afro-American Autobiography, 1760–1865* (University of Illinois Press, 1988); Robert B. Stepto, *From Behind the Veil: A Study of Afro-American Narrative* (University of Illinois Press, 1979).

53. On speculation in a similar context, Kazanjian writes, "This more speculative approach to the archives has revealed to me rich scenes of speculative, heterodox thought about freedom in the pores of quotidian, nineteenth-century documents, thought that questions many of our basic presuppositions about the

meaning of freedom and the modes in which it can or should be lived." See David Kazanjian, "Scenes of Speculation," *Social Text* 125 (December 2015): 79. More recently, he expanded upon these thoughts in his book *The Brink of Freedom: Improvising Life in the Nineteenth-Century Atlantic World* (Duke University Press, 2016).

54. Kazanjian, "Scenes," 79.

55. Angela Y. Davis, *Lectures on Liberation* (United Committee to Free Angela Davis, ca. 1971), 1.

Chapter One

1. Another noteworthy example of such a poem by a major nineteenth-century American writer, one that portrays the maroon mainly as pitiful, is Henry Wadsworth Longfellow's "The Slave in the Dismal Swamp." See Henry Wadsworth Longfellow, "The Slave in the Dismal Swamp," in *Poems on Slavery*, by Longfellow, 18–20 (J. Owen, 1842).

2. Herman Melville, "The Swamp Angel," in *Battle-Pieces and Aspects of the War*, by Melville, 107 (Harper, 1866).

3. Melville, "Swamp Angel," 107.

4. Robert S. Levine, introduction to *Dred: A Tale of the Great Dismal Swamp*, by Harriet Beecher Stowe, ed. Levine (University of North Carolina Press, 2000), xvi.

5. Robert S. Levine, *Martin Delany, Frederick Douglass, and the Politics of Representative Identity* (University of North Carolina Press, 1997), 174.

6. Martha Schoolman, *Abolitionist Geographies* (University of Minnesota Press, 2014), 163.

7. Jared Hickman, *Black Prometheus: Race and Radicalism in the Age of Atlantic Slavery* (Oxford University Press, 2016), 17.

8. Herman Melville, *Benito Cereno*, *Putnam's Monthly Magazine*, no. 34, October 1855 / no. 35, November 1855 / no. 36, December 1855.

9. Thomas Wentworth Higginson also wrote and published on slave revolts and on maroons in the Caribbean, but the work was released after the end of the American Civil War.

10. James Redpath, *The Roving Editor; or, Talks with Slaves in the Southern States* (A. B. Burdick, 1859), 269–70.

11. For a recent consideration of Denmark Vesey in the context of marronage, see James O'Neil Spady, "Belonging and Alienation: Gullah Jack and Some Maroon Dimensions of the 'Denmark Vesey Conspiracy,'" in *Maroons and the Marooned: Runaways and Castaways in the Americas*, eds. Richard Bodek and Joseph Kelly (University Press of Mississippi, 2020).

12. For more on Americans' changing views of swamp environments and landscapes during the pre-Civil War period and afterward, see David C. Miller, *Dark Eden: The Swamp in Nineteenth-Century American Literature and Culture* (Cambridge University Press, 1989); and Anthony Wilson, *Shadow and Shelter: The Swamp in Southern Culture* (University Press of Mississippi, 2005).

13. See the introduction to Anthony Kaye, *Joining Places: Slave Neighborhoods in the Old South* (University of North Carolina Press, 2008).

14. Harriet Beecher Stowe, *Dred: A Tale of the Great Dismal Swamp*, ed. Robert S. Levine (University of North Carolina Press, 2006), 254–55.

15. Stowe, *Dred*, 255.

16. Stowe, 262.

17. Martin R. Delany, *Blake; or, The Huts of America*, ed. Jerome McGann (Harvard University Press, 2017), 313.

18. Rebecca Ginsburg, "Escaping Through a Black Landscape," in *Cabin, Quarter, Plantation: Architecture and Landscapes of North American Slavery*, ed. Clifton Ellis and Ginsburg (Yale University Press, 2010), 52–54.

19. Stowe, *Dred*, 270.

20. Stowe, 270.

21. Stowe, 340–41.

22. I refer here to an excerpt from Irène Mathieu's poem "maron (circa 1735)" that serves as one of the epigraphs to chapter 3. The poem explores the intertwined nature of Black bodies and their environments, specifically here that of a swamp. Irène Mathieu, "maron (circa 1735)," in *Grand Marronage*, by Mathieu (Switchback Books, 2019).

23. Stowe, *Dred*, 341.

24. For recent work arguing that fugitive slaves, maroons, and insurrections real and imagined played a significant role in the movement toward abolition in the United States and British colonies, see Gerald Horne, *The Counter-Revolution of 1776: Slave Resistance and the Origins of the United States of America* (NYU Press, 2014); and Manisha Sinha, *The Slave's Cause: A History of Abolition* (Yale University Press, 2017).

25. Allison L. Hurst, "Beyond the Pale: Poor Whites as Uncontrolled Social Contagion in Harriet Beecher Stowe's *Dred*," *The Mississippi Quarterly* 63, no. 4 (2010): 637.

26. The concept of "masterless men" was first introduced in another context by A. L. Beier in *Masterless Men: The Vagrancy Problem in England, 1560–1640* (Methuen, 1985). Beier defines masterless men as "a large landless element with no firm roots and few prospects" (1) and analyzes this class of people as a unique challenge in the realm of social control during this particular period in England's history. More recently, Keri Leigh Merritt has studied the concept in the context of poor whites in the US South prior to the Civil War. See Keri Leigh Merritt,

Masterless Men: Poor Whites and Slavery in the Antebellum South (Cambridge University Press, 2017).

27. Stowe, *Dred*, 105.
28. Stowe, 105.
29. Stowe, 106.
30. Stowe, 190.
31. Stowe, 190.
32. Stowe, 240.
33. Stowe, 240–41.
34. While some critical attention has been given to operations of the law in relation to slavery in *Dred*, none of it has focused on the law as it relates to maroons or, as it would have been more accurately described in the parlance of the time, the practice of outlawing slaves for "lying out" or "truancy." Several chapters of *Dred* not discussed here focus on a local trial taken up pro bono and prosecuted by the attorney Edward Clayton. The case centers around the murder of an enslaved man by his owner. Clayton attempts to argue that the murder was unlawful and initially wins the case, but on appeal it is overturned by none other than his father, Judge Clayton, who, although he too abhors the institution of slavery and the violences it encourages, is a purist who is compelled to rule in favor of the defendant on the grounds that, in short, enslaved persons are property and the enslaver in question did not break the law by executing lethal punishment of said property. For work that focuses on this trial and other aspects of the law in *Dred* and antebellum US culture, see Jeffory A. Clymer, "Family Money: Race and Economic Rights in Antebellum US Law and Fiction," *American Literary History* 21, no. 2 (Summer 2009): 211–38; Jeannine Marie DeLombard, "Representing the Slave: White Advocacy and Black Testimony in Harriet Beecher Stowe's *Dred*," *New England Quarterly* 75, no. 1 (March 2002): 80–106; Laura H. Korobkin, "Appropriating Law in Harriet Beecher Stowe's *Dred*," *Nineteenth-Century Literature* 62, no. 3 (December 2007): 380–406; Keiko Noguchi, "Harriet Beecher Stowe's *Dred*: Legal Exploration in a Sentimental Novel," *Tsuda Review* 55 (November 2010): 1–24; Gail K. Smith, "Reading with the Other: Hermeneutics and the Politics of Difference in Stowe's *Dred*," *American Literature* 69, no. 2 (June 1997): 289–313.
35. "Revised Code—No. 105: Slaves and Free Persons of Color: An Act Concerning Slaves and Free Persons of Color," 1831, *Documenting the American South*, North Carolina Collection, University Library, University of North Carolina at Chapel Hill, https://docsouth.unc.edu/nc/slavesfree/slavesfree.html.
36. Stowe, *Dred*, 85.
37. Stowe, 85.
38. Stowe, 401.
39. Byrd's collected writings and observations on the Great Dismal Swamp first appeared in William Byrd and Edmund Ruffin, *The Westover Manuscripts* (Edmund and Julian C. Ruffin, 1841).

40. Stowe, *Dred*, 406.
41. Stowe, 168.
42. Stowe, 171.
43. Stowe, 231.
44. Stowe, 212.
45. Stowe, 211.
46. Stowe, 233.
47. Stowe, 247.
48. Stowe, 479.
49. Stowe, 478.
50. Stowe, 479.
51. Stowe, 481.
52. Stowe, 481.
53. Stowe, 389.
54. Stowe, 389.
55. Stowe, 492.
56. Stowe, 493.
57. Stowe, 493.
58. Stowe, 493.
59. Stowe, 494.
60. Stowe, 499.
61. Hagar Kotef, *Movement and the Ordering of Freedom: On Liberal Governances of Mobility* (Duke University Press, 2015), 9.
62. Kotef, *Movement*, 15; emphasis in original.
63. Kotef, 5.

Chapter Two

1. Martha Schoolman, "Martin Delany, *Blake; or, the Huts of America* (1859–1862)," in *Handbook of the American Novel of the Nineteenth Century*, ed. Christine Gerhardt (Walter de Gruyter, 2018), 340.
2. Martha Schoolman, *Abolitionist Geographies* (University of Minnesota Press, 2014), 1.
3. See Koritha Mitchell, "Identifying White Mediocrity and Know-Your-Place Aggression: A Form of Self-Care," *African American Review* 51, no. 4 (Winter 2018): 253–62.
4. Martin R. Delany, *Blake; or, The Huts of America*, ed. Floyd J. Miller (Beacon Press, 1970).
5. Jerome McGann, introduction to *Blake; or, The Huts of America*, by Martin R. Delany, ed. McGann (Harvard University Press, 2017), xiv, xxvi.
6. Floyd Miller, introduction to Delany, *Blake* (ed. Floyd Miller), xxv.

7. Schoolman, *Abolitionist Geographies*, 6.

8. Andy Doolen, "'Be Cautious of the Word "Rebel"': Race, Revolution, and Transnational History in Martin Delany's *Blake; or, The Huts of America*," *American Literature* 81, no. 1 (2009): 157.

9. Eugene Genovese, *From Rebellion to Revolution: Afro-American Slave Revolts in the Making of the Modern World* (Louisiana State University Press, 1979), 76–77.

10. Genovese, *From Rebellion*, 77.

11. All quotations from *Blake* in this chapter are from Jerome McGann's corrected edition, Delany, *Blake* (ed. McGann).

12. McGann, introduction to Delany, *Blake* (ed. McGann), xiii.

13. McGann, introduction, xiii.

14. Walter Johnson, "On Agency," *Journal of Social History* 37, no. 1 (Fall 2003): 117.

15. Gad Heuman, ed., *Out of the House of Bondage: Runaways, Resistance, and Marronage in Africa and the New World* (Routledge, 1986) includes chapters on practices of marronage in Africa in part 2 of the book. Notably, it includes chapters on enslaved resistance in the US and on marronage in the Caribbean but does not address marronage in the US.

16. Neil Roberts, *Freedom as Marronage* (University of Chicago Press, 2015), 13.

17. See note 53 in the introduction to the present volume on David Kazanjian's work on challenges to nineteenth-century liberalism.

18. Angela Davis, *Lectures on Liberation* (United Committee to Free Angela Davis, ca. 1971), 1.

19. Rebecca Skidmore Biggio, "The Specter of Conspiracy in Martin Delany's *Blake*," *African American Review* 42, vol. 3/4 (Fall–Winter 2008): 440.

20. Jeffory A. Clymer, "Martin Delany's *Blake* and the Transnational Politics of Property," *American Literary History* 15, vol. 4 (2003): 710.

21. Jean Lee Cole, "Theresa and Blake: Mobility and Resistance in Antebellum American Serialized Fiction," *Callaloo* 34, no. 1 (2011): 158–75.

22. Jo-Ann Marx, "The Language of Liberation in Martin R. Delany's *Blake; or, The Huts of America*," *Griot* 18, vol. 1 (Spring 1999): 19.

23. Doolen, "'Be Cautious'"; Gregory Pierrot, "Writing over Haiti: Black Avengers in Martin Delany's *Blake*," *Studies in American Fiction* 41, no. 2 (2014): 175–99. See also Pierrot's excellent book, in which his arguments about *Blake* are further elaborated in chapter 4, "Fear of a Black America: Literary Racial Uprisings in the Antebellum United States." Gregory Pierrot, *The Black Avenger in Atlantic Culture* (University of Georgia Press, 2019).

24. Britt Rusert, "Delany's Comet: Fugitive Science and the Speculative Imaginary of Emancipation," *American Quarterly* 65, no. 4 (December 2013): 801.

25. Katy Chiles, "Within and Without Raced Nations: Intertextuality, Martin Delany, and *Blake; or, The Huts of America*," *American Literature* 80, no. 2 (2008): 325.

26. Chiles, "Within and Without," 325.

27. Sharada Balachandran Orihuela, "The Black Market: Property, Freedom, and Piracy in Martin Delany's *Blake; or, The Huts of America*," *J19: The Journal of Nineteenth-Century Americanists* 2, no. 2 (Fall 2014): 273.

28. Orihuela, "Black Market," 275.

29. Piracy and marronage have been compared by critics such as Marcus Rediker and Peter Linebaugh. See Marcus Rediker, *Outlaws of the Atlantic: Sailors, Pirates, and Motley Crews in the Age of Sail* (Beacon Press, 2014); Peter Linebaugh and Marcus Rediker, *The Many-Headed Hydra: Sailors, Slaves, Commoners, and the Hidden History of the Revolutionary Atlantic* (Beacon Press, 2013).

30. Judith Madera, *Black Atlas: Geography and Flow in Nineteenth-Century African American Literature* (Duke University Press, 2015), 83.

31. Delany, *Blake* (ed. McGann), 22.

32. Henry Highland Garnet, "An Address to the Slaves of the United States of America, Buffalo, N.Y., 1843," in *A Memorial Discourse*, by Garnet (J. M. Wilson, 1865), 44–51.

33. Delany, *Blake*, 22.

34. Delany, 23.

35. Delany, 4.

36. For a representative example, see Thomas Dixon. *The Clansman: A Historical Romance of the Ku Klux Klan* (Doubleday, Page, 1905). This is the second work in a trilogy by Dixon.

37. Delany, *Blake*, 18.

38. Ifeoma Kiddoe Nwankwo, *Black Cosmopolitanism: Racial Consciousness and Transnational Identity in the Nineteenth-Century Americas* (University of Pennsylvania Press, 2014), 7.

39. Gabino La Rosa Corzo, *Runaway Slave Settlements in Cuba: Resistance and Repression*, trans. Mary Todd (University of North Carolina Press, 2003).

40. La Rosa Corzo, *Runaway*, 8.

41. La Rosa Corzo, 8.

42. La Rosa Corzo, 8.

43. Delany, *Blake*, 27.

44. This quotation appears on the back cover of Floyd Miller's 1970 edition of *Blake*. See Delany, *Blake* (ed. Floyd J. Miller). The book was reprinted by Beacon Press in 2016, a year before Miller's corrected version came out.

45. Laurent Dubois, *Avengers of the New World: The Story of the Haitian Revolution* (Harvard University Press, 2004), 199.

46. Dubois, *Avengers*, 199.

47. Dubois, 100.

48. See Jean Fouchard, *The Haitian Maroons: Liberty or Death* (Edward W. Blyden Press, 1981); and Carolyn Fick, *The Making of Haiti: The Saint Domingue Revolution from Below* (University of Tennessee Press, 1990).

49. Pierrot, *Black Avenger*, 145.

50. Pierrot, 146.

51. Both Boukman and Blake are also dismissive of Christianity when figured as the religion of their oppressors. While Blake does not dismiss it entirely, he interprets scripture according to the needs of his particular liberatory project, just as slaveholders interpreted it according to their own desire to inure African-descended peoples to their enforced condition of bondage.

52. Delany, *Blake*, 39.

53. Delany, 40.

54. Delany, 21.

55. Roberts, *Freedom*, 11.

56. Delany, *Blake*, 21.

57. Rebecca Ginsburg, "Escaping Through a Black Landscape," in *Cabin, Quarter, Plantation: Architecture and Landscapes of North American Slavery*, ed. Clifton Ellis and Ginsburg (Yale University Press, 2010), 54.

58. Ginsburg, "Escaping," 52.

59. It should be noted that the women on the Franks plantation (and, we must imagine, on surrounding plantations), especially Mammy Judy, are active participants in the network of subversive and dissembling speech acts that assist in the runaways' marronage. The distinctive roles of women in marronage are further explored in chapter 3.

60. Delany, *Blake*, 33.

61. Sylviane A. Diouf, *Slavery's Exiles: The Story of the American Maroons* (NYU Press, 2014), 11.

62. Delany, *Blake*, 42.

63. Roberts, *Freedom*, 9.

64. Delany, *Blake*, 42.

65. Delany, 42.

66. James C. Scott, *Seeing Like a State: How Certain Schemes to Improve the Human Condition Have Failed* (Yale University Press, 1999), 54.

67. Alvin O. Thompson, *Flight to Freedom: African Runaways and Maroons in the Americas* (University of the West Indies Press, 2006), 13.

68. Stephanie LeMenager, "Marginal Landscapes: Revolutionary Abolitionists and Environmental Imagination," *Interdisciplinary Literary Studies* 7, no. 1 (Fall 2005): 50–51.

69. Delany, *Blake*, 111.

70. Diouf, *Slavery's Exiles*, 3.

71. Delany, *Blake*, 69.
72. Solomon Northup, *Twelve Years a Slave* (Sampson Low, Son, 1853), 241.
73. Northup, *Twelve*, 248.
74. Northup, 246–48.
75. Northup, 247–48.
76. Northup, 248.
77. Delany, *Blake*, 98.
78. Delany, 91.
79. Delany, 107.
80. Delany, 107–8.
81. Delany, 109.
82. For more on the 1811 German Coast Uprising, see Eugene Genovese, *Roll, Jordan, Roll: The World the Slaves Made* (Vintage, 1976), 52; Daniel Rasmussen, *American Uprising: The Untold Story of America's Largest Slave Revolt* (Harper Perennial, 2012); and Herbert Aptheker, *American Negro Slave Revolts* (International Publishers, 1983).
83. Alice L. Baumgartner, *South to Freedom: Runaway Slaves to Mexico and the Road to the Civil War* (Basic Books, 2020), 2.
84. Delany, *Blake*, 110.
85. Delany, 113.
86. Delany, 115.
87. Delany, 113.
88. Delany, 115.
89. Delany, 115.
90. Delany, 113.
91. Steven Hahn, *The Political Worlds of Slavery and Freedom* (Harvard University Press, 2009), 30.
92. Hahn, *Political Worlds*, 34.
93. Hahn, 36.
94. Ted Maris-Wolf, "Hidden in Plain Sight: Maroon Life and Labor in Virginia's Dismal Swamp," *Slavery & Abolition* 34, no. 3 (2013): 446.
95. Delany, *Blake*, 127.
96. Delany, 131.
97. Delany, 131.
98. Delany, 136.
99. Delany, 135.
100. Delany, 141.
101. Delany, 143.
102. Delany, 144.
103. Delany, 145.
104. Delany, 154.

105. Delany, 154.

106. Floyd J. Miller, letter to the editor, in "An Exchange on Black History," *The New York Review of Books*, May 21, 1970, www.nybooks.com/articles/1970/05/21/an-exchange-on-black-history/.

107. Fernanda Bretones Lane, "Free to Bury Their Dead: Baptism and the Meanings of Freedom in the Eighteenth-Century Caribbean," *Slavery & Abolition* 42, no. 3 (2021): 449.

108. Julius S. Scott, *The Common Wind: Afro-American Currents in the Age of the Haitian Revolution* (Verso, 2018).

109. Delany, *Blake*, 186.

110. Delany, 313.

Chapter Three

1. Harriet Jacobs, "Cruelty to Slaves," *New York Tribune*, July 25, 1853, 3.

2. Her first letter to the *New York Daily Tribune*, entitled "LETTER FROM A FUGITIVE SLAVE. Slaves Sold Under Peculiar Circumstances," was published on June 21, 1853, at which time Jacobs was also legally free. Yellin explains that Jacobs refers to a third letter to the *Tribune* in a letter from Harriet Jacobs to Amy Post, dated October 9, 1853, but this one has not been found. See Jean Fagan Yellin, *Harriet Jacobs: A Life* (Basic Books, 2004), 306.

3. The full text of the law Jacobs is referring to can be found in the North Carolina Slave Code (1741). Terri L. Snyder's *The Power to Die: Slavery and Suicide in British North America* (University of Chicago Press, 2015), chapter 4, contains an excellent discussion of the legal history of outlawing slaves.

4. Hereafter referred to by the shortened form *Incidents*.

5. Joanne Braxton has suggested the idea that we might imagine Linda as a maroon in the narrative but did not elaborate further on the point. My argument builds directly on her observation. Braxton writes, "As in Jamaica and elsewhere in the African diaspora, maroonage or running away from slavery, proved a viable form of rebellion for many enslaved in the United States. Like Grandy Nanny, Linda takes to the woods, and becomes, for a brief period, an American maroon, a rebel and a fugitive from slavery. With the help of her maternal grandmother, Aunt Marthy, a free woman, and another outraged mother, 'Linda' was disguised as a sailor and taken to the 'Snaky Swamp,' a location she found more hospitable than landed slave culture." Joanne M. Braxton, "Ancestral Presence: The Outraged Mother Figure in Contemporary Afra-American Writing," in *Wild Women in the Whirlwind: Afra-American Culture and the Contemporary Literary Renaissance*, ed. Joanne M. Braxton and Andree Nicola McLaughlin (Rutgers University Press, 1990), 301.

6. Carolyn Sorisio, " 'There Is Might in Each': Conceptions of Self in Harriet Jacobs's *Incidents in the Life of a Slave Girl, Written by Herself*," *Legacy: A Journal of American Women Writers* 13, no. 1 (1996): 2.

7. See Sylviane A. Diouf, *Slavery's Exiles: The Story of the American Maroons* (NYU Press, 2014); Daniel O. Sayers, *A Desolate Place for a Defiant People: The Archaeology of Maroons, Indigenous Americans, and Enslaved Laborers in the Great Dismal Swamp* (University of Florida Press, 2014); Neil Roberts, *Freedom as Marronage* (University of Chicago Press, 2015); Marcus Nevius, *City of Refuge: Slavery and Petit Marronage in the Great Dismal Swamp, 1763–1856* (University of Georgia Press, 2020).

8. See, for example, Hazel Carby, *Reconstructing Womanhood: The Emergence of the Afro-American Woman Novelist* (Oxford University Press, 1989); Valerie Smith, " 'Loopholes of Retreat': Architecture and Ideology in Harriet Jacobs's *Incidents in the Life of a Slave Girl*," in *Reading Black, Reading Feminist: A Critical Anthology*, ed. Henry Louis Gates, Jr., 212–26 (New American Library, 1990); Jenny Sharpe, *Ghosts of Slavery: A Literary Archaeology of Black Women's Lives* (University of Minnesota Press, 2002); Hortense J. Spillers, "Mama's Baby, Papa's Maybe: An American Grammar Book," *Diacritics* 17, no. 2 (1987): 64–81.

9. Joy James, "Afrarealism and the Black Matrix: Maroon Philosophy at Democracy's Border," *Black Scholar* 43, no. 4 (2013): 124.

10. Julius Scott, *The Common Wind: Afro-American Currents in the Age of the Haitian Revolution* (Verso, 2018), 14.

11. Stephanie M. H. Camp, *Closer to Freedom: Enslaved Women and Everyday Resistance in the Plantation South* (University of North Carolina Press, 2004), 37.

12. Camp, *Closer*, 37.

13. Camp, 54.

14. Marisa J. Fuentes, *Dispossessed Lives: Enslaved Women, Violence, and the Archive* (University of Pennsylvania Press, 2016), 5.

15. Jean Fagan Yellin, *Harriet Jacobs: A Life* (Basic Books, 2004). While Yellin cites and briefly discusses the excerpts about marronage from the *Edenton Gazette*, she does not address how marronage might function in the narrative.

16. Diouf, *Slavery's Exiles*, 260.

17. Diouf, 260.

18. Diouf, 260.

19. See, for example, Ashli White, *Encountering Revolution: Haiti and the Making of the Early Republic* (Johns Hopkins University Press, 2010).

20. Yellin, *Harriet Jacobs*, 6.

21. Yellin, 6.

22. Yellin, 9.

23. Yellin, 10.

24. Yellin, 10.

25. Yellin, 10.
26. Yellin, 11.
27. Yellin, 11.
28. Diouf, *Slavery's Exiles*, 265.
29. Diouf, 271.
30. Diouf, 270.
31. Diouf, 273.
32. Saidiya V. Hartman, *Scenes of Subjection: Terror, Slavery, and Self-Making in Nineteenth-Century America* (Oxford University Press, 1997), 110.
33. Jacobs, *Incidents*, 34.
34. Jacobs, 45.
35. Yuko Miki, "Fleeing into Slavery: The Insurgent Geographies of Brazilian Quilombolas (Maroons), 1880–1881," *Americas* 68, no. 4 (April 2012): 497.
36. Jacobs, *Incidents*, 56.
37. Thomas R. Gray, *The Confessions of Nat Turner, the Leader of the Late Insurrection in Southampton, VA* (Thomas R. Gray, 1831), 16, 17.
38. Spillers, "Mama's Baby," 80.
39. Jacobs, *Incidents*, 56.
40. Jacobs, 83.
41. Jacobs, 83.
42. Rebecca Ginsburg, "Escaping Through a Black Landscape," in *Cabin, Quarter, Plantation: Architecture and Landscapes of North American Slavery*, ed. Clifton Ellis and Ginsburg (Yale University Press, 2010), 52.
43. Jacobs, *Incidents*, 85.
44. Jacobs, 95.
45. William Tynes Cowan, *The Slave in the Swamp: Disrupting the Plantation Narrative* (Routledge, 2005), 45.
46. Judith Madera, *Black Atlas: Geography and Flow in Nineteenth-Century African American Literature* (Duke University Press, 2015), 5.
47. Stephanie LeMenager, *Manifest and Other Destinies: Territorial Fictions of the Nineteenth-Century United States* (University of Nebraska Press, 2008), 1.
48. Jacobs, *Incidents*, 95.
49. Jacobs, 131.
50. Jacobs, 131.
51. Michelle Burnham, "Loopholes of Resistance: Harriet Jacobs' Slave Narrative and the Critique of Agency in Foucault," *Arizona Quarterly* 49, no. 2 (1993): 55.
52. See Jean Fagan Yellin, "Written by Herself: Harriet Jacobs' Slave Narrative," *American Literature* 53, no. 3 (November 1981): 479–86.
53. See Keith Michael Green, *Bound to Respect: Antebellum Narratives of Black Imprisonment, Servitude, and Bondage, 1816–1861* (University of Alabama Press, 2015); Caleb Smith, *The Prison and the American Imagination* (Yale University Press, 2009), 18; Douglas Taylor, "From Slavery to Prison: Benjamin Rush, Harriet Jacobs, and the Ideology of Reformative Incarceration," *Genre* 35, nos. 3–4 (2002): 429–47.

54. Georgia Krieger, "Playing Dead: Harriet Jacobs's Survival Strategy in *Incidents in the Life of a Slave Girl*," *African American Review* 42, nos. 3–4 (2008): 607.

55. Gloria T. Randle, "Between the Rock and the Hard Place: Mediating Spaces in Harriet Jacobs's *Incidents in the Life of a Slave Girl*," *African American Review* 33, no. 1 (1999): 43.

56. Katherine McKittrick, *Demonic Grounds: Black Women and the Cartographies of Struggle* (University of Minnesota Press, 2006), 41.

57. Miranda A. Green-Barteet, "'The Loophole of Retreat': Interstitial Spaces in Harriet Jacobs's *Incidents in the Life of a Slave Girl*," *South Central Review* 30, no. 2 (2013): 53–54.

58. Fuentes, *Dispossessed*, 5.

59. Jacobs, *Incidents*, 98.

60. Roberts, *Freedom*, 9.

61. Jacobs, *Incidents*, 95–96.

62. *Merriam-Webster Dictionary*, "dismal," accessed August 25, 2023, https://www.merriam-webster.com/dictionary/dismal.

63. Jacobs, *Incidents*, 97.

64. Jacobs, 98.

65. Diouf, *Slavery's Exiles*, 99.

66. These interviews and transcripts can be found on the Library of Congress website in the *Born in Slavery: Slave Narratives from the Federal Writers' Project, 1936 to 1938* collection, https://www.loc.gov/collections/slave-narratives-from-the-federal-writers-project-1936-to-1938/about-this-collection/.

67. Diouf, *Slavery's Exiles*, 101.

68. Jacobs, *Incidents*, 96.

69. Jacobs, 98.

70. Jacobs, 98.

71. Stephanie Li, "Motherhood as Resistance in Harriet Jacobs's *Incidents in the Life of a Slave Girl*," *Legacy: A Journal of American Women Writers* 23, no. 1 (2006): 14.

72. Angela Davis, "Reflections on the Black Woman's Role in the Community of Slaves," *Massachusetts Review* 13, nos. 1/2 (1972): 84.

73. James, "Afrarealism," 124.

74. Carol E. Henderson, "Borderlands: The Critical Matrix of Caste, Class, and Color in *Incidents in the Life of a Slave Girl*," *Legacy: A Journal of American Women Writers* 16, no. 2 (1999): 49.

Chapter Four

1. Frederick Douglass, *The Heroic Slave*, in *Autographs for Freedom*, ed. Julia Griffiths (John P. Jewett, 1853). All citations refer to this edition of the book.

2. For a recent, comprehensive historical analysis of the *Creole* rebellion, see Bruce Chadwick, *The Creole Rebellion: The Most Successful Slave Revolt in American History* (University of New Mexico Press, 2022).

3. Robert S. Levine, *Martin Delany, Frederick Douglass, and the Politics of Representative Identity* (University of North Carolina Press, 1997), 4.

4. Krista Walter, "Trappings of Nationalism in Frederick Douglass's *The Heroic Slave*," *African American Review* 34, no. 2 (Summer 2000): 245.

5. Robert S. Levine et al., introduction to *The Heroic Slave: A Cultural and Critical Edition*, by Frederick Douglass, ed. Levine et al. (Yale University Press, 2015), xxxi.

6. Thomas Koenigs, "The 'Mysterious Depths' of Slave Interiority: Fiction and Intersubjective Knowledge in *The Heroic Slave*," *J19: The Journal of Nineteenth-Century Americanists* 8, no. 2 (Fall 2020): 196.

7. In some of the earliest scholarship on *The Heroic Slave*, Robert B. Stepto argues that Douglass drew deliberately from conventions of the slave narrative, being intimately familiar with them himself, in order to develop the fictional strategies present in the novel. See Robert B. Stepto, "Storytelling in Early Afro-American Fiction: Frederick Douglass's 'The Heroic Slave,'" *Georgia Review* 36, no. 2 (Summer 1982): 355–68. Importantly to my own arguments here, Stepto acknowledges Douglass's unique and developed facility as a writer of fiction despite it being his only published work in that genre.

8. Martha Schoolman makes the case that "the practice and experience of geography in the nineteenth-century United States should . . . be seen as marked by deep contingency. But we would likely not know this from the more or less unwitting emergence of the critical narrative of abolitionist geography. Rather, abolitionist geography as it has emerged piecemeal has been less interested in discovering the clear possibility of tension between spatial coverage and political significance than in fixing the identity between space and meaning with the greatest possible consistency." Martha Schoolman, *Abolitionist Geographies* (University of Minnesota Press, 2014), 5.

9. Eric Foner offers these thoughts on the Underground Railroad in the popular and scholarly imaginations: "The picture that emerges from recent studies is not of the highly organized system with tunnels, codes, and clearly defined stations and routes of popular lore, but of an interlocking series of local networks, each of whose fortunes rose and fell over time." "The 'underground railroad,'" he concludes, "should be understood not as a single entity but as an umbrella term for local groups that employed numerous methods to assist fugitives, some public and entirely legal, some flagrant violations of the law." Eric Foner, *Gateway to Freedom: The Hidden History of the Underground Railroad* (Norton, 2015), 15.

10. Booker T. Washington, *Up from Slavery: An Autobiography* (Doubleday, 1901).

11. See Julia Griffiths, ed., *Autographs for Freedom* (John P. Jewett, 1853). Douglass's story was included in this volume after being published first as a

serial in Douglass's *North Star* magazine in 1852. The citations in this chapter, however, come from the more easily available version printed by Griffiths (which is unchanged from the original).

12. James B. Haile III, "Frederick Douglass and the Black Infrahuman Surreal: A Story of Origins," *MLN* 137, no. 5 (December 2022): 856.

13. Haile, "Black Infrahuman Surreal," 857.

14. William Wells Brown, *The Black Man, His Antecedents, His Genius, and His Achievements* (Thomas Hamilton, 1863), 78.

15. Lydia Maria Child, ed., *The Freedmen's Book* (Ticknor and Fields, 1866), 147.

16. Child, *Freedmen's*, 148.

17. Douglass, *Heroic*, 177.

18. See note 6 in the introduction for sources discussing this aspect of US marronage. See also Herbert Aptheker, "Maroons Within the Present Limits of the United States," *Journal of Negro History* 24 (1939): 167–84. This was one of the first articles to take seriously the study of marronage in the United States context.

19. It should be noted that in later iterations of his autobiography, after the Civil War and emancipation, Douglass did include more details about his escape from slavery once he deemed it safe to do so.

20. Douglass, *Heroic*, 194.

21. Frederick Douglass, *My Bondage and My Freedom* (Penguin, 2003), 282–83.

22. Douglass, *Heroic*, 196.

23. Douglass, 175.

24. Douglass, 175–76.

25. Douglass, 175.

26. Douglass, 176.

27. Douglass, 180.

28. Douglass, 180.

29. Douglass, 180.

30. Douglass, 178.

31. Douglass, 178.

32. Douglass, 179.

33. Douglass, 179.

34. I broadly borrow the term "structure of feeling" from Raymond Williams, *Marxism and Literature* (Oxford University Press, 1977).

35. My thinking here on Black cognitive landscapes is informed by Rebecca Ginsburg, "Escaping Through a Black Landscape," in *Cabin, Quarter, Plantation: Architecture and Landscapes of North American Slavery*, ed. Clifton Ellis and Ginsburg (Yale University Press, 2010).

36. Carolyn Cooper, *Noises in the Blood: Orality, Gender, and the "Vulgar" Body of Jamaican Popular Culture* (Duke University Press, 1995), 4; Greg Thomas, "*Marronnons* / Let's Maroon: Sylvia Wynter's 'Black Metamorphosis' as a Species of Maroonage," *small axe* 20, no. 1 (2016): 70.

37. Douglass, *Heroic*, 182.

38. Douglass, 189–90.

39. See Herbert Aptheker, "Maroons Within the Present Limits of the United States," in *Maroon Societies: Rebel Slave Communities in the Americas*, ed. Richard Price, 151–68 (Johns Hopkins University Press, 1973).

40. Richard Price, ed., *Maroon Societies: Rebel Slave Communities in the Americas* (Johns Hopkins University Press, 1973).

41. See chapter 2, "Forms of Marronage," in Alvin O. Thompson, *Flight to Freedom: African Runaways and Maroons in the Americas* (University of the West Indies Press, 2006), wherein Thompson offers a valuable historiography of the terms *petit marronage* and *grand marronage* and the various meanings attached to them in different places and times.

42. Douglass, *Heroic*, 190–91.

43. John Hope Franklin and Loren Schweninger, *Runaway Slaves: Rebels on the Plantation* (Oxford University Press, 1999), xiv.

44. Franklin and Schweninger, *Runaway*, xv. The facts outlined in this book are crucial to reorienting the way we think about where enslaved people actually ran away to and why. They push back against the primacy of the idea, particularly in the public imagination, that most enslaved people who ran away did so in an attempt to reach the Northern "free" states. Their ideas and this greater reorientation are key underpinnings of the arguments made in this book.

45. Harriet Tubman's narrative cannot be properly called a "slave narrative" because it is a biography rather than an autobiography. See Sarah H. Bradford, *Scenes in the Life of Harriet Tubman* (W. J. Moses, 1869). Significantly, it was also published *after* the conclusion of the American Civil War.

46. Sylviane A. Diouf, *Slavery's Exiles: The Story of the American Maroons* (NYU Press, 2014), 12.

47. Diouf, *Slavery's Exiles*, 12.

48. Carla Peterson, *"Doers of the Word": African-American Women Speakers and Writers in the North (1830–1880)* (Rutgers University Press, 1998), 5.

49. Douglass, *Heroic*, 193–94.

50. Douglass, 193.

51. I am thinking here in terms proffered by Ginsburg, who argues that "enslaved workers knew the land through a different set of cognitive processes than did whites." Ginsburg, "Escaping," 52.

52. Douglass, *Heroic*, 193–94.

53. I discuss incidents such as this at more length in my consideration of *Incidents in the Life of a Slave Girl* in chapter 3.

54. See Richard Price, *Maroon Societies*, 3.

55. Douglass, *Heroic*, 193.

56. "Borderland maroons" is Diouf's term from *Slavery's Exiles*. See her elaboration on it in the book's introduction.

57. Thompson, *Flight*, 58–59.
58. Douglass, *Heroic*, 195.
59. See Diouf, *Slavery's Exiles*, 99.
60. Douglass, *Heroic*, 193.
61. Jean Fouchard, *The Haitian Maroons: Liberty or Death* (Edward W. Blyden Press, 1981), 339; Orlando Patterson, *Freedom in the Making of Western Culture*, vol. 1 (Basic Books, 1991), 10.
62. Douglass, *Heroic*, 226.
63. Douglass, 227.
64. Douglass, 230.
65. Douglass, 231.
66. Douglass, 231.
67. Douglass, 239.
68. George W. Perkins, "Can Slaves Rightfully Resist?," in Griffiths, *Autographs*, 33.
69. Perkins, "Can Slaves Rightfully Resist?," 33.
70. Perkins, 34.
71. Perkins, 39.
72. S. J. May, "The Heroic Slave Woman," in Griffiths, *Autographs*, 162.
73. May, "Heroic Slave Woman," 163.
74. May, 164.
75. May, 163.
76. Douglass, *Heroic*, 227–28.
77. Douglass, 229.
78. Hakim Bey, *T.A.Z.: The Temporary Autonomous Zone, Ontological Anarchy, Poetic Terrorism*, 2nd ed. (Autonomedia, 2003).
79. Frederick Douglass, "Slavery, the Slumbering Volcano: An Address Delivered in New York, New York on 23 April 1849," *National Anti-Slavery Standard*, May 3, 1849.
80. Kim Dovey, *Becoming Places: Urbanism/Identity/Architecture/Power* (Routledge, 2010).
81. Paul Gilroy, *The Black Atlantic: Modernity and Double-Consciousness* (Harvard University Press, 1993).
82. Bey, *T.A.Z.*, 97.
83. Bey, 106. For theorizations of the concept of "third spaces," see Homi Bhabha, *The Location of Culture* (Routledge, 2004); and Edward Soja, *Thirdspace: Journeys to Los Angeles and Other Real-and-Imagined Places* (Blackwell, 1996).
84. Bey, *T.A.Z.*, 100.
85. Bey, 100.
86. Douglass, *Heroic*, 233–34.
87. Douglass, 235.
88. Douglass, 235.

89. See Marcus Rediker, *The Slave Ship: A Human History* (Penguin, 2008) for an analysis of the architecture of slave ships as it relates to regimes of forced captivity and migration as well as potential opportunities for resistance and revolt.

90. Fouchard, *Haitian*, 339.

91. Bey, *T.A.Z.*, 99.

92. I borrow and loosely apply the term "rhizomatic" here from Gilles Deleuze and Félix Guattari, *A Thousand Plateaus: Capitalism and Schizophrenia* (University of Minnesota Press, 1987).

93. Douglass, *Heroic*, 239–40.

94. Ifeoma Kiddoe Nwankwo, *Black Cosmopolitanism: Racial Consciousness and Transnational Identity in the Nineteenth-Century Americas* (University of Pennsylvania Press, 2014), 35.

95. Ivy Wilson, "On Native Ground: Transnationalism, Frederick Douglass, and 'The Heroic Slave,'" *PMLA* 121, no. 2 (March 2006): 446.

Coda

1. "Event to Honor Dismal Swamp Ancestors," *Suffolk News-Herald*, August 2, 2022, https://www.suffolknewsherald.com/2022/08/02/event-to-honor-dismal-swamp-ancestors/.

2. "Event."

3. Moses Grandy, *Narrative of the Life of Moses Grandy; Late a Slave in the United States of America* (C. Gilpin, 1843), 8.

4. Grandy, *Narrative*, 8.

5. Saidiya Hartman, *Scenes of Subjection: Terror, Slavery, and Self-Making in Nineteenth-Century America* (Oxford University Press, 1997), 115.

Bibliography

Allewaert, Monique. *Ariel's Ecology: Plantations, Personhood, and Colonialism in the American Tropics*. University of Minnesota Press, 2013.
Andrews, William L. *To Tell a Free Story: The First Century of Afro-American Autobiography, 1760–1865*. University of Illinois Press, 1988.
Aptheker, Herbert. *American Negro Slave Revolts*. International Publishers, 1983.
Aptheker, Herbert. "Maroons Within the Present Limits of the United States." *The Journal of Negro History* 24, no. 2 (April 1939): 167–84.
Aptheker, Herbert. "Maroons Within the Present Limits of the United States." In Price, *Maroon Societies*, 151–68.
Baumgartner, Alice L. *South to Freedom: Runaway Slaves to Mexico and the Road to the Civil War*. Basic Books, 2020.
Beier, A. L. *Masterless Men: The Vagrancy Problem in England, 1560–1640*. Methuen, 1985.
Bey, Hakim. *T.A.Z.: The Temporary Autonomous Zone, Ontological Anarchy, Poetic Terrorism*. 2nd ed. Autonomedia, 2003.
Bhabha, Homi. *The Location of Culture*. Routledge, 2004.
Bibler, Michael P. "Introduction: Smash the Mason-Dixon! or, Manifesting the Southern United States." *PMLA* 131, no. 1 (January 2016): 153–56.
Biggio, Rebecca Skidmore. "The Specter of Conspiracy in Martin Delany's *Blake*." *African American Review* 42, vol. 3/4 (Fall–Winter 2008): 439–53.
Bledsoe, Adam. "Marronage as a Past and Present Geography in the Americas." *Southeastern Geographer* 57, no. 1 (2017): 30–50.
Bodek, Richard, and Joseph Kelly, editors. *Maroons and the Marooned: Runaways and Castaways in the Americas*. University Press of Mississippi, 2020.
Bradford, Sarah H. *Scenes in the Life of Harriet Tubman*. W. J. Moses, 1869.
Braxton, Joanne M. "Ancestral Presence: The Outraged Mother Figure in Contemporary Afra-American Writing." In *Wild Women in the Whirlwind: Afra-American Culture and the Contemporary Literary Renaissance*, edited by Joanne M. Braxton and Andree Nicola McLaughlin. Rutgers University Press, 1990.

Bretones Lane, Fernanda. "Free to Bury Their Dead: Baptism and the Meanings of Freedom in the Eighteenth-Century Caribbean." *Slavery & Abolition* 42, no. 3 (2021): 449–65.

Brown, William Wells. *The Black Man, His Antecedents, His Genius, and His Achievements*. Thomas Hamilton, 1863.

Burnham, Michelle. "Loopholes of Resistance: Harriet Jacobs' Slave Narrative and the Critique of Agency in Foucault." *Arizona Quarterly* 49, no. 2 (1993): 53–73.

Byrd, William, II. *The Westover Manuscripts: Containing the History of the Dividing Line Betwixt Virginia and North Carolina; A Journey to the Land of Eden, A.D. 1733; and A Progress to the Mines. Written from 1728 to 1736, and Now First Published*. Edmund and Julian C. Ruffin, 1841.

Caldwell, Titcomb, et al. "An Exchange on Black History." *The New York Review of Books*, May 21, 1970. www.nybooks.com/articles/1970/05/21/an-exchange-on-black-history/.

Camp, Stephanie. *Closer to Freedom: Enslaved Women and Everyday Resistance in the Plantation South*. University of North Carolina Press, 2004.

Campbell, Mavis. *The Maroons of Jamaica: A History of Resistance, Collaboration and Betrayal*. Bloomsbury, 1988.

Carby, Hazel. *Reconstructing Womanhood: The Emergence of the Afro-American Woman Novelist*. Oxford University Press, 1989.

Carretta, Vincent. *Unchained Voices: An Anthology of Black Authors in the English-Speaking World of the Eighteenth Century*. University of Kentucky Press, 2003.

Chadwick, Bruce. *The Creole Rebellion: The Most Successful Slave Revolt in American History*. University of New Mexico Press, 2022.

Chemerinsky, Erwin. *Constitutional Law: Principles and Policies*. 6th ed. Walters Kluwer, 2015.

Child, Lydia Maria, editor. *The Freedmen's Book*. Ticknor and Fields, 1866.

Chiles, Katy. "Within and Without Raced Nations: Intertextuality, Martin Delany, and *Blake; or the Huts of America*." *American Literature* 80, no. 2 (2008): 323–52.

Clymer, Jeffory A. "Family Money: Race and Economic Rights in Antebellum US Law and Fiction." *American Literary History* 21, no. 2 (Summer 2009): 211–38.

Clymer, Jeffory A. "Martin Delany's *Blake* and the Transnational Politics of Property." *American Literary History* 15, no. 4 (2003): 709–31.

Cole, Jean Lee. "Theresa and Blake: Mobility and Resistance in Antebellum American Serialized Fiction." *Callaloo* 34, no. 1 (2011): 158–75.

Cooper, Carolyn. *Noises in the Blood: Orality, Gender, and the "Vulgar" Body of Jamaican Popular Culture*. Duke University Press, 1995.

Cowan, William Tynes. *The Slave in the Swamp: Disrupting the Plantation Narrative*. Routledge, 2006.

Davis, Angela Y. *Lectures on Liberation*. United Committee to Free Angela Davis, ca. 1971.

Davis, Angela Y. "Reflections on the Black Woman's Role in the Community of Slaves." *Massachusetts Review* 13, nos. 1/2 (1972): 81–100.

Delany, Martin R. *Blake; or, The Huts of America*. Edited by Jerome McGann. Harvard University Press, 2017.

Delany, Martin R. *Blake; or, The Huts of America*. Edited by Floyd J. Miller. Beacon Press, 1970.

Deleuze, Gilles, and Guattari, Félix. *A Thousand Plateaus: Capitalism and Schizophrenia*. University of Minnesota Press, 1987.

DeLombard, Jeannine Marie. "Representing the Slave: White Advocacy and Black Testimony in Harriet Beecher Stowe's *Dred*." *New England Quarterly* 75, no. 1 (March 2002): 80–106.

Diouf, Sylviane A. *Slavery's Exiles: The Story of the American Maroons*. NYU Press, 2014.

Dixon, Thomas. *The Clansman: A Historical Romance of the Ku Klux Klan*. Doubleday, Page, 1905.

Doolen, Andy. "'Be Cautious of the Word "Rebel"': Race, Revolution, and Transnational History in Martin Delany's *Blake; or, The Huts of America*." *American Literature* 81, no. 1 (2009): 153–79.

Douglass, Frederick. *The Heroic Slave*. In Griffiths, *Autographs*.

Douglass, Frederick. "Inhumanity of Slavery." Extract from a lecture on slavery at Rochester, December 8, 1850. In Douglass, *My Bondage*.

Douglass, Frederick. *My Bondage and My Freedom*. Penguin, 2003. Originally published in 1855 by Miller, Orton & Mulligan.

Douglass, Frederick. "Slavery, the Slumbering Volcano: An Address Delivered in New York, New York on 23 April 1849." *National Anti-Slavery Standard*, May 3, 1849.

Dovey, Kim. *Becoming Places: Urbanism/Identity/Architecture/Power*. Routledge, 2010.

Dubois, Laurent. *Avengers of the New World: The Story of the Haitian Revolution*. Harvard University Press, 2004.

Ellison, Ralph. *Invisible Man*. Vintage, 1995.

"Event to Honor Dismal Swamp Ancestors." *Suffolk News-Herald*, August 2, 2022. https://www.suffolknewsherald.com/2022/08/02/event-to-honor-dismal-swamp-ancestors/.

Fick, Carolyn. *The Making of Haiti: The Saint Domingue Revolution from Below*. University of Tennessee Press, 1990.

Foner, Eric. *Gateway to Freedom: The Hidden History of the Underground Railroad*. Norton, 2015.

Fouchard, Jean. *The Haitian Maroons: Liberty or Death*. Edward W. Blyden Press, 1981.

Franklin, John Hope, and Loren Schweninger. *Runaway Slaves: Rebels on the Plantation*. Oxford University Press, 1999.

Fuentes, Marisa J. *Dispossessed Lives: Enslaved Women, Violence, and the Archive*. University of Pennsylvania Press, 2016.

Gardner, Eric. *Unexpected Places: Relocating Nineteenth-Century African American Literature*. University Press of Mississippi, 2009.

Garnet, Henry Highland. "An Address to the Slaves of the United States of America, Buffalo, N.Y., 1843." In *A Memorial Discourse*, by Henry Highland Garnet. J. M. Wilson, 1865.

Genovese, Eugene. *From Rebellion to Revolution: Afro-American Slave Revolts in the Making of the Modern World*. Louisiana State University Press, 1979.

Genovese, Eugene. *Roll, Jordan, Roll: The World the Slaves Made*. Vintage, 1976.

Gerrity, Sean. "Maroons and Marronage in Antebellum African American Literature." In *A History of the Literature of the U.S. South*, edited by Harilaos Stecopoulos. Cambridge University Press, 2021.

Gilroy, Paul. *The Black Atlantic: Modernity and Double Consciousness*. Harvard University Press, 1993.

Ginsburg, Rebecca. "Escaping Through a Black Landscape." In *Cabin, Quarter, Plantation: Architecture and Landscapes of North American Slavery*, edited by Clifton Ellis and Rebecca Ginsburg. Yale University Press, 2010.

Golden, Kathryn E. B. "Through the Muck and Mire: Marronage, Representation, and Memory in the Great Dismal Swamp." PhD diss., University of California, Berkeley, 2018.

Grandy, Moses. *Narrative of the Life of Moses Grandy; Late a Slave in the United States of America*. C. Gilpin, 1843.

Gray, Thomas R. *The Confessions of Nat Turner, the Leader of the Late Insurrection in Southampton, VA*. Thomas R. Gray, 1831.

Green, Keith Michael. *Bound to Respect: Antebellum Narratives of Black Imprisonment, Servitude, and Bondage, 1816–1861*. University of Alabama Press, 2015.

Green-Barteet, Miranda A. "'The Loophole of Retreat': Interstitial Spaces in Harriet Jacobs's *Incidents in the Life of a Slave Girl*." *South Central Review* 30, no. 2 (2013): 53–72.

Greeson, Jennifer Rae. *Our South: Geographic Fantasy and the Rise of National Literature*. Harvard University Press, 2010.

Griffiths, Julia, editor. *Autographs for Freedom*. John P. Jewett, 1853.

Hahn, Steven. *The Political Worlds of Slavery and Freedom*. Harvard University Press, 2009.

Haile, James B., III. "Frederick Douglass and the Black Infrahuman Surreal: A Story of Origins." *MLN* 137, no. 5 (December 2022): 855–71.

Hartman, Saidiya V. *Scenes of Subjection: Terror, Slavery, and Self-Making in Nineteenth Century America*. Oxford University Press, 1997.

Henderson, Carol E. "Borderlands: The Critical Matrix of Caste, Class, and Color in *Incidents in the Life of a Slave Girl.*" *Legacy: A Journal of American Women Writers* 16, no. 2 (1999): 49–58.
Heuman, Gad, editor. *Out of the House of Bondage: Runaways, Resistance, and Marronage in Africa and the New World.* Routledge, 1986.
Hickman, Jared. *Black Prometheus: Race and Radicalism in the Age of Atlantic Slavery.* Oxford University Press, 2016.
Higginson, Thomas Wentworth. *Travellers and Outlaws: Episodes in American History.* Lee and Shepard, 1888.
Horne, Gerald. *The Counter-Revolution of 1776: Slave Resistance and the Origins of the United States of America.* NYU Press, 2014.
Hosbey, Justin, and J. T. Roane. "A Totally Different Form of Living: On the Legacies of Displacement and Marronage as Black Ecologies." *Southern Cultures* 27, no. 1 (2021): 68–73.
Hurst, Allison L. "Beyond the Pale: Poor Whites as Uncontrolled Social Contagion in Harriet Beecher Stowe's *Dred.*" *The Mississippi Quarterly* 63, no. 4 (2010): 635–53.
Hyman, Christy. "To Render a Landscape of Trauma: Deep Mapping a Historical Landscape of Domination—The Great Dismal Swamp." In *Expanding the Boundaries of Black Intellectual History*, edited by Leslie Alexander, Brandon Byrd, and Russell Rickford. Northwestern University Press, 2021.
Jackson, Edmund. "The Virginia Maroons." *National Anti-Slavery Standard*, February 12, 1852, 152. *Slavery and Anti-Slavery: A Transnational Archive*, Gale.
Jacobs, Harriet. "Cruelty to Slaves." *New York Tribune*, July 25, 1853.
Jacobs, Harriet. *Incidents in the Life of a Slave Girl.* Dover, 2001.
James, Joy. "Afrarealism and the Black Matrix: Maroon Philosophy at Democracy's Border." *Black Scholar* 43, no. 4 (2013): 124–31.
Johnson, Walter. "On Agency." *Journal of Social History* 37, no. 1 (Fall 2003): 113–24.
Kaye, Anthony. *Joining Places: Slave Neighborhoods in the Old South.* University of North Carolina Press, 2008.
Kazanjian, David. *The Brink of Freedom: Improvising Life in the Nineteenth-Century Atlantic World.* Duke University Press, 2016.
Kazanjian, David. "Scenes of Speculation." *Social Text* 125 (December 2015): 77–83.
Koenigs, Thomas. "The 'Mysterious Depths' of Slave Interiority: Fiction and Intersubjective Knowledge in *The Heroic Slave.*" *J19: The Journal of Nineteenth-Century Americanists* 8, no. 2 (Fall 2020): 193–217.
Korobkin, Laura H. "Appropriating Law in Harriet Beecher Stowe's *Dred.*" *Nineteenth-Century Literature* 62, no. 3 (December 2007): 380–406.
Kotef, Hagar. *Movement and the Ordering of Freedom: On Liberal Governances of Mobility.* Duke University Press, 2015.

Krieger, Georgia. "Playing Dead: Harriet Jacobs's Survival Strategy in *Incidents in the Life of a Slave Girl.*" *African American Review* 42, nos. 3–4 (2008): 607–21.

La Rosa Corzo, Gabino. *Runaway Slave Settlements in Cuba: Resistance and Repression.* Translated by Mary Todd. University of North Carolina Press, 2003.

Leaming, Hugo Prosper. *Hidden Americans: Maroons of Virginia and the Carolinas.* Garland Publishing, 1995.

LeMenager, Stephanie. *Manifest and Other Destinies: Territorial Fictions of the Nineteenth Century United States.* University of Nebraska Press, 2008.

LeMenager, Stephanie. "Marginal Landscapes: Revolutionary Abolitionists and Environmental Imagination." *Interdisciplinary Literary Studies* 7, no. 1 (Fall 2005): 49–56.

Levine, Robert S. Introduction to *Dred: A Tale of the Great Dismal Swamp*, by Harriet Beecher Stowe, edited by Levine. University of North Carolina Press, 2000.

Levine, Robert S. *Dislocating Race and Nation: Episodes in Nineteenth-Century American Literary Nationalism.* University of North Carolina Press, 2008.

Levine, Robert S. *Martin R. Delany: A Documentary Reader.* University of North Carolina Press, 2003.

Levine, Robert S. *Martin Delany, Frederick Douglass, and the Politics of Representative Identity.* University of North Carolina Press, 1997.

Levine, Robert S., John Stauffer, and John R. McKivigan. Introduction to *The Heroic Slave: A Cultural and Critical Edition*, by Frederick Douglass, edited by Levine, Stauffer, and McKivigan. Yale University Press, 2015.

Li, Stephanie. "Motherhood as Resistance in Harriet Jacobs's *Incidents in the Life of a Slave Girl.*" *Legacy: A Journal of American Women Writers* 23, no. 1 (2006): 14–29.

Linebaugh, Peter, and Marcus Rediker. *The Many-Headed Hydra: Sailors, Slaves, Commoners, and the Hidden History of the Revolutionary Atlantic.* Beacon Press, 2013.

Lockley, Timothy James, editor. *Maroon Communities in South Carolina: A Documentary Record.* University of South Carolina Press, 2009.

Longfellow, Henry Wadsworth. "The Slave in the Dismal Swamp." In *Poems on Slavery*, by Henry Wadsworth Longfellow, 18–20. J. Owen, 1842.

Madera, Judith. *Black Atlas: Geography and Flow in Nineteenth-Century African American Literature.* Duke University Press, 2015.

Maris-Wolf, Ted. "Hidden in Plain Sight: Maroon Life and Labor in Virginia's Dismal Swamp." *Slavery & Abolition* 34, no. 3 (2013): 446–64.

Marshall, Yannick. "An Appeal—Bring the Maroon to the Foreground in Black Intellectual History." *Black Perspectives*, June 19, 2020. https://www.aaihs.org/an-appeal-bring-the maroon-to-the-foreground-in-black-intellectual-history/.

Marx, Jo-Ann. "The Language of Liberation in Martin R. Delany's *Blake; or, The Huts of America.*" *Griot* 18, no. 1 (Spring 1999): 19–25.

Mathieu, Irène. *Grand Marronage*. Switchback Books, 2019.
May, S. J. "The Heroic Slave Woman." In Griffiths, *Autographs*.
McKittrick, Katherine. *Demonic Grounds: Black Women and the Cartographies of Struggle*. University of Minnesota Press, 2006.
Melville, Herman. *Benito Cereno*. Putnam's Monthly Magazine, no. 34, October 1855 / no. 35, November 1855 / no. 36, December 1855.
Melville, Herman. "The Swamp Angel." In *Battle-Pieces and Aspects of the War*, by Herman Melville, 107. Harper, 1866.
Merritt, Keri Leigh. *Masterless Men: Poor Whites and Slavery in the Antebellum South*. Cambridge University Press, 2017.
Miki, Yuko. "Fleeing into Slavery: The Insurgent Geographies of Brazilian Quilombolas (Maroons), 1880–1881." *Americas* 68, no. 4 (April 2012): 495–528.
Miller, David C. *Dark Eden: The Swamp in Nineteenth-Century American Literature and Culture*. Cambridge University Press, 1989.
Miller, Floyd J. Letter to the editor, in "An Exchange on Black History." *The New York Review of Books*, May 21, 1970. www.nybooks.com/articles/1970/05/21/an-exchange-on-black-history/.
Mitchell, Koritha. "Identifying White Mediocrity and Know-Your-Place Aggression: A Form of Self-Care." *African American Review* 51, no. 4 (Winter 2018): 253–62.
Morris, J. Brent. *Dismal Freedom: A History of the Maroons of the Great Dismal Swamp*. University of North Carolina Press, 2022.
Moten, Fred. *In the Break: The Aesthetics of the Black Radical Tradition*. University of Minnesota Press, 2003.
Moten, Fred, and Stefano Harney. *The Undercommons: Fugitive Planning and Black Study*. Minor Compositions, 2013.
Nevius, Marcus. *City of Refuge: Slavery and Petit Marronage in the Great Dismal Swamp, 1763–1856*. University of Georgia Press, 2020.
Noguchi, Keiko. "Harriet Beecher Stowe's *Dred*: Legal Exploration in a Sentimental Novel." *Tsuda Review* 55 (November 2010): 1–24.
Northup, Solomon. *Twelve Years a Slave*. Sampson Low, Son, 1853.
Nwankwo, Ifeoma Kiddoe. *Black Cosmopolitanism: Racial Consciousness and Transnational Identity in the Nineteenth-Century Americas*. University of Pennsylvania Press, 2014.
Olmsted, Frederick Law. *A Journey in the Seaboard Slave States, with Remarks on Their Economy*. Dix and Edwards, 1856.
Orihuela, Sharada Balachandran. "The Black Market: Property, Freedom, and Piracy in Martin Delany's *Blake; or, The Huts of America*." *J19: The Journal of Nineteenth-Century Americanists* 2, no. 2 (Fall 2014): 273–300.
Pargas, Damian Alan, editor. *Fugitive Slaves and Spaces of Freedom in North America*. University Press of Florida, 2018.
Patterson, Orlando. *Freedom in the Making of Western Culture*. Vol. 1. Basic Books, 1991.

Patterson, Orlando. "Slavery and Slave Revolts: A Socio-Historical Analysis of the First Maroon War in Jamaica, 1655–1740." *Social and Economic Studies* 19, no. 3 (September 1970): 289–325.

Perkins, George W. "Can Slaves Rightfully Resist?" In Griffiths, *Autographs*.

Peterson, Carla L. *"Doers of the Word": African-American Women Speakers and Writers in the North (1830–1880)*. Rutgers University Press, 1998.

Pierrot, Gregory. *The Black Avenger in Atlantic Culture*. University of Georgia Press, 2019.

Pierrot, Gregory. "Writing over Haiti: Black Avengers in Martin Delany's *Blake*." *Studies in American Fiction* 41, no. 2 (2014): 175–99.

Price, Richard, editor. *Maroon Societies: Rebel Slave Communities in the Americas*. Johns Hopkins University Press, 1979.

Randle, Gloria T. "Between the Rock and the Hard Place: Mediating Spaces in Harriet Jacobs's *Incidents in the Life of a Slave Girl*." *African American Review* 33, no. 1 (1999): 43–56.

Rasmussen, Daniel. *American Uprising: The Untold Story of America's Largest Slave Revolt*. Harper Perennial, 2012.

Rediker, Marcus. *Outlaws of the Atlantic: Sailors, Pirates, and Motley Crews in the Age of Sail*. Beacon Press, 2014.

Rediker, Marcus. *The Slave Ship: A Human History*. Penguin, 2008.

Redpath, James. *The Roving Editor; or, Talks with Slaves in the Southern States*. A. B. Burdick, 1859.

"Revised Code—No. 105: Slaves and Free Persons of Color: An Act Concerning Slaves and Free Persons of Color." 1831. *Documenting the American South*, North Carolina Collection, University Library, University of North Carolina at Chapel Hill. https://docsouth.unc.edu/nc/slavesfree/slavesfree.html.

Reynolds, David S. *John Brown, Abolitionist: The Man Who Killed Slavery, Sparked the Civil War, and Seeded Civil Rights*. Vintage, 2006.

Roberts, Neil. *Freedom as Marronage*. University of Chicago Press, 2015.

Rogers, Melvin L., and Jack Turner, editors. *African American Political Thought: A Collected History*. University of Chicago Press, 2021.

Rusert, Britt. "Delany's Comet: Fugitive Science and the Speculative Imaginary of Emancipation." *American Quarterly* 65, no. 4 (December 2013): 799–829.

Sayers, Daniel O. *A Desolate Place for a Defiant People: The Archaeology of Maroons, Indigenous Americans, and Enslaved Laborers in the Great Dismal Swamp*. University Press of Florida, 2014.

Schoolman, Martha. *Abolitionist Geographies*. University of Minnesota Press, 2014.

Schoolman, Martha. "Martin Delany, *Blake; or, the Huts of America* (1859–1862)." In *Handbook of the American Novel of the Nineteenth Century*, edited by Christine Gerhardt. Walter de Gruyter, 2018.

Scott, James C. *Seeing Like a State: How Certain Schemes to Improve the Human Condition Have Failed*. Yale University Press, 1999.

Scott, Julius S. *The Common Wind: Afro-American Currents in the Age of the Haitian Revolution*. Verso, 2018.
Sharpe, Christina. *In the Wake: On Blackness and Being*. Duke University Press, 2016.
Sharpe, Jenny. *Ghosts of Slavery: A Literary Archaeology of Black Women's Lives*. University of Minnesota Press, 2002.
Sinha, Manisha. *The Slave's Cause: A History of Abolition*. Yale University Press, 2017.
Smith, Caleb. *The Prison and the American Imagination*. Yale University Press, 2009.
Smith, Gail K. "Reading with the Other: Hermeneutics and the Politics of Difference in Stowe's *Dred*." *American Literature* 69, no. 2 (June 1997): 289–313.
Smith, Valerie. " 'Loopholes of Retreat': Architecture and Ideology in Harriet Jacobs's *Incidents in the Life of a Slave Girl*." In *Reading Black, Reading Feminist: A Critical Anthology*, edited by Henry Louis Gates, Jr., 212–26. New American Library, 1990.
Snyder, Terri L. *The Power to Die: Slavery and Suicide in British North America*. University of Chicago Press, 2015.
Soja, Edward. *Thirdspace: Journeys to Los Angeles and Other Real-and-Imagined Places*. Blackwell, 1996.
Sorisio, Carolyn. " 'There Is Might in Each': Conceptions of Self in Harriet Jacobs's *Incidents in the Life of a Slave Girl, Written by Herself*." *Legacy: A Journal of American Women Writers* 13, no. 1 (1996): 1–18.
Spady, James O'Neil. "Belonging and Alienation: Gullah Jack and Some Maroon Dimensions of the 'Denmark Vesey Conspiracy.' " In Bodek and Kelly, *Maroons and the Marooned*.
Spillers, Hortense J. "Mama's Baby, Papa's Maybe: An American Grammar Book." *Diacritics* 17, no. 2 (1987): 64–81.
Stepto, Robert B. *From Behind the Veil: A Study of Afro-American Narrative*. University of Illinois Press, 1979.
Stepto, Robert B. "Storytelling in Early Afro-American Fiction: Frederick Douglass's 'The Heroic Slave.' " *Georgia Review* 36, no. 2 (Summer 1982): 355–68.
Stowe, Harriet Beecher. *Dred: A Tale of the Great Dismal Swamp*. Edited with an introduction and notes by Robert S. Levine. University of North Carolina Press, 2006.
Stowe, Harriet Beecher. *Uncle Tom's Cabin*. Jewett, 1852. http://utc.iath.virginia.edu/uncletom/uteshbsbt.html.
Stowe, Harriet Beecher. *Uncle Tom's Cabin; or, Life Among the Lowly: Arranged for Young Readers*. Altemus Young People's Library. Henry Altemus, 1900.
Strother, David Hunter [Porte Crayon, pseud.]. *Virginia Illustrated: Containing a Visit to the Virginian Canaan, and the Adventures of Porte Crayon and His Cousins*. Harper & Brothers Publishers, 1857.
Taylor, Christopher. *Empire of Neglect: The West Indies in the Wake of British Liberalism*. Duke University Press, 2018.

Taylor, Douglas. "From Slavery to Prison: Benjamin Rush, Harriet Jacobs, and the Ideology of Reformative Incarceration." *Genre* 35, nos. 3–4 (2002): 429–47.

Thomas, Greg. "*Marronnons* / Let's Maroon: Sylvia Wynter's 'Black Metamorphosis' as a Species of Maroonage." *small axe* 20, no. 1 (2016): 62–78.

Thompson, Alvin O. *Flight to Freedom: African Runaways and Maroons in the Americas*. University of the West Indies Press, 2006.

Walker, David. *Walker's Appeal, in Four Articles; Together with a Preamble, to the Coloured Citizens of the World, but in Particular, and Very Expressly, to Those of the United States of America, Written in Boston, State of Massachusetts, September 28, 1829*, 3rd ed. David Walker, 1829.

Walter, Krista. "Trappings of Nationalism in Frederick Douglass's *The Heroic Slave*." *African American Review* 34, no. 2 (Summer 2000): 233–47.

Washington, Booker T. *Up from Slavery: An Autobiography*. Doubleday, 1901.

White, Ashli. *Encountering Revolution: Haiti and the Making of the Early Republic*. Johns Hopkins University Press, 2010.

Williams, Raymond. *Marxism and Literature*. Oxford University Press, 1977.

Williams, Roland Leander. *Smooth Operating and Other Social Acts*. State University of New York Press, 2022.

Wilson, Anthony. *Shadow and Shelter: The Swamp in Southern Culture*. University Press of Mississippi, 2005.

Wilson, Ivy. "On Native Ground: Transnationalism, Frederick Douglass, and 'The Heroic Slave.'" *PMLA* 121, no. 2 (March 2006): 453–68.

Winston, Celeste. *How to Lose the Hounds: Maroon Geographies and a World Beyond Policing*. Duke University Press, 2023.

Yellin, Jean Fagan. *Harriet Jacobs: A Life*. Basic Books, 2004.

Yellin, Jean Fagan. "Written by Herself: Harriet Jacobs' Slave Narrative." *American Literature* 53, vol. 3 (November 1981): 479–86.

Index

"Address to the Slaves of the United States." *See* Garnet, Henry Highland
agency (to resist or obtain freedom), 3, 14–15, 23, 34, 48, 73–74, 92–93, 101, 106, 108, 117–20, 138, 140, 144, 153, 158, 160
antinationalism. *See* counternationalism
Appeal to the Coloured Citizens of the World. *See* Walker, David
Aptheker, Herbert, 4, 6, 8, 137
asylum, 1–6, 42, 48, 53, 55, 76, 83, 107–9, 113, 136, 139–40, 143–44, 158. *See also* forests, swamps
assimilation, 18, 20, 23, 56, 59, 139. *See also* integration
Autographs for Freedom. *See* Griffiths, Julia; *see also* Douglass, Frederick: *The Heroic Slave*; *and* Perkins, George W.
autonomy: 7, 14, 19, 23, 25, 34, 38, 79, 86, 108, 115, 118, 136, 142, 144, 153; "Temporary Autonomous Zone," *see* Bey, Hakim

Bahamas, 122, 126, 136, 151, 153–55
Benito Cereno. *See* Melville, Herman
Bey, Hakim, 150–153
Black Man, His Antecedents, His Genius, and His Achievements. *See* Brown, William Wells
Blake; or, The Huts of America. *See* Delany, Martin
borderlands; *see* liminal spaces
Boukman, Dutty, 73–75, 82–83, 172n51. *See also* Revolution: Haitian
Brazil, 65, 86, 108, 143
Brent, Linda; *see* Jacobs, Harriet
bribery, 89–91
Brown, John, 2, 31–32, 161n3
Brown, William Wells, 127–28; *The Black Man*, 127–30

"Can Slaves Rightfully Resist and Fight?" *See* Perkins, George W.
Canada: 13, 16–17, 24–25, 76, 84, 89–91, 121–22, 125, 128, 130, 133, 139, 163n18; as symbolic refuge, 1–3, 90–91, 99, 108, 128, 137, 139
capitalism: 18, 43, 66, 112, 117–18, 135, 153; environmental effects, 8, 43, 112, 135
Carolina: North, 36, 42, 44–45, 48, 54, 97–99, 101–4, 107, 116; South, 33, 85, 116
Cheney, Lew, 81–82, 84
Child, Lydia Maria, 19–20, 27, 101, 127, 129–30; *Freedmen's Book*, 129–30
children, 42–43, 46–50, 106, 114, 117–19, 138, 150, 158

Index

Christianity. *See* religion
citizenship, 10, 12, 18, 26, 58–59, 68, 155, 163n19
Colombia, 65
colonization: of the Americas, 4–10, 14, 18, 93–95, 101–3, 112, 143, 158; of Liberia, *see* Liberia. *See also* emigration, Great Dismal Swamp
communication (means and networks), 50, 52, 73, 76–78, 80, 83, 89, 117–18, 143
communities, 3, 5, 7, 13–14, 16–17, 23, 34, 36, 38, 47–48, 55, 57, 61–62, 64–65, 67, 71, 78–79, 81, 85–89, 104, 143–44, 151, 158
Compromise of 1850, 8, 69–70, 98
concealment, 5–6, 14, 19, 24, 44, 47–48, 57, 72, 79–81, 82, 85, 98–100, 103, 106–17, 119–20, 130–33, 136, 141, 144
Confessions of Nat Turner. *See* Gray, Thomas R.
conspiracy, 41, 64, 67, 72, 102, 143
counternationalism, 11, 31–32, 131, 148, 151, 156
Creole (ship). *See* Douglass, Frederick: *Heroic Slave*
Cuba, 7, 63, 65, 71–73, 93–94

Delany, Martin, 16, 18, 30, 70, 92, 95: *Blake; or, the Huts of America*, 10, 16–17, 20, 23, 32, 39, 61–95
diaspora, 10, 12, 65–67, 108, 120, 125, 154–55, 174n5
Dismal Swamp. *See* Great Dismal Swamp
Diouf, Sylviane, 4–6, 13, 15–16, 36, 47, 62, 77, 80, 85–86, 100, 104, 116, 139–40
dogs, 6, 21, 42, 45, 52, 77, 83, 85
Dominican Republic. *See* Santo Domingo

Douglass, Frederick, 10, 30, 122–123, 131; *Heroic Slave*, 19, 24–25, 32, 35, 64, 121–48, 150–56; "Inhumanity of Slavery," 121, 134; *My Bondage and My Freedom*, 131; *Narrative of the Life of Frederick Douglass*, 22, 130; "Slavery, the Slumbering Volcano," 145
Dred: A Tale of the Great Dismal Swamp. *See* Stowe, Harriet Beecher
Dred Scott (*v. Sandford* decision), 9, 11, 23, 163n19

economy: capitalist, 8, 50–51, 122; slave, 17, 66, 70, 89, 122, 126
Edenton Gazette, 103–4
education/literacy, 42, 55, 71–73, 117–18, 139
emancipation (*spec.* state-sponsored), 2, 11, 17, 19, 23, 25, 32, 63, 91, 93, 100, 123, 131, 140, 144, 146, 149, 153, 155–56, 159
emigration, 16, 61. *See also* Liberia
encroachment. *See* colonization
exile, 3, 31, 34, 40, 55, 65, 77. *See also* Great Dismal Swamp

family, 19, 37, 40–41, 55, 65, 75, 94, 101, 114, 128, 138, 141–43, 158
fear (of violence, insurrection), 29, 35, 41, 46, 53, 71, 75, 79–80, 83–84, 88, 94, 102–6, 116, 128, 133, 138, 142
fictionalization (as narrative), 2, 19, 33, 44, 56, 124, 126–28, 130
forests (as refuge, hiding places), 3, 14, 47, 89, 107, 109, 116, 121–22, 128, 130–37, 141–45
Freedmen's Book, *see* Child, Lydia Maria
Fugitive Slave Act, 8–9, 11, 21, 23, 71, 84, 88–91, 93, 98, 125, 131, 168n34
Fuentes, Marisa, 101, 114

fugitive (status), 2, 10–11, 48–49, 57–58, 65, 68–71, 77, 84, 88–91, 94, 97–98, 103, 108, 117–18, 121, 125, 131–34, 140, 143–44, 178n9. *See also* Fugitive Slave Act *and* outlaw status

Garnet, Henry Highland, 20, 69
Garrison, William Lloyd, 27, 121–22, 147
Goober Jack, 116–17
Grandy, Moses: *Narrative of the Life of Moses Grandy*, 7, 157–60
Gray, Thomas R.: *Confessions of Nat Turner*, 107
Great Dismal Swamp, 1–8, 15, 32–36, 42, 57, 62, 85–88, 101, 107, 112, 115, 121, 151, 157. *See also* swamps *and* Stowe, Harriet Beecher
Griffiths, Julia: 126, *Autographs for Freedom*, 126, 148, 149, 178n11

Haiti, 20, 67, 71, 73–75, 82–84, 86, 100, 102, 108. *See also* Revolution: Haitian
Harper's New Monthly Magazine, 7
Heroic Slave. *See* Douglass, Frederick
"Heroic Slave Woman." *See* May, S. J.
hiding. *See* concealment
Higginson, Thomas Wentworth, 7, 13, 36
Hopkins, Pauline, 127
hunting (subsistence), 5, 72, 142, 144
Hyman, Christy, 4, 8, 159

immobility. *See* stillness
Incidents in the Life of a Slave Girl. *See* Jacobs, Harriet
"Inhumanity of Slavery." *See* Douglass, Frederick
insurrection, 16, 19–20, 23–24, 31–33, 36, 41, 56–57, 59, 61–63, 65, 71, 73–74, 77–78, 80–81, 83, 85–87, 94–95, 101–4, 116, 121–22, 126, 128–29, 138 144–54. *See also* Revolution
integration, 18, 23, 25, 56, 123, 139, 144. *See also* assimilation
isolation. *See under* maroons/marronage

Jackson, Edmund: "The Virginia Maroons," 7, 13, 36
Jacobs, Harriet, 91, 97–99: *Incidents in the Life of a Slave Girl*, 8, 10, 19–20, 22, 24, 35, 80–81, 91, 98–120
Jamaica, 7, 13–14, 47, 71, 80, 86, 100–1, 108, 143, 174n5
James, Joy, 97, 100, 120

Knox: Andrew, 102; Elijah, 102

legibility/illegibility, 30, 37–38, 50, 69, 76, 79–80, 117, 141
Levine, Robert, 11, 30–31, 63–64, 122–23, 164n
liberalism, 1, 3, 13–14, 16–18, 20–21, 25–26, 30, 42, 57–59, 61, 66, 68, 84–85, 88, 92, 93, 95, 100, 112, 123–26, 131, 136, 140, 144, 155, 159
Liberia, 16, 26, 30, 61; *see also* emigration
liminal spaces, 5, 37, 47, 51, 57, 64, 79–80, 85–86, 99, 104, 110, 112–20, 142–44, 150–53, 158. *See also* plantations *and* swamps
Louisiana, 4, 81–84, 116

manumission, 25, 94, 140, 153
marginal landscapes. *See* liminal spaces

maroons/marronage: as choice/ political act, 25, 35, 80, 128, 138; industry/industriousness, 5, 72, 117–118; isolation, 5, 47, 112; maritime, 93–94, 136, 150–55; representation of by/for whites, 7, 10–11, 14–15, 23, 29–30, 34, 47–48, 50, 54, 57, 59, 133–34, 147, 150 (*see also* Stowe, Harriet Beecher; Douglass, Frederick); as resistance practice, 19, 24, 32, 63, 75–81, 84–87, 91–92, 101, 107–10, 116–17, 123, 133, 137–38, 141, 158, 174n5; romanticization of, 2, 7, 29, 134; short-term, 24–25, 45, 47, 72, 79, 85, 99–101, 106–7, 111–12, 129–30, 137–38, 141, 143, 158; spatial conceptions, 13–15, 24, 31, 37–43, 47, 49–51, 55, 58, 65–66, 72, 77, 99, 106, 109–10, 112–17, 135–37, 141, 150; in the West Indies, 7, 13–14, 47, 71–73, 86, 151
Mathieu, Irène, 41, 97
May, S. J.: "The Heroic Slave Woman," 149–50
Melville, Herman: *Benito Cereno*, 32–33, 39, "The Swamp Angel," 29
Mexico, 81, 84, 108, 140
Miller, Floyd J., 63–64, 67, 73, 92
mobility/movement, 14, 18, 23, 38, 55, 57–59, 64, 66–69, 72, 76–78, 82, 85, 106, 109, 111, 120, 125, 136, 151
Moten, Fred, 1, 12–13, 18
My Bondage and My Freedom; see Douglass, Frederick

narrative (as genre), 1–2, 11–12, 15–16, 19–22, 25, 32, 35–36, 42, 45, 50, 57, 67, 70, 81, 100, 108–9, 113, 119, 124, 130, 139–40, 147–48, 165n50, 178n7, 180n45

Narrative of the Life of Frederick Douglass. See Douglass, Frederick
Nassau. *See* Bahamas
National Anti-Slavery Standard, 7
Nevius, Marcus: 4–5, 8, 13, 85, 100
New Orleans. *See* slave trade: American; Louisiana
New York, 91, 98–99, 120, 163n18
New York Review of Books, 92
New York Tribune, 98–99, 174n2
North Carolina. *See under* Carolina
North Star, 126
Northup, Solomon: *Twelve Years a Slave*, 81–82

Olmsted, Frederick Law, 7
outlaw (status), 35, 44–46, 48, 55, 58, 69, 80, 97–98, 103–5, 144, 168n34
Owen, John, 104

paternalism, 66, 80, 140, 144
patrols/hunting, 6, 21, 44–46, 48, 52–53, 77, 83, 90–91, 98, 103–4, 116–17, 166
Patterson, Orlando: "Slavery and Slave Revolts," 61, 64, 75 144
Perkins, George W.: "Can Slaves Rightfully Resist and Fight?" 148
petit-marronage. See maroons/marronage: short-term
planning/plotting (as resistance), 33, 41, 56–57, 59, 62–67, 71–80, 82–83, 85, 89, 93, 101–3, 107, 128–30, 158
plantations: as non-liberal/ordered spaces, 5, 14, 23, 32, 34, 40, 43, 47, 49, 50–51, 55–59, 76, 79, 84–86, 105, 109–10, 113, 118, 132, 136–37, 143, 161n3, 164n30; romanticization of, 36, 42. *See also* swamps
poor whites, 23, 34, 36, 39–40, 42–44, 46–48, 50–53, 106

publishing: industry, 2, 10, 29, 52, 62–63; editorial influence, 22–23
punishment (for marronage), 5, 45, 114, 142, 168n34

Queen Nanny, 101

rape. *See* violence, sexual
Rebellion: Gabriel's 87, 101–102; Turner's, 45; 87, 107; *see also* insurrection
Redpath, James: *Roving Editor; or, Talks with Slaves in the Southern States*, 1–2, 33, 38
refuge. *See* asylum
religion: 39–41, 56, 62, 74, 87, 172n51; Catholic conversion, 93–94
relocation; *see* emigration
resistance practices (general), 6–7, 10–11, 14, 17, 19, 23, 25, 37, 39, 41, 46, 57, 62, 65, 73, 76, 101, 113, 118–19, 130, 144, 153–154. *See also* insurrection
revolt. *See* insurrection
Revolution: American, 67, 87, 124–26, 128, 147–49, 154; Haitian, 67, 71, 74–75, 84, 100, 102–3, 142
Roberts, Neil, 8, 26, 62, 66, 75–76, 78, 87, 100, 115
romanticization. *See* maroons/marronage; plantations; swamps
Roving Editor; or, Talks with Slaves in the Southern States. See Redpath, James
runaways, 11, 18, 21, 43–45, 53, 72, 76–84, 87, 89–90, 97–98, 103–4, 108, 118, 133, 135, 139, 142, 180n44

Saint-Domingue. *See* Haiti
Santo Domingo (Dominican Republic), 7, 71
Sayers, Daniel, 5, 7–8, 85, 100
Schoolman, Martha, 31, 61–64, 126
secrecy, 50, 74–78, 113, 130
self-liberation, 37, 41, 59, 69, 78, 136, 154
self-reliance/sufficiency, 63, 66, 69, 86, 92, 143–144. *See also* autonomy
sentimentalism, 18, 20, 30, 48, 109, 129
settlements encampments: of maroons, 5, 15, 21, 33, 38, 48, 50, 86, 161n3. *See also* swamps as refuge
slave trade: American, 75–76, 104, 106, 121, 128, 130, 135, 141–42, 145–47, 158; transatlantic, 4, 66, 137, 146, 153
"Slavery and Slave Revolts," *see* Patterson, Orlando
"Slavery, the Slumbering Volcano." *See* Douglass, Frederick
South Carolina. *See* Carolina
stillness, 14, 24, 69, 77, 100–1, 105–11, 113–16
stereotypes (of Blacks, maroons), 42, 47. *See also* maroons/marronage: representation of
Stowe, Harriet Beecher: 7, 10, 14, 29, 32, 36; *Dred*, 7, 15–16, 20–23, 30–44, 46–59; *Uncle Tom's Cabin*, 20–21, 30–31, 36, 42–43, 61, 81
subjectivity, 9–10, 12–13, 15, 18, 26, 30, 37, 42, 46–48, 58–59, 62, 66, 68–69, 75, 77, 92, 99, 101, 105–7, 110, 116, 118–20, 131, 144, 151, 153, 160
support networks, 66, 76, 81, 85, 91–92, 108, 118, 131
Suriname, 13, 47, 65, 80, 86, 100, 108, 143, 162n7
survival strategies, 5–6, 23, 37–38, 46, 79, 85–86, 107–8, 111–12, 117, 129–31, 142–43, 158. *See also* subsistence hunting

198 | Index

swamps: encroachment/settlement by whites, 5–6, 8, 43, 53, 83, 112; as disordered/liberal space, 58–59, 84, 111–13 (*see also* marginal landscapes); industry within, 8, 36, 46, 49–51, 112; in literature, 7, 32–35, 42–43, 47–51, 79; as refuge/hiding place, 1–6, 14–15, 20–21, 29, 30–31, 34–37, 40–42, 44–45, 47–49, 51–53, 55–56, 58–59, 61–62, 79, 82–83, 85–86, 103–4, 109, 111–15; romanticization of, 49

"Swamp Angel." *See* Melville, Herman

theft, 51, 72, 82, 104
trade (networks), 5, 46, 50–51, 67
Tubman, Harriet, 139, 180n45
Turner, Nat, 31, 41, 45, 73, 82–87, 106–7, 142
Twelve Years a Slave. See Northup, Solomon

Uncle Tom's Cabin. See Stowe, Harriet Beecher
Underground Railroad, 12, 21, 125, 132, 157; (as paradigm), 16, 21, 84–85, 138–39, 178n9

Venezuela, 65, 108
Vesey, Denmark, 31, 33, 41

violence, 20–21, 29, 32–33, 35, 37, 44, 54–56, 64, 66–67, 71–73, 82–84, 94, 98, 102–4, 107–8, 114–16, 137, 139, 142, 145, 148, 150, 168n34; sexual, 20, 37, 40–41, 101, 108, 129–30, 149–50, 152

Virginia, 2–4, 7, 45, 101–2, 106–7, 116, 121–22, 128, 130–32, 134, 137, 146, 153, 157. *See also* Dismal Swamp

"Virginia Maroons." *See* Jackson, Edmund

Walker, David: *Walker's Appeal in Four Articles,* 20, 45, 69, 104
Washington, Booker T., 125
Washington, George, 8
Washington, Madison (historical fig.), 121–22, 124, 126–31. *See also* Douglass: *Heroic Slave*
Weekly Anglo-African, 63
West Indies, 7, 9, 16, 61, 71, 151. *See also* Cuba, Jamaica, Santo Domingo, *etc.*
Willis, Nathaniel Parker, 99
women (enslaved): 58, 99–101, 105–13, 118–20, 150, 172n59; domestic roles, 105, 109–11, 118, 143, 149–50. *See also* Jacobs, Harriet

Yellin, Jean Fagan, 20, 101, 113, 174n2

www.ingramcontent.com/pod-product-compliance
Lightning Source LLC
Chambersburg PA
CBHW030623230426
43661CB00053B/2122